FOLLOWERS OF THE TRAIL

David Leviatin

Followers of the Trail

Jewish Working-Class Radicals in America

Yale University Press : New Haven and London

Ethel G.

Published with assistance from the Louis Stern Memorial Fund.

Designed by Sally Harris/Summer Hill Books and set in Linotron
Plantin type by Brevis Press, Bethany, Connecticut. Printed in the
United States of America by Murray Printing Company, Westford,
Massachusetts.

Library of Congress Cataloging-in-Publication Data

Leviatin, David, 1961–
Followers of the trail: Jewish working-class radicals in America /
David Leviatin.
    p.   cm.
Bibliography: p.
Includes index.
ISBN 0–300–04354–6 (alk. paper)
1. Jews—New York (N.Y.)—Interviews. 2. Jewish radicals—
New York (N.Y.)—Interviews. 3. Jewish communists—New
York (N.Y.)—Interviews. 4. Immigrants—New York (N.Y.)—
Interviews. 5. Oral history. 6. New York (N.Y.)—Social life
and customs. I. Title.
F128.9.J5L47   1989
974.7'1004924—dc19   88–27766
                      CIP

The paper in this book meets the guidelines for permanence and
durability of the Committee on Production Guidelines for Book
Longevity of the Council on Library Resources.

10 9 8 7 6 5 4 3 2 1

This book is dedicated to my parents,
Rosalind and Victor, my brother, Daniel, my
grandparents, Jenya, Rubin, Rachel, and
Harry, and to all the Followers of the Trail.
Thank you.

Contents

Acknowledgments

This book would not have been possible without the unbelievable amount of time, energy, and skill my mother devoted to it from its inception. Her typing, transcribing, translating, and editorial assistance have proven essential and invaluable to this work. My father's unrelenting optimism, support, and advice helped keep me on the Followers' trail. My brother's friendship provided me with a source of encouragement and entertainment—thanks for all the bowling and pool. My grandparents have been an inspiration to me throughout.

I would also like to thank: Daniel Aaron, Miriam Chrisman, Robert Coles, Andrew Courtney, Ruth DiPietro, David Donald, Donald Fleming, Greenburgh Central 7 School District, Charles Grench, Maurice Isserman, Leslie Jean-Bart, Julius Lester, Herb Levart, Don Levine, Jerome Liebling, Mark Naison, the National Endowment for the Humanities, Northeast Scanning Technology, Abraham Ravett, Carl Rosen, Alice Rossi, Eric Rothschild, John Shearer, Werner Sollors, Stephan Thernstrom, the Woodlands Individualized Senior Experience, and special thanks to the students and faculty in the American Civilization Program at Harvard University.

Introduction

Mostly no one there was conscious of a
grandfather unless as remembering one as an
old man living in the house with them or as
living in another place and being written to
sometimes by them and then having died and
that was the end of grandfathers to them.
—Gertrude Stein, The Making of Americans

"Why so many questions, so many pictures. . . . What's going to be with all this?"

I turned off the tape recorder and tried to explain to my grandmother that I wasn't sure what would happen with the interviews I was recording and the pictures I was taking.

"So then why bother? What's the use of it?"

Uncertain of what it was I was doing and why, I sought desperately for an answer. "For history," I finally responded. "All of this is important to do for history."

It was as if I had uttered some magical word. My grandmother sat back in her chair and sighed deeply. Her hand gestured awkwardly toward the tape recorder.

"All right, all right," she said impatiently. "Go ahead, make the machine. . . . It's for history."

In January 1980 I applied for a Youth Grant from the National Endowment for the Humanities (NEH). On the four lines of the NEH application requesting that I summarize my project, I wrote: "I plan to photograph and interview the remaining members of a Communist Jewish workers' camp established in 1929. The project will examine various aspects of immigration, assimilation, radical political activity, and

Jewish culture." Five months later, I received a brief letter of congratulations, a thick packet of guidelines, and a check for $2,500.

At the time, I was an eighteen-year-old University of Massachusetts freshman with some experience as a photographer and none as an oral historian. What I knew of Marx and historical materialism came from a confused but ambitious reading of *Capital*. I knew little about the relationship between Jews and communism in New York City in the 1930s. I could not tell the difference between a Trotskyist and a Trotskyite. The *Freiheit* and the *Forward* meant nothing to me. "Boring from within" sounded like something having to do with a nuclear reactor.

The major advantage I had in documenting the history of the camp known as "Followers of the Trail" was a personal connection. Both sets of my grandparents were members. My mother's parents became actively involved with the camp soon after its founding in 1929. My father's parents became "Followers" in the mid-fifties. Moreover, since many of the Followers had refused to bring children into what they considered to be a "cruel world" (thirties America), my younger brother and I became something akin to communal grandchildren. We spent our first thirteen summers in the camp being coddled and fed, our backs slapped, our faces continually plastered with kisses, our hands always busy wiping away lipstick. We were shuttled from bungalow to bungalow, asked to determine if Bertha's "mandelbread" was better than Reva's or if we wanted Jack's "barely used" bathing suit or Harry's "almost like new swim trunks." We were loved, we were shared. Consequently, years later I was well-liked and trusted.

When I arrived in May 1980 to spend the summer with the camp's remaining members, they were delighted and surprised. "It's very nice to see you, David, but what do you want to stay among us old people for? You're young, go have fun. It's only old people here. Go on, what do you want here?" I wasn't exactly sure.

I moved in with my mother's parents. They had already "prepared" the upstairs of their two-story bungalow—a bungalow my grandfather pieced together throughout the thirties and forties. When I told him I would need a darkroom, his eyes beamed with mischievous delight. "But, naturally, what kind of a photographer is it that has no darkroom?"

After transforming the bathroom into a darkroom and filling the refrigerator with more film than my grandmother thought necessary, I was ready to begin working. From the outset I considered the project to be primarily photographic; pictures were what interested me, not interviews. It was images I thought I was after, not words.

My camera equipment consisted of two Nikon bodies, three lenses—24-mm, 35-mm, 85-mm—and a small Vivitar strobe. A cumbersome and thoroughly battered Sanyo AM-FM cassette deck played the role of tape recorder.

Photographically, my plan was simple. Photograph everything and everyone. I had an almost mystical sense of the power of blanket coverage. Within quantity, I thought, one could always find some quality. My photographic heroes were the giants of the documentary tradition: Paul Strand, Henri Cartier-Bresson, W. Eugene Smith, Bruce Davidson. I looked at their work over and over again. I tried to photograph my subjects with the same passion, concern, and humanity, with the same straightforward black and white vision. I felt confident and excited with what I would be trying to do with my camera.

The only clue I had for conducting the interviews was Studs Terkel's *Working*,[1] a book my father more than suggested I read. After "experiencing" the lives Terkel presented, I became fascinated with the possibility of listening to someone relive his or her life story. History did not have to be boring, beaten of feeling and immediacy, entombed in stale textbooks. It could be brought to life, unlocked and directly experienced. Oral history was the key. I realized that I was in an extraordinary position. I would be able to do my own interviews, to see and hear history replayed, feel its pulse and power. I would be listening to my grandparents and their friends as they reconstructed their past—my past.

I worked up an extensive and "exhausting" questionnaire. Again, coverage, coverage. It began with questions that dealt with European life at the turn of the twentieth century and ended by eliciting commentary on that morning's *New York Times*. I asked about religion, school, family life, social life, antisemitism, recipes, clothing, weather, transportation, immigration, assimilation, work, unions, strikes, politics, disillusionment, old age—absolutely everything I could think of. I did not want to take the chance of missing anything. The questionnaire was cumbersome, suffocating.

The first ten interviews were more like interrogations—stiff and awkward. I knew something was wrong. I asked my grandfather for advice. He told me that I had too many questions. "Let them talk, let them think. There's not even room to breathe here. It's too many questions. Listen to them. Be patient. Be quiet. Listen. Always listen. We know what happened. We don't forget, we never forget, never. Remember, we lived through it all."

I trimmed the questionnaire drastically and perhaps just as importantly accustomed myself to the lengthy pauses I had earlier combatted with rapid-fire follow-up questions. "Don't worry," my grandfather said. "The quiet means they're thinking. We're old. It takes longer. You're young. You can't sit still, be patient."

The interviews improved immediately. They became intimate conversations over coffee and cake—relaxed and revealing. I drank, ate, and listened. They talked, reliving their lives before my eyes: laughing, crying, pounding on the table, holding my hand as we walked back along the dirt roads of small villages, running from stones thrown by Gentile children, traveling miles to trains and boats that rocked and rolled toward America, waiting nervously and impatiently at Ellis Island, walking the streets of New York's Lower East Side looking for work; we sewed, stitched, and sweated, sent money home, learned English, went to concerts and lectures, joined unions, read Marx, read Lenin, demonstrated, struck, picketed, fought and struggled for a better world.

After listening to countless stories, I began to understand the Followers' experiences and identify with their values. There seemed to be a bond that bridged the gap of generations, that transcended the obstacles of thick accents and poor English. Their words struck several untouched chords in my life.

I was raised in a fundamentally secular household in which the cultural and humanistic aspects of Judaism were stressed. Being Jewish meant being socially conscious: aware, concerned, and active. The environment in which I grew up was also politically charged—intellectually rather than dogmatically. The existence of progressive politics in my family's life was taken for granted, there was nothing strange about the stuff of everyday life. I remember overhearing stories about strikes and scabs, listening to heated discussions emphasizing the need for racial justice and equality, sitting atop my father's shoulders at demonstrations, trying to explain to my friends, with a great deal of confusion, why I could not eat lettuce or grapes. Secular Judaism and progressive politics appeared to intersect and interact. The stories the Followers told put my upbringing in perspective, linking their lives with what there was of mine. I stopped thinking of the oral histories as simply their stories; they were also my story—our history.

The Followers' life histories were presented to me as valuable heirlooms. I was almost always asked what I was going to do with the material, would I "take good care of it." Sometimes I was advised to "put the material away in a safe place." Each interview was an event, a lesson, a transfer of knowledge from past to present. The Followers understood and appreciated the importance of history. They approached the interviews as if they wanted to make sure that their stories would not only be heard but remembered, their lives not simply listened to but woven into the fabric of history. They knew that they had worked alongside history, attempting to change its course; they also knew that their struggles were of only marginal interest to historians. Their lives were not in textbooks, or in academic monographs, or in the popular catalogs of Jewish life like Irving Howe's *World of Our Fathers*.[2] The Followers were forgotten people, Communist rank and filers, whom historians have written around. Talking to me provided them with an audience and a student. They taught while I listened and learned about pogroms, the Russian Revolution, the Lower East Side, the needle trades, the Communist Party, the Spanish Civil War; about fighting for what one believes in, and about aging with grace and dignity—never being bitter or vindictive, always proud of a life lived with purpose, excitement, and energy.

In September, I packed my bags, said my goodbyes, sent the NEH Youth Grant evaluation form to Washington and returned to the University of Massachusetts with a suitcase full of tapes and pictures. In four months I had learned a great deal about immigration and assimilation, radical politics and Judaism, oral history and photography; as far as I was concerned the project was finished. Julius Lester, my advisor at the University of Massachusetts, thought otherwise. After looking at the pictures and listening to the tapes, he told me that he thought the Followers' stories could be shaped into a book. I laughed. He explained the material's significance and originality, suggested how to edit and organize, stressed the importance of sharing the Followers' lives with others. I was overwhelmed with the prospect of having a book published. I told Julius that I would have the manuscript ready in six months. He laughed. "Try six years."

Yale University Press exhibited interest in the raw, six-month-old manuscript but asked for substantial revisions that, at the time, I felt unprepared to make. For the next two years I only occasionally tinkered with the material, devoting the bulk of my time to working as a freelance photographer. During this period, many of the Followers I had interviewed passed away; the death of a friend became an almost monthly occurrence in my life. I gradually began to feel responsible for keeping the Followers' stories, their legacy and spirit, alive.

I decided to reorganize the manuscript, moving away from short quotations grouped into numerous categories—such as family life, schooling, religion, anti-semitism, work—and toward the creation of a more unified narrative divided into three parts: "Europe," "America," and "A Shtetl on a Hill." The result read more smoothly; it gave the reader a better sense of the people behind the words rather than my burying their individuality in topics that I created by chopping up and sorting out their lives.

In the summer of 1984, I sent the revised manuscript to Yale and decided to apply to Harvard's graduate program in American Civilization. The commercial aspects of photography had tempered my romance with practicing the medium professionally. Working closely with the oral histories convinced me of their value.

As a student at the graduate school at Harvard, I was drawn to the study of immigration, assimilation, and ethnicity. Reading Oscar Handlin's *The Uprooted* and Moses Rischin's *Promised City* enabled me to see the academic potential of the Followers' life stories.[3] Historians had written about immigrants, but I thought it was necessary to read their own words, to "hear" them describe Europe, the trip to America, their attempt to adapt to a new world. Similarly, after surveying the literature devoted to American communism, I was surprised to discover that the lives of rank-and-file Communists were rarely dealt with. In addition, aside from a few exceptions—most notably *The Narrative of Hosea Hudson*—oral history was employed infrequently, even by those social historians busy reexamining and revising an older generation's institutional and political history of the American Communist movement.[4]

The Followers' stories, useful for students of immigration, ethnicity, and politics, also proved a valuable source for the study of European and American social history. Their detailed discussion of clothing and food, housing and transportation, religious activity and medical practices, work and entertainment, economic, geographic, and social mobility, all vividly portray many aspects of "everyday life" too often overlooked by historians.

For example, a careful study of the Followers' discussion of living patterns in America reveals an interesting case of the intersection of economic, geographic, and social mobility. The Followers indicate that the cheapest apartments were on the top floors of tenement buildings located on the Lower East Side. The more steps one had to climb, the less rent one had to pay. These apartments were usually occupied by newly arrived immigrants. As the inhabitants of these upper floors made more money, they moved down to apartments on lower floors of the same building or in buildings nearby. Those more fortunate economically were able to move up to the Bronx, where one could find elevator apartments and private toilets. The few children of the Followers extended this pattern, leaving apartment buildings in the Bronx to purchase private homes in the suburbs of Long Island and Westchester. It would not be implausible to suggest, considering the recent reversal of urban flight, that someday soon the handful of Followers' grandchildren will journey back into the city and live in remodeled apartments on the Lower East Side.

Finally, the Followers' stories are a contribution to the little known genre of immigrant autobiography. The 1901 serial publication of Jacob Riis's autobiography, *The Making of an American,* marked the beginning of an American literary form inspired directly by the circumstances surrounding immigration to the United States between 1881 and 1925 and indirectly by Benjamin Franklin's *Autobiography.* First person narratives by immigrants such as Riis, Mary Antin (*The Promised Land,* 1912), S. S. McClure (*My Autobiography,* 1914), Edward Steiner (*From Alien to Citizen,* 1914), Marcus Ravage (*An American in the Making,* 1917), Edward Bok (*The Americanization of Edward Bok,* 1920), and many others are imbued with Benjamin Franklin's spirit of individualism and Theodore Roosevelt's ethic of "Americanism." The people behind these tales of American idealism and individual achievement attempt to pacify those worried about their presence by championing the virtues of America and casting themselves as the hard-working beneficiaries of the gift of opportunity. They are "model citizens," rarely critical and easily assimilable.[5]

The Followers, arriving in America at the same time as these autobiographers, are "new immigrants" who present themselves differently. In doing so, they provide a more complete picture of the immigrants who came to America between 1881 and 1925. The Followers' "collective autobiography," told to another rather than written by themselves and recorded near the end of their lives rather than as young adults, emphasizes the maintenance of ethnic identity rather than its abandonment and the importance of cooperation rather than individualism. America is still perceived to be "the land of opportunity" and for essentially the same reason championed by the autobiographers mentioned above—freedom. The Followers, however, chose to exercise America's offer of freedom by refusing to "melt" their ethnic identity and by challenging the spirit of individualism with one of cooperation.

In February 1986, Yale agreed that the manuscript was publishable. I began the process of reediting and refining, inserting a number of previously unedited interviews as well as researching and preparing materials for an introduction that I began working on in Donald Fleming's intellectual history seminar. Fleming, through the works of Perry Miller, Eric Auerbach, and Arthur Lovejoy, stressed the importance of tracing *unit-ideas,* of locating the essential blocks upon which systems of thought are built. I attempted to identify the forces that made a group of young immigrants into a group of committed Communist Party members and fellow travelers.

My intellectual adventure led me to the three factors that directed the Followers' political development: oppression, curiosity, and hope. The suffering that they endured daily as European Jews helped nurture their longing for a world in which they would be treated equally: economically, socially, and politically. America was believed to be the Promised Land where dreams could be realized; emigration was the first step in their journey of hope. After arriving in New York City and encountering economic exploitation as well as difficult living conditions, communism appeared to provide an avenue toward salvation. America and communism, immigration and radical politics, symbolized the Followers' desire for freedom and equality. Their political ideology grew naturally from their belief that a better world could be created, that men and women working collectively could control and improve their lives. Hunting for unit-ideas proved to be a useful academic exercise, revealing the complex interaction among a group of people, a series of events and circumstances, and an ideology. Perhaps the most valuable lesson the Followers' life stories have to offer, however, is the importance of listening to voices outside of the academy—in this case, the voices of people who attempted to change the course of history with dreams and with sweat.

Road to Followers of the Trail

Entrance

Bungalow

Bungalow

ONE

The Followers of the Trail

Beginning in 1881, the nature of European immigration to the United States changed significantly. In the years up to and including 1880, immigrants from northwestern Europe had outnumbered those from central, eastern, and southern Europe. From 1881 through 1925, 26,067,288 men, women, and children emigrated to the United States—22,297,969 were European; 16,049,808, more than half of the all-countries total and almost three-quarters of the European total, were central, eastern, and southern Europeans.

From 1881 to 1894, the central European country of Germany set the pace, consistently providing the largest number of immigrants, from any one country, bound for the United States. In 1895, immigrants from Russia, Italy, Hungary, and Austria began to dominate. This trend continued. From 1901 through 1925 the number of immigrants from central, eastern, and southern Europe—especially from Russia, Italy, Hungary, Austria—was staggering: from all countries, 17,160,110 immigrants; the total from Europe, 14,011,945; and from central, eastern, and southern Europe, 11,473,104.[1]

This huge movement of central, eastern, and southern Europeans was commonly referred to as "a wave," "a tide," "a flood," or "an invasion." It was what the Dillingham Commission's (1907–1910) forty-two volume report called "the New Immigration." The majority of "New Immigrants" were single males between the ages of sixteen and forty-four. They spoke very little or no English, were probably Jewish or Catholic, and were likely unemployed or unskilled laborers in Europe.[2] They were thought to be dangerous: intellectually inferior, sexually promiscuous, religiously deviant, politically radical.

Native-born Americans and assimilated immigrants were concerned and worried.

Some saw the New Immigrant and the prospect of his assimilation as a challenge, others saw him as a threat to the fabric of American society. Differing plans designed to integrate and exclude the newcomers were widespread.

Anglo-Conformists, like Theodore Roosevelt, welcomed the immigrant as long as he left his past in Europe. Advocates of the cosmopolitanism popularized by Israel Zangwill's play *The Melting Pot* (1908) argued that "the American Crucible" could produce a new man, "a superman." Cultural pluralists, following Horace Kallen, suggested that immigrants could maintain their old identity within a new context. Restrictionists such as Albert Johnson, Prescott F. Hall, and Madison Grant rejected all attempts to assimilate the New Immigrant and instead devoted their energy to keeping him out of the country.

The Followers of the Trail, coming to the United States between 1905 and 1925, were New Immigrants who integrated themselves into the American scene on their own terms—politically and culturally. They successfully managed to create a community built upon the tenets of political internationalism and the tradition of Jewish culture.

In 1929, '30, when I still worked in the [fur] industry . . . I found out about an organization called Followers of the Trail. It was known as a left-wing camp. Some people called it a Communist camp. I considered myself a left-winger, which meant trying to obtain better conditions for the working people. . . . I came here, spent a couple of weekends, and I enjoyed it. I liked the life here, the lectures, the entertainment.

It was an entirely different life than being in the city, with the tuml *[noise; commotion]. . . . After a week working in the shop . . . it was a pleasure to be here.*

It was a place out of heaven. . . . Everyone accepted you with open arms.

Throughout the twenties and thirties, several predominantly Jewish left-wing summer camps were established along the Hudson River in upstate New York. They were designed to function as workers' resorts where people with similar backgrounds, concerns, and political convictions could come to rest their bodies and exercise their minds at an affordable price in what was termed a "proletarian environment." Recreational and intellectual activities were strongly intertwined—softball and Stalin, swimming and Sholom Aleichem, hiking and historical materialism all competed for the campers' time and attention. This book tells the story of one of these camps.

In 1929 a small group of young Jewish immigrants who lived and worked in New York City pooled their meager resources and raised one thousand dollars to put down toward the purchase of twenty-three acres of land, valued at eighteen thousand five hundred dollars, atop a hill overlooking the Hudson River in Peekskill, New York. They called themselves and the workers' camp they created "The Followers of the Trail." Those who contributed fifty dollars for the initial purchase of the property were considered members of the camp. Future members were required to pay an initiation fee of one dollar and a monthly dues fee of twenty-five cents. Members had to be proposed by an already existing member and approved by a membership committee. According to a number of the founders, there was only one membership restriction: bosses were not welcome. The by-laws of the camp, printed in 1929, stated: "In case of doubt as to the character of the prospective member, he or she shall be requested to participate in our out-door activities for at least a period of one month, before being admitted to our organization" (Article 4, Section 3). In addition to members, the camp accepted "campers" and "privileged campers." Campers paid by the night, the weekend, the week, or the month. Privileged campers paid for the summer and were permitted to use the facilities every weekend. The camp was administered by an executive committee, a financial committee, a management committee, and a grounds committee. Each committee was chaired by a secretary. The by-laws followed the system outlined in *Robert's Rules of Order.*

The camp began with a few tents and a communal dining room. As the summer business prospered, the tents were replaced by small one- and two-room bungalows. In 1939 twenty-eight more acres were purchased for six thousand dollars. The camp provided three meals daily, sleeping quarters, and athletic and educational activities. The camp's speakers included Earl Browder and Mike Gold; Zero Mostel and Pete Seeger were frequent performers. The camp attracted workers from New York City, primarily those in the needle trades, but also some radical professionals. Camp members supported the Bolshevik Revolution of 1917 and the Communist Party. They took part in countless demonstrations—most notably those rallying for unemployment insurance and social security and those that attempted to prevent the executions of the Scottsboro Boys and the Rosenbergs. In 1937 they raised enough money to buy an ambulance for the Abraham Lincoln Brigade in Spain. During World War II, many members were actively involved with the Russian War Relief. On August 27, 1949, Paul Robeson was scheduled to perform in Peekskill. Before the concert began, a riot broke out between progressives who had come to listen to Robeson and conservatives from the surrounding community. The concert was rescheduled for September 4, 1949. After Robeson completed his performance, violence followed. Many people, including camp members, were injured. After "the Robeson affair" the camp was referred to by outsiders in the area as a "Communist colony." Campers were constantly harassed and threatened.

The summer seasons of 1950 and 1951 were business disasters for the camp. Joseph McCarthy's "witchhunt" frightened previously dedicated guests away. Some members claim that FBI agents were found snooping around the premises. A few of the members were called to testify before the House Un-American Activities Committee. A number of other camps were forced to close down. In 1952, Camp Followers of the Trail could no longer afford to stay in business. The bungalows were sold to interested members and the camp was incorporated as the Reynolds Hills Colony. The new colony has attempted to maintain a low political profile.

Some of the camp's members and guests belonged to the Communist Party. Most can best be described as fellow travelers. Both followed the Communist Party line until as late as 1956, when Khrushchev exposed and denounced Stalin's crimes in a secret speech delivered to a Closed Session of the Twentieth Congress of the Communist Party of the Soviet Union.[3]

An examination of how the Followers became Party members and fellow travelers will help provide the historical background needed to understand and more fully appreciate their histories as well as the world in which they moved. To begin, one must go back to eastern Europe, specifically to Russia, and find out why the Followers of the Trail decided to leave their homes and come to America.

After the Russian revolution of 1905, hostility toward Jews increased dramatically. They were economically oppressed, politically ignored, and physically persecuted. The pursuit of higher education was restricted. Conditions in Russia were desperate, opportunities bleak.[4] A consistent theme in the interviews conducted with the Followers is their desire to leave Russia "to develop" and to "better their condition."

Life was too narrow for me. I wanted to have more activities and see more. There you get married right away. It wasn't, somehow, enough for my aspirations.

We lived in a very small town near Kiev. Life was very dull, particularly for young people. . . . I was growing up in this atmosphere of nothingness.

When you undertook a trip to America by yourself, not knowing anybody, not knowing what encounter you may have, whom you may meet on the way, what advantage they may take of you—you took all those chances because you wanted to develop, to find out what's in the world, what is it next door that's locked up to me.

And, finally, "a lot of people came here [to the United States] because they wanted to better their condition." The Followers, interested in improving the quality of their lives, believed that emigrating to America would help. In addition, a few of the Followers while still in Europe and the majority after arriving in America, were attracted to the ideals of communism, convinced that the ideology would also enable them to realize their dreams.

The question of where the Followers became radicalized is a complicated one. Some of them were politically engaged before coming to the United States.

In 1917, when the Revolution broke out, I knew that the Bolsheviks are those that are fighting for the interests of the working class, whereas the others were for the rich. Lenin was one of the greatest men in those days to us. We always admired him, and we tried to get some literature of Lenin and read a little bit, and discuss. . . . We used to get together and have little meetings, and start reading radical newspapers, progressive newspapers. . . . We used to get together, we used to smoke on Saturday, and talk about helping the working people.

In 1917 the Revolution came. There was a tremendous joy and a tremendous friendship between the Gentiles and the Jews. We thought that this was like the Messiah came. "Frei geboiren." . . . We youngsters got together, we had meetings, and we organized groups to visit the Council of Soviets. It was really a joy. The citizens were friendly to each other, Gentile and Jew, they went to meetings to listen to the different parties that were established—the Socialists, Socialist Mensheviks, Bolsheviks—all different parties, revolutionary parties.

I was too young to participate in making the Revolution, but I was old enough when it came time to fight to defend it. When I was fourteen years old, I joined the Komsomol and I happened to be the Secretary of the unit. I had a rifle that was twice my size, and I was afraid of it.

Aside from the exceptions cited above, most of the Followers became politically radical only after coming to the United States. It was in the shops and in the streets, in the clubs and coffeehouses that the Followers absorbed a systematic radical political philosophy. However, all of the Followers appear to have undergone a series of pivotal radicalizing experiences, not necessarily political, while still youngsters in Europe. These general experiences may have influenced the Followers' political development.

One of the Followers bitterly remembers the day his mother told him that she could not afford to pay to have him bar mitzvahed. From then on, he was painfully aware that some would have and some would not, that rites and passages were more often bought than earned.

Another Follower, the daughter of a middleman, or a "broker," recalls her feelings after discovering the significance of her father's line of work. "At a very young age, when I started to observe and see how our life is being provided by my father and by what means, I began to rebel. I began to rebel inside me that here is a man, doing nothing with his hands, not producing anything, and yet he makes a living."

In addition to their discovery of class dynamics, the Followers discussed the difficult condition of Jews in Europe. Jews were discriminated against at every step, their place of residence severely circumscribed, their choice of occupation carefully restricted. Antisemitism appears to have been commonplace, covering a spectrum from spontaneous name calling and rock throwing to calculated acts of pillage and murder. As Jews, the Followers experienced a world of hostility and violence. The constant and systematic inequality they observed and suffered may have led them to communism.

Arthur Liebman, in *Jews and the Left*, suggests that the reason large numbers of Jews embraced radical political programs was because of the oppressive nature of the Czarist government:

The role of the Czarist government in the economic and ethnic oppression of Jews facilitated the focusing of their hostility onto the political arena and back upon the state, the ultimate source of their misery. For many, a radical political movement that attacked both the state and capitalism was considered an effective vehicle for the expression of the anger that flowed from their treatment as workers and as Jews. The attraction was even greater when these radical movements also included as objectives the elimination of ethnic discrimination.[5]

One of the Followers, accounting for the belief in communism he developed after coming to America, echoes the points made by Liebman:

The ideas of communism attracted me first of all because I had a worker's background and I felt that the worker was being exploited. I felt that the worker should be compensated for the work that he is doing. The main attraction was the idea of the equality of people—that everyone is alike, Jews, black people, Indians—there is one human being. This was the main attraction.

While there may be no definitive answer to the question, Why did the Followers choose communism? it seems reasonable to assume that, after living and working in America, the Followers perceived communism to be the solution to their recent oppression as workers and their historical oppression as Jews. Strikingly more ambitious and messianic than the Socialist agenda, perhaps considered more realistic and less apocalyptic than the anarchist message, the Communist program, promising justice and equality as well as a rich and varied cultural life, helped satisfy the Followers' desire to live in a new world—physically and spiritually. However, before the majority of the Followers embraced communism, they traveled to America, politically curious and extremely hopeful. They believed that they would be respected as workers, that they would be able to develop themselves intellectually, and, above all, that as Jews they would be free from persecution. Although their situation improved, their myth of America was quickly shattered. One of the Followers describes her reaction after arriving in New York: "When I came to Ellis Island, we were on one side of a fence and my sister and brother [who were already in America and had come to meet her] were on the other side. At first I felt, 'I'm in America. It's a free country. Why is that fence there? Why can't I go over from the boat straight to my brother?' That sort of puzzled me." Another was picked up at the boat by his father: "My father didn't have a car . . . so we went to his house by subway. To take a cab would have been too expensive. When I went down in the subway station at Bowling Green, I saw a black man sweeping the floor. I didn't like it. I said to myself, 'This reminds me of *Uncle Tom's Cabin*'—I had read it so many years before in Russian. 'Is this the kind of job that is allotted to a black person? To sweep the floor?' I thought there was something wrong."

The Followers were also struck by the living and working conditions they experienced. Those who did not have the good fortune of living in the Bronx or Brooklyn were crammed into overcrowded, poorly constructed tenement buildings on New York's Lower East Side. Most worked long hours in shops and factories.

A number of organizations and institutions that the Followers became involved with in the United States helped channel and refine their hopes and experiences into a political ideology.

The Unions

After settling down in New York, the majority of the Followers began working in the needle and fur trades. These industries were controlled by Socialist and Communist unions. Throughout the twenties, intense battles were waged between the Socialists and the Communists for control of the unions. According to one of the Followers:

At that time there were two unions. There was a left-wing union and a right-wing union. My shop wanted to take the left-wing union. So the right-wing union sent gangsters with blackjacks, and they were after me because I was the chairlady. It was a rainy day and a few girls got into the car and we were sitting there. They surrounded the car and they said, "There she is." But before they could get me, I ran out of the car through the other door. They were running after me, so I grabbed an umbrella and I hit them with the umbrella. But one girl was beaten up badly then.

In November 1920, William Z. Foster, a trade unionist later to become an influential figure in the Communist Party, founded the Trade Union Educational League. "The League was not a union. It issued no charters and collected no dues or taxes. Financially the organization depended on voluntary contributions of individuals and labor unions, and the sale of its organ *The Labor Herald*."[6] The League was designed as a tool to transform existing American Federation of Labor (AFL) unions into revolutionary unions. Foster followed a plan of action devised in Moscow and referred to as "boring from within." The idea behind the League was to organize workers to bore from within their existing AFL unions and transform them into revolutionary Communist unions. This strategy was opposed by the Socialists, who, satisfied with their AFL affiliation, fought a bitter struggle against the "boring" of their Communist counterparts. After the factional fighting was over, the Socialists were in control of the ILGWU and the Communists controlled the International Fur Workers' Union.[7]

The Followers working in these industries received a steady diet of left-wing political propaganda. It is important to emphasize that the Followers did not come to America and consciously decide that they wanted to work in the needle and fur trades because they harbored revolutionary aspirations. These were the jobs available, and they took them. One of the Followers says: "Where could they send a girl without any experience to work if not to a dress shop? There are so many variations in a dress . . . [that] you don't have to have any knowledge or any sense . . . , it's the place where you sent girls to work." Another reason the Followers worked in the needle and fur trades was because they were considered to be "Jewish industries": "When I became a furrier, 90 percent of the people in the furriers were Jewish. The bosses were also Jewish. You could go on the East Side and hardly hear an English-speaking person." The Followers who began working in the needle and fur trades did so because these industries were receptive to unskilled immigrants and because they were predominantly Jewish. Their political values were shaped by the daily debates between the Socialist and Communist union leaders.

Why did the Followers adopt the position and principles of the Communist union leaders rather than those of the Socialists? Irving Howe, in *World of Our Fathers*, suggests that "One major reason for the success of the Communists in gaining support among garment workers was that a good part of the traditional leadership—socialist, nominally socialist, ex-socialist, or nonpolitical—had been losing its spiritual élan."[8] The traditional leadership's loss of spiritual élan no doubt played its part in enhancing the appeal and the message of Communist union leaders. However, another reason for the garment and fur trade workers' support of the Communists exists, and it is one Howe ignores. The Communists were calling for concrete and dramatic changes in the needle and fur trades that were designed to improve working and living conditions. The traditional union leaders were perceived by the rank and file as increasingly bureaucratic and more interested in maintaining the status quo than in fighting for workers' rights.

Beginning in January 1926 the fur workers, led by Ben Gold—manager of the Furriers' New York Joint Board and also a Communist—went out on a general strike that lasted seventeen weeks. Philip Foner notes that the manufacturers, the *Forward*, and the right-wing Socialists argued that the strike was a "Moscow-inspired revolution."[9] Among the Furriers' demands were: (1) a forty-hour five-day week; (2) unemployment insurance; (3) that the first day of May be observed as a holiday with full pay; and (4) that shops be inspected by union representatives. In June, settlement was finally achieved. The Furriers, led by Communist union officials, secured, among other things, a forty-hour week of five eight-hour days—the first in the needle and fur trades—and a 10 percent wage increase above the existing minimum wage scale.[10]

One of the Followers, who was a furrier, describes the differences between the right-wing Socialists and the left-wing Communists and why he supported the Communist-controlled union:

There was such a thing as a left-winger and a right-winger, and I asked people in the market, in the fur market, "what is the difference between a right-winger and a left-winger?" I didn't know what it meant. "Well, the right-wingers are ready to sell everything to the boss. They don't care for the workers, they're just interested in working a lot of overtime, no matter how little or how much they get in the shop. They're not interested in having the union come in and sort of dictate to you what you're supposed to do." I said to them, "What is a left-winger?" "Well, a left-winger is more for the workers than the others. They are interested in building unions and becoming leaders of the union, not to allow the old-time leaders to maintain superiority forever." I said, "Well, that means I'm a left-winger." That's how I named myself a left-winger, and I stuck with that all these years. For years I followed not just the Socialist Party line, I followed the Communist Party line. From each according to his ability, to each according to his need. Integration. Everything. We all followed the line.

In addition to the influence of the radical union movement, the Followers' political development—especially that of those who did not work in the needle and fur trades—was shaped and directed, perhaps most significantly, by the newspaper they read.

The Morning Freiheit

The *Morning Freiheit* was founded on April 2, 1922. Its first issue appeared three weeks later. It was organized by a group of workers from the *Jewish Daily Forward* who were upset with what they perceived to be the Socialist paper's move to the right politically. They accused the *Forward* of being more concerned with the interests of the bosses in the needle and fur trades than with the workers in those industries. They were opposed to the *Forward*'s policy toward the Soviet Union. The *Forward* supported the Russian Revolution of 1917, but it did not support the complete Bolshevization of the country being undertaken by Lenin. The *Forward* wanted to see a union of all the Russian Socialist parties in command. The *Freiheit* founders thought this idea to be heretical and counterrevolutionary. They supported the Bolsheviks and Lenin faithfully.[11]

The *Freiheit*, although it claimed not to be a direct organ of the Communist Party (like the *Daily Worker*, founded two years after the *Freiheit* and read religiously by the Followers), did have strong ties to the Party. In fact, two incidents in the newspaper's history suggest that even if the *Freiheit* did not consider itself a direct organ of the Party, the Party treated it as if it were.

In the early 1920s a great debate raged within the Communist Party. After pressure from the Comintern in Moscow, the illegal American underground Communist Party was encouraged to form a legal aboveground party. The Workers Party was founded to meet this demand on December 23, 1922. (The underground party was known as "Number One" and the Workers Party, "Number Two.") The decision to create the party faced strong opposition. A faction within the underground thought the timing of the legal party's creation was premature. However, not wanting to disagree with the Comintern's orders, this faction—known as the "Left Opposition"—created its own aboveground party on February 18, 1923, calling themselves the "United Toilers." There were now two contending legal parties and one sharply divided illegal party. The Workers Party was the much more influential and powerful of the two legal parties. The underground Number One party was sharply divided about how the legal (Workers) party should exist. The underground was split into three factions over this issue. There were the Liquidators, who wanted to do away with the underground party and make the Workers Party the only Communist Party in the United States. There were the Geese, who wanted to use the Workers Party as a front organization designed to recruit people into the underground party. And, finally, there was a faction known as the Conciliators, who wanted to leave things as they were, using Number Two as a legal front for Number One.[12]

The *Freiheit,* led by its editor, Moissaye J. Olgin, supported the position of the Liquidators. The Geese, who were more powerful at the time, felt the *Freiheit*'s stand to be threatening. In 1923, Benjamin Gitlow, an extremely important figure in the Communist Party and a member of the Geese, was sent to edit the *Freiheit.* Olgin was encouraged to take an extended vacation. He did so. Since Gitlow was not fluent in Yiddish, Melech Epstein carried out the duties of editor under Gitlow's close scrutiny until Olgin's return in 1929.[13]

The second incident occurred on August 23, 1929. A number of Jewish settlers in Palestine were killed by Arabs. The *Freiheit* originally reported the incident as a pogrom. They blamed the Arab violence on British imperialist policies in Palestine. The Communist Party was not pleased with the *Freiheit*'s description of the Arab-Jewish conflict. The Party Secretariat wrote a biting critique of the *Freiheit* and encouraged the paper to publish it.

The roots of the revolt of the Arabian masses are to be found in the economic exploitation of the Arab peasantry, whose land has been expropriated by British imperialism, through the reactionary Jewish Zionism. . . . We sharply condemn the position of our

Communist Jewish daily, the Morning Freiheit *as absolutely opportunist and hardly, if at all, different from the stand of the Jewish nationalist, Zionist and the capitalist press.*[14]

The *Freiheit*, after a brief internal battle, published the Secretariat's critique.

The *Freiheit* was also closely connected with the Communist controlled International Fur Workers' Union. Moissaye Olgin, in a written "Greeting" prepared for the Twenty-fifth Anniversary of the Furriers' Joint Council of New York in 1937, stated:

The "Morning Freiheit" does not feel an outsider in relation to the life and struggles of the fur workers. From the very first day the "Freiheit" was organized, fifteen years ago, it made it one of its major tasks to fight for better conditions for the workers of every industry, particularly of the needle trades in which so many Jewish workers are engaged. . . . The "Morning Freiheit" has witnessed and helped carry out the great historical struggles of the fur workers in New York. It has helped expose the enemies of the fur workers in New York.[15]

The Followers, primarily needle and fur trade workers interested in bettering their working and living conditions, were dedicated readers of the *Freiheit*. One of the Followers describes why he read the newspaper:

I read the Freiheit *because I was a worker, and it represented the views of the working class. The* Forward *was supposed to be a working paper, but it attracted middle-class manufacturers. It catered more toward the middle class than the cause of the workers. They always took the side of the right-wing union. Also, the* Forward *always attacked the Soviet Union and communism and those in the left-wing union supported the Soviet Union and communism.*

The Followers looked to the Soviet Union as the culmination of all their dreams and hopes for workers around the world:

Our shining star was the Soviet Union—that was our shining star, and whatever they did was right.

We placed so much faith in the Soviet Union. We saw that as the beacon of light for the world.

Stalin was like a God to everybody. Some people used to say, "How could Stalin be wrong? How could the Soviet Union be wrong?"

I was a great admirer of the Soviet Union. I used to go to all the meetings. I used to subscribe to the working class periodicals and newspapers. I used to go listening to some speakers talking about the Russian Revolution. . . . I was a great admirer—I supported it a hundred percent.

In addition to being concerned about the lives of New York's needle and fur trade workers and championing the cause of the Soviet Union, the *Freiheit* was interested in encouraging cultural activity of all kinds. The *Freiheit* successfully combined the inspiring political message of the Communist-run unions with an emphasis on culture. The Followers thought of cultural activity as a way of improving themselves, of making themselves better people:

When I came here as a young fellow, I was right away interested in many things, many more useful things than some of the American boys were interested in. For instance, I couldn't understand somehow why young people are so crazy about certain things, which to me didn't look interesting at all. I was very much puzzled why I can't see many young fellows at a concert when a symphony was playing, or at a good literary play on Broadway. They would rather go and see a ball game. To them, a ball game was more important than to see a good literary play on Broadway. Somehow, I couldn't grasp it. I couldn't see the reason for it.

After work, I used to go a lot to concerts and a lot to operas. I went with another girl or two. Naturally, we couldn't get tickets for a seat. So we went standing—it was a dollar. We went straight from work to the opera, standing, all the way up in the old opera house. . . . Whether I understood it well or not, I wouldn't complain. I wouldn't claim that I understood it so much, but I loved it.

I read Turgenev, I read Tolstoi, I read Chekhov, I read Dostoevski, a few plays of Shakespeare, and some French authors—Maupassant, Dumas. I also read a lot of books in Hebrew, because I studied that language when I was in Russia. And then the main thing—Marx, Lenin.

The Followers had an insatiable appetite for culture. The *Freiheit* was able to meet their demand with an incredibly varied array of Jewish and proletarian cultural activities. The paper created and supported mandolin ensembles, Yiddish language choruses, theater groups and schools, all emphasizing Jewish ethnicity and culture. The paper also stressed the importance of proletarian culture, which was designed to be a workers' form of culture. *Proletcult,* as it was called, distinguished itself from bourgeois middle-class culture. It attempted to dramatize Communist political ideology, especially the concept of class struggle. It did this most effectively through theater groups and choruses.

In the *Daily Worker* of January 17, 1934, an article discusses the importance of the chorus as a medium to transmit proletarian culture: "The chorus is one of the most popular mediums for reaching the masses. The capitalist class, through the churches and so-called people's choruses, use this medium for lulling the workers. The revolutionary movement uses it for rousing the workers against their oppressors."[16] And Moissaye J. Olgin, speaking in 1938 at the Tenth Convention of the Communist Party, New York State, said in reference to the *Freiheit*: "We are creating culture. Therefore it is necessary that we Communists should create Communist culture. . . . We are interested in the Jewish people, but more interested in the Jewish workers, in the revolutionary traditions of the Jewish masses."[17]

The Followers, interested in bettering their condition as workers and improving themselves culturally, turned to the *Freiheit,* which promised to help them do both daily. The *Forward,* under Abraham Cahan, was thought to be aimed at a more affluent audience. It was attacked by Communists because of its alleged failure to deal with issues that concerned workers. The *Freiheit* claimed that the *Forward* was responsible for the adulteration of the Jewish language by using such English words as *potato, chicken,* and *kitchen* instead of their Yiddish equivalents. Consequently, the *Forward's* Yiddish was known as "potato Yiddish."[18]

Paul Novick, at ninety-three still the editor of the *Freiheit,* describes the differences between the *Freiheit* and the *Forward* during the twenties, thirties, and forties:

We were a fighting paper, and that was not the nature of the other papers, the Forvertz *[Forward], you know. They were more sedate, more rich. The* Forvertz *had a circulation of a quarter million and they were very, very rich. So in this respect, they were a different paper altogether. We were progressive, fighting—fighting for the interests of the workers in the shops, against bureaucracy, fighting for Jewish culture, fighting against the assimilation. . . . Those who were for Jewish culture were against the assimilationism of the* Forvertz. *And the* Forvertz *was not a fighting paper. We worked for change a great deal. On the basis of struggle for workers' conditions and the basis of Jewish culture. We had people that came to us just because of culture.*[19]

The left-wingers who supported the *Freiheit* thought of themselves as internationalist-cosmopolitan thinkers interested in promoting dynamic cultural interaction, as well as fighting for the rights of workers. Their opponents, the more politically moderate supporters of the *Forward*, thought otherwise. Left-wingers were accused of being: anti-religious—conducting lectures on Jewish holy days; anti-Zionist—withholding support for an independent Jewish nation; and being dangerous political extremists—blindly following all Soviet dictates. As Arthur Liebman points out, to readers of the *Forward*, "the Communists, both domestic and international, were depicted as the major enemies of the Jewish people and of Israel as well as the United States and the free world. Those who knowingly or not sympathized with communism or advocated policies that the *Forvertz* interpreted as being similar to or supportive of the Communists were also attacked."[20]

Despite, or perhaps because of, the relentless battles with their socialist opponents, the Followers of the Trail remained faithful to the *Freiheit* and the radical political-cultural world it represented. The *Freiheit* embraced and attempted to realize the ideals of economic and racial equality, social justice and international peace that the Followers dreamed of achieving. In doing so, the paper also helped establish an important sense of community. "The *Freiheit*," according to Arthur Liebman, "stood at the center of a network of Yiddish proletarian institutions. In this subculture, the Yiddish Communists and pro-Communists found a world that offered them identity, meaning, friendship, and understanding. It was simply not possible for them to forsake the *Freiheit* and retain membership in this subculture."[21] By combining Communist political ideology with elements of Jewish and proletarian culture, the *Freiheit* emphasized, with a more alluring cultural twist, the political message espoused by the radical union movement. The *Freiheit*, through its effective blend of political ideology and cultural activity, played an instrumental role in transforming a group of young immigrants into a group of committed Party members and fellow travelers.

The International Workers' Order

A number of the Followers were members of the International Workers' Order (IWO). The IWO was the Communist counterpart of the Socialist-run Workmen's Circle. It was a fraternal organization and mutual aid society that was designed to provide insurance to its members. The IWO, like the *Freiheit*, combined cultural activity with Communist political ideology, making the latter more easily palatable. The IWO was founded in 1930 in similar fashion to the *Freiheit*. After the Russian Revolution of 1917 and the creation of the American Communist Party in 1919, the Workmen's Circle was split into two factions—the left, or Communist, faction, and the right, or Socialist. Throughout the twenties, there was a battle between the left and the right for control of the Workmen's Circle. The left claimed that the Workmen's Circle was abandoning its Socialist principles as it took on more members and became a more lucrative business. The left wanted to come out in support of the Soviet Union. They wanted to pursue what they called cultural work, and they wanted the Workmen's Circle to pay more attention to the needs of the workers rather than the bosses. They accused the right of "distributing thousands of dollars to every reactionary organization in the fold and to reactionary party organs, both in America and in Europe. It did not lend support to the extent of even a single penny to any of the progressive movements."[22] The left said that the major problem with the Workmen's Circle was that it "fell under the complete domination of the '*Forward*' machine, the most brutal force in the Jewish labor movement—a machine whose deadly hand was felt by every vital movement which disagreed with it and whose touch was withering and annihilating."[23]

Finally, after a bitter struggle in which both groups accused one another of persecution, the left-wing faction left the Workmen's Circle and founded the International Workers' Order in 1930. A pamphlet, published six months after the creation of the IWO, explained what the organization was and what it stood for. The pamphlet first establishes the IWO's political beliefs and then links these beliefs to the pursuit of culture:

The International Workers' Order assumes the point of view of the class struggle. . . . The International Workers' Order maintains that capitalism is bankrupt. . . . The International Workers' Order realizes that the only Party that leads the working class in its struggle against capitalism, is the Communist Party. . . . It follows therefore that the International Workers' Order is part of the battle-front of the working class. . . . We find that the Communist Party is the only Party that fights for the workers' interests. We therefore endorse the Communist Party. We appeal to all workers to vote for the Communist Party. We aid the Party in its struggles. At the same time, however, we remain a non-Party organization.[24]

Later in the pamphlet, the importance of culture is noted:

The International Workers' Order holds aloft the banner of culture. . . . The I.W.O. wishes to furnish its membership with rich and many-sided culture. But there is culture and culture. There is that kind of culture which befogs the brains of the workers with the lie of class unity and weakens their will with the lie of hopelessness. Such culture is poison for the working class. There is another culture which opens the eyes of the workers, strengthens their will and unites them for the struggle. This is proletarian culture. Such culture is necessary for the working class, and this is the kind of culture the I.W.O. wishes to help create.[25]

In a pamphlet published in 1932, entitled *Youth Section, International Workers' Order, Insurance, Dramatics, Athletics, Cultural, Social Activities,* the type of culture the IWO wants to create is outlined. "All of our cultural activity is based upon the problems of the working class and student youth in shop and classroom." The pamphlet emphasizes the beneficial aspects of athletic activity—basketball, soccer, baseball, swimming, and track and field—stating that "the youth need sports to build itself up physically, to offset drudgery and fatigue, the effect of long hours of work under sped-up conditions." The pamphlet mentions that the IWO is "affiliated with the labor sports union—the only working class sports organization." It goes on to state that "the crowning feature of our entire sporting activity is the participation of our membership in the Spartakiade." The Spartakiade was designed to be a workers' version of the Olympics. There was one held in Berlin in 1931 and one in Chicago in 1932. The IWO agreed to sponsor those of its members who qualified.[26]

In addition to sporting activity, the IWO promoted and sponsored a number of choruses, bands, orchestras, concerts, and dances. They had "pianos, phonographs, and radios at branch headquarters for the use of their members." They published a monthly magazine known as the *New Order,* and "branches have libraries containing all the important proletarian literature." The IWO stressed the importance of workers' theater as a means of reaching the masses and raising their level of political consciousness. The plays "deal with our own lives and problems, our homes, our schools, our shops, and shop matters; people you live and work with are placed behind the footlights." The pamphlet goes on to say that "the cultural committee has on hand a complete file of all working class plays which are placed at the disposal of the branches." The IWO also held lectures, forums, and discussions dealing with "the general struggles of the youth and adult workers."[27]

The IWO was broken down into a number of semi-independent national and language groups. The Jewish section of the IWO was the largest of these groups. Many of the Followers, because of their working class background, their desire to speak

Yiddish, and their passion for cultural activities, joined the Jewish section of the IWO. One of the Followers described his reasons for joining:

I was a member of the IWO, which was a fraternal organization, and they had different groups from different nationalities. They also had a Jewish group. I was a member, and an active member. Besides taking care in case somebody dies, and funerals, and all that, they had different cultural activities. It was the same thing like the clubs. They participated in demonstrations, they participated in all the progressive movements, and it was interesting to be there.

The Prospect Workers' Club

The Communist workers' clubs of New York performed a function similar to that of the *Freiheit* and the IWO. They combined Communist political ideology with an enticing array of cultural activities, from choruses to sports teams. They also raised considerable sums of money for the Communist Party, the *Freiheit*, and the *Daily Worker*. There were three clubs in the Bronx—the Middle Bronx Workers' Club, the Bronx Jewish Workers' Club, the Prospect Workers' Club; three in Brooklyn—the Brownsville Workers' Club, the East New York Workers' Club, the Williamsburgh Workers' Club; and two in Manhattan—the East Side Workers' Club and the Harlem Workers' Club. All eight of these clubs were run by a coordinating committee made up of two members selected from each club. The coordinating committee was responsible for hiring lecturers to speak at clubs, for organizing inter-club outings and events, and for establishing financial quotas for the various clubs.[28]

The largest of all the clubs and the one that a number of the Followers either belonged to or frequented was the Prospect Workers' Club, located in the Bronx at 1257 Southern Boulevard. The club had a chorus, a dramatic group, a mandolin orchestra, a band, a modern dance group, and a soccer team. Dues were fifty cents a month. Various committees oversaw the club's day-to-day operations. There was a library committee to take care of the books, a house committee to take care of the building, a press committee established to distribute the *Freiheit*, the *Daily Worker*, and the *Liberator*. The club invited a number of influential Communist leaders to lecture to its members—most notable were William Z. Foster, the powerful trade unionist and Communist Party leader, and Earl Browder, the General Secretary of the Communist Party.

The club's credo, embodying its political position, was found in its anthem, entitled *The Builders*:

We are the builders,
We build the future,
The future world lies in our hands.
We swing our hammers,
We use our weapons,
Against our foe in every land.
And we are the workers,
Who are the builders,
We fight, we do not fear to die.
All power and freedom unto the workers
Is our defiant battle cry.[29]

The Prospect Workers' Club, through its cultural activities, its speakers, and its political ideology, tried to create a workers' or proletarian culture that also emphasized the importance of Jewish ethnicity. Many of the Followers were drawn to the club for its cultural activities and its comfortable Jewish atmosphere. Once members or visitors, they were exposed to Communist political ideology night and day. The Communists promised that they alone would better the conditions of workers. Their message appealed to a group of people who left Europe precisely to improve their way of life. The Communists seemed to promise them the world culturally and politically. Consequently, the club proved to be a fertile recruiting ground for the Communist Party. Those who were not persuaded to join the Party became fellow travelers. Club members, whether Party members or not, proved useful to the Party because they could be counted on to demonstrate, picket, boycott, sell newspapers, and hand out leaflets.

Two of the Followers, both members of the Prospect Workers' Club, described the nature of the club. Their description illustrates the attraction the club had, first as a social entity and second as a political organization:

RACHEL: *First of all, it was a social club, and a workers' club. It was a big organization of a thousand members. We participated in all kinds of demonstrations—May first demonstrations, and when there were picket lines, we were participating in strikes. It was made up of mainly immigrants. There were very few Americans, if there were any. There was a lot of things doing there. There was a chorus and all kinds of other groups. We were all young, and we used to have picnics, and we used to go swimming together—big crowds—and we used to do a lot of singing. We had a very nice time. . . . Every Friday there was a lecture, every Saturday there was a concert, every Sunday there was dancing. . . . We used to sell tickets, and we had money. We were to the left. We raised a lot of money for different organizations. When they had strikes, we supported them. We used to give money to the* Daily Worker.

HARRY: *To the* Freiheit, *to the Communist Party.*

RACHEL: *To the left-wing organizations. We had a lot of fun. We had a wonderful time.*

The *Freiheit*, the IWO, and the Prospect Workers' Club were able to meet the cultural demands, both Jewish and proletarian, of the Followers, while at the same time exposing them to Communist ideology. These three organizations convinced the Followers that it was in their best interest as Jews and workers to sympathize actively with the goals of the Party. Those who did not join the Party followed the Communist political trail as fellow travelers.

Camp Followers of the Trail

Throughout the twenties, thirties, and forties, workers' camps were popular as vacation spots for those on the Jewish left. These camps were designed as proletarian resorts, places where a worker could afford to enjoy his or her weekends in the country with people of the same background. One camp described itself as "A Resting Place for Proletarians."[30] There was swimming, boating, hiking, basketball, volleyball, wholesome food, and clean air. There was also a fair amount of political propagandizing undertaken at the camps. Like the clubs, the camps invited influential figures on the Communist left to speak on the weekends. Teachers from the Jefferson School of Social Science (a workers' school in New York City) led discussions on the Soviet Union and the "Principles of Communism, Leninism, Dialectical Materialism, Revolutionary Parliamentarism." The *Freiheit* and *Daily Worker* were sold to guests. A significant portion of the money the camps raised, after the cost of upkeep and maintenance, went to the Communist Party, the *Freiheit*, and the *Daily Worker*. The first of these Jewish proletarian camps to emerge was "Nitgedaiget" (no worries), founded in 1923 near Beacon, New York. Camp Unity (Wingdale, New York), Camp Wocolona (Monroe, New York), designed for English-speakers, and Camp

Kinderland (Hopewell Junction, New York), a Jewish Communist children's camp, followed soon after.

Advertisements for the camps appeared frequently in the *New Masses*, the *Freiheit*, and the *Daily Worker*. On Tuesday, July 1, 1930, an ad for Camp Unity appeared in the *Daily Worker*:

UNITY CAMP. A COOPERATIVE CAMP FOR WORKERS. Gather Strength for the Looming Fight! Good Food, Comradely Atmosphere, Proletarian Sports, Recreation and Cultural Activities, Bathing, Boating, and Fishing in Lake Unity.[31]

On Monday, September 14, 1931, a piece of proletcult poetry titled "Red Front" was published in the *Daily Worker* to entice readers to spend their vacation at the proletarian camps.

OUR BATTLE IS GREAT, OUR FIGHTING IS VITAL
PROLETARIAN CAMPS MAKE US READY AND STRONG
PROLETARIAN CULTURE, SPORT AND RECITAL
TEACH US TO FIGHT WITH A SONG
COME TO WOCOLONA
COME TO NITGEDAIGET
COME TO UNITY AND KINDERLAND—
THEY ARE ALL WITHIN THE REACH OF YOUR HAND.[32]

And, on Tuesday, June 14, 1932, the following advertisement in the *Daily Worker* struck an authoritarian tone:

YOUR VACATION SHOULD BE SPENT IN A PROLETARIAN CAMP ONLY. The Month of June is ideal for vacation in the Proletarian Camps. Every dollar spent by a worker on rest and vacation must go to the institutions of our movement. GO TO YOUR THREE PROLETARIAN CAMPS. Nitgedaiget, Kinderland, Unity. ALL CAMPS HAVE UNIFORM RATES. $16.50 Per Week, Including Organization and Press Tax. NO COLLECTIONS.[33]

The Followers' decision to start their own camp was, no doubt, influenced by their experience with and support for the Stalinist politics and proletarian culture of the original camps. However, there was another factor—the work of Bernarr Macfadden. One of the original Followers recalls: "In 1920 there was a man named Macfadden who wrote in the newspaper *The World*. His idea was that we have to live outdoors, that we are too much confined to the inside—we live in the shop or the office or the factory. When you have free time, he said, be outdoors. This appealed to us a great deal. So we organized a group and we started to go hiking."

Bernarr Macfadden was born on August 16, 1868, in Mill Spring, Missouri. He was one of the most influential newspapermen of his time. He was the owner of the *New York Evening Graphic,* the *Automotive Daily News,* the *Investment Daily News,* and the publisher of *True Story Magazine* and *True Romances.* Macfadden is credited as the first to illustrate stories with photographs and as the inventor of the composite photograph. He was also the founder and editor of *Physical Culture* magazine. His articles on health were printed in a number of newspapers around the country. He wrote forty-two books dealing with health topics, ranging from *Asthma and Hay Fever* to *Womanhood and Marriage.* In addition to his extremely popular "How-To" books, he wrote two novels related to issues of health—*The Athlete's Conquest* and *The Strenuous Lover.* He also wrote and published a five-volume *Encyclopedia of Physical Culture.*[34] Clement Wood, in his biography of Bernarr Macfadden, compares him to a "guardian of the temple": "The human body, from the religious standpoint, is the temple of God. Judging by his entire life, his unaltering aim, and his wide achievement, Bernarr Macfadden, from this point of view, may be rightly regarded as the restorer, rebuilder, and guardian of the temple of the living God."[35] Macfadden was a champion of hiking and of the pure air found in the country. "The proper place to walk is in the country, away from the foul air and the dirt, dust and smoke incidental to urban life. If you live in the city your walk can be made more pleasurable and beneficial if you will ride out into the country before beginning it."[36] In *The Virile Powers of Superb Manhood: How Developed, How Lost, How Regained,* Macfadden emphasizes the importance of fresh country air. "Pure air is absolutely essential to life, to health. One can exist on bad air, but to exist does not necessarily mean living."[37]

Throughout Macfadden's work there is a consistent theme of bettering oneself through vigorous physical exercise. "THERE IS A WAY OF CHANGING YOUR UNHAPPY CONDITION FOR THE BETTER AS SURELY AS THERE IS A SUN IN THE HEAVENS!"[38] Macfadden's books urge his readers to take their lives into their own hands and make the best of them by embracing his regimen of physical culture. "DON'T BE A CHRONIC GRUMBLER! Cultivate the happy faculty of getting as much out of life as you can. Remember that your life after all is of your own making."[39] "Do not be satisfied with mediocrity: Push onward and upward."[40]

This upbeat message, emphasizing limitless possibilities, appealed to the Followers, all of whom originally left Europe to improve the quality of their lives. Macfadden's pitch to "take control of your life" and "change conditions for the better" echoed the revolutionary call to action that the Followers were exposed to, and for the most part absorbed at work, as readers of the *Freiheit* and as members of the IWO and the Prospect Workers' Club. Camp Followers of the Trail was influenced by the Communist Party's proletarian culture (the cornerstone on which Camps Nitgedaiget, Unity, and Wocolona were built), by a strong emphasis on the preservation of Jewish culture, and also by the physical culture of Bernarr Macfadden. The culture that the Followers managed to stitch together is revealed in their founding manifesto.

In a document titled "Camping as Our Ideal," one of the original members of Followers of the Trail establishes the multifaceted culture of the camp. She begins by discussing "the new movement of camping." She explains how factory workers in New York City started hiking out to the country to "find relief in Mother Nature." "We, the 'Followers of the Trail,' began to spend our best leisure time out in the open, close to Mother Nature's shrine, bathing our bodies in the silver rays of the sun, drinking to intoxication the air which is full of perfume from the plants and flowers surrounding us." The first three paragraphs of the document deal with the beneficial aspects of life with Mother Nature. The fourth paragraph establishes the Followers' political position: "'It is true,' we said, 'in the lap of nature we are children, but we are also children of a definite class—the working class. As devoted children we dare not forget the duties we owe to our class.'" Foremost among them is to "promote the struggle," "organize workers' cultural centers," and "see that our press is kept going."

We out here in the lap of Mother Nature, freed from the poisons of the city can more readily crystallize our aims, our ideals, bring ourselves up to the level of some of our dreams.

Our ideal, therefore, of camping is and should be a combination of both conscientiousness as members of a definite class and outdoor activities.[41]

The first advertisement that the Followers placed in *The Daily Worker* on August 4, 1933 is revealing. Far less politically strident than the advertisements placed by other camps, the Followers describe their camp's beautiful natural setting, its athletic facilities, and its easy access from New York City. The camp's political orientation is clear, but subtly mentioned—"Comradely Atmosphere," a lecture to be given by A. J. Muste on "Fascism in Germany."[42]

The Followers created their own camp to meet the increased demand made by workers for affordable vacation spots.[43] Perhaps more importantly, the establishment of Camp Followers of the Trail presented workers with a less dogmatic but no less politically committed alternative to the camps run by the Communist Party, such as Unity and Nitgedaiget. The Followers were interested in fresh air and radical politics, in maintaining their ethnic identity and fighting for equality, and above all, dedicated to improving their cultural standard of living. They were Followers of more than one trail.

Today many of the original Followers have become disillusioned with the radical politics of their past. A good number are passionate supporters of Israel as well as angry critics of the Soviet Union. Zionism, although rarely referred to as such, is now more acceptable. Communism is dealt with gingerly and somewhat suspiciously. The word, for many, conjures up bitter memories and shattered dreams.

For the Followers, the Hitler-Stalin pact of 1939, the exposure of Soviet antisemitism, and Khrushchev's shocking denunciation of Stalin at the Twentieth Party Congress in 1956 initially all proved to be the confusing pieces of what later became a devastating puzzle. It began to appear—slowly and unbelievably at first, all too real and painful later—that the very source of salvation—the Soviet Union—was riddled with the ugly sores of antisemitism. The evolution of Soviet antisemitism was a process that ultimately crushed the radical political spirit of many of the Followers.

The Followers, like the majority of rank-and-file Communists, were stunned to learn that the Soviets had negotiated with the Fascists in 1939. As Jews they were shaken and horrified. The anger and resentment that surfaced was quickly contained but not extinguished by the official Communist line. Molotov's dealing with Ribbentrop was presented as a necessary tactical move. Dedicated Communists—Party members and sympathizers—were expected to understand and defend the actions of the Soviet Union; they were instructed to do so by speakers, pamphlets, and newspapers that explained the necessity of a pact that appeared to be hammered out with the devil. Torn between political faith and ethnic allegiance, the Followers adhered closely to the word from Moscow. Despite this apparent political dedication, the Followers were confused and disturbed; the Hitler-Stalin pact was the first of a series of major events that set the process of doubt and eventual disillusionment in motion.

Rumors throughout the forties of Stalin's war on Jewish culture in the Soviet Union, the grim reality of Hitler's final solution in Germany, the traumatic nature of Senator McCarthy's witchhunt in the United States, Khrushchev's exposure and attack upon "the cult" and excesses of Stalin, were all factors that forced the Followers to critically reevaluate their lives as Jewish Communists and fellow travelers. They had embraced the ideals of internationalism because they believed that when realized the world would be much safer and more equitable for all of those who had been oppressed and exploited—especially Jewish workers. Their interest in radical politics was intimately tied to their ethnic and occupational identity. Communism seemed to promise relief from the historical oppression of antisemitism and the economic exploitation of capitalism. For the Followers, the fight for internationalism was their attempt to simultaneously affirm and protect their rights as Jewish workers.

When the dream became a nightmare, the ideological world that the Followers attempted to realize and hoped to perfect simply fell apart; they were isolated and attacked—accused by hard-line Communists of being potential Zionists, denounced by conservative, politically moderate, and socialist Jews for being anti-Jewish—religiously and culturally. Angry and disillusioned about the connection between the Soviet Union and antisemitism, thoroughly shaken by Hitler's selective barbarism, seriously frightened by McCarthyism—especially the politically charged execution of Julius and Ethel Rosenberg—it is not difficult to understand why the majority of the Followers became, in their words, "more Jewish conscious" and why they eventually turned toward Israel—a symbol of Jewish hope, unity, and survival.

In the years since 1952, when Camp Followers of the Trail was reorganized and renamed Reynolds Hills, a number of the original members have passed away and been replaced by predominantly American-born Jews who were managers rather than workers, liberals rather than radicals, and Zionists rather than internationalists. The arrival of these new members, often a generation younger than the original Followers, has transformed the community's collective spirit and energy. A small group of Party members and fellow travelers still exists. They receive the *Daily World*, formerly the *Daily Worker*, regularly. They are referred to by the camp's politically moderate faction as revolutionists and fanatics.

However, despite political differences, the camp remains a vibrant and supportive community. Lectures, concerts, and readings—all followed by folk dancing—continue to be well attended weekly events. The remaining members, most of whom are in their eighties, live together like family. Unlike many elderly people, who face growing older alone, the Followers have had the good fortune of growing old with those they know and trust in a community of their own design that keeps them actively engaged intellectually and physically. For over sixty years the camp has successfully met the needs of its members, initially providing the young Followers with the chance to realize some of their dreams and later allowing them to age with grace and dignity among friends.

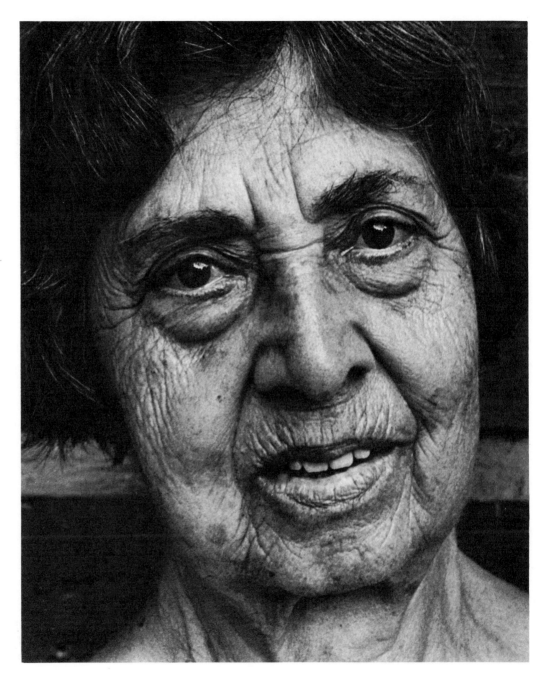

Anna T.

Morris H.

Sol S.

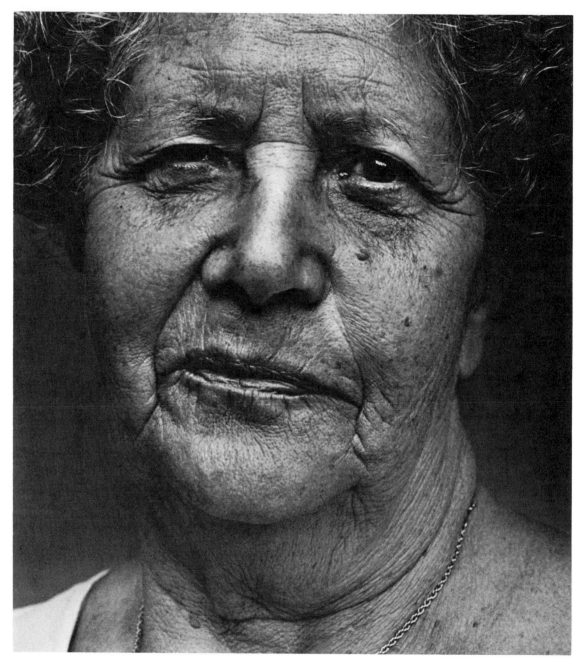

Bertha S.

Europe

Introduction

Regardless of where the Followers grew up—Russia, Austria, in the bustling streets of Minsk or along the dirt roads of a Galician village—they portray European life as circumscribed, unfulfilling, and without promise. Europe is remembered as a place in which youth's potential was stifled by antisemitism and orthodox Judaism.

Virulent antisemitism prevented Jews from traveling freely, pursuing higher education, and residing or doing business in certain cities and towns. Pogroms made life nerve-wracking; death was in the air, always lingering, a possibility at any time. Antisemitism served as a clearly defined external boundary, confining and hindering physical, economic, and intellectual mobility.

However, in addition to the restrictions imposed upon Jews by others, the Followers also reveal the ways in which Jews imposed restrictions upon themselves. Aspects of traditional Jewish culture, deeply rooted in orthodox religion, are recalled by the Followers as frustrating old world obstacles that limited ambitions and dreams. Almost all of the Followers were raised religiously, those who were not were nevertheless part of an overwhelmingly religious environment. Orthodox Judaism was not a force that any of the Followers could have ignored. A rigorous routine had to be maintained: from memorizing the Talmud, going to synagogue, and observing the holidays to keeping kosher and dressing according to established custom. All aspects of life, including what one ate, wore, and thought, were carefully outlined. There was virtually no alternative to, and even less tolerance for, deviating from the designated path.

Gender roles were rigidly defined. Men were expected to pray first, work later, and then pray again before eating and going to sleep. Education, almost exclusively reserved for males, stressed the importance of memorizing biblical passages rather than encouraging imagination and creativity. Women were expected to work as mothers, housewives, and more often than not, as breadwinners too. They were provided with only the most rudimentary education. Their religious experience was considered to be perfunctory rather than essential—their main task, lighting candles. Men and women were expected to marry young, raise children (usually between six and eight), and live, if not directly according to religious law, in deference to it. The Followers discuss the ways in which aspects of Orthodox Judaism made life simple, predictable, and essentially hopeless.

The externally imposed boundaries of antisemitism along with the internally imposed boundaries of religious tradition created a community of severe physical and intellectual limitations. The Followers describe this community as frightened and distrustful, primarily concerned with the rudiments of survival. Coming of age when revolutionary ideas and activity questioned all aspects of traditional European life, the Followers challenged an increasingly antiquated and fruitless world by leaving it behind. In doing so, they sought to overcome the external boundaries of antisemitism as well as the internal boundaries erected by their ancestors. By rejecting the limited nature of their community in Europe they initiated a search for a new sense of community based upon equality and promise rather than bigotry and superstition. They hoped to become part of a community that would explore possibilities rather than impose boundaries.

Jenya L.

Sol S.

Morris and Tecia H.

Reva Y.

Wolf U.

I was born at the dawn of the twentieth century. It's better not to be so precise. When you're precise, it's no good.

I was brought up in a village which had a couple of hundred families. At the entrance of the village they used to enumerate how many people lived there, how many horses they had, how many sheep. The village was Derevichi. I was one of those primitive little kids. I used to cry when I had to put on shoes. When I went to town, I had to put on shoes and that was a torture for me, because I always went barefoot.

We had horses, and I used to fly with the wind. I used to love to go. I worked in the field, swinging a big scythe all day, helping out a friend of mine. It was clean— flowers in the summer, orchards with all kinds of trees, apples, pears, plums, cherries. And we also had a big garden for vegetables, which was more or less sufficient for us for the winter. I took care of the cow. We usually used to have one cow that supplied us with enough milk and butter and sourcream.

Whenever people used to cross over from a little town known as Ostropol (which is known particularly for one of the legendary folk heroes of the Jewish nation—Hershl Ostropoler) they always used to stop in our house to be treated. They always liked sour milk and cream and whenever they offered something to pay, my mother used to be insulted. We always used to offer everybody something to eat, something to drink, and then they passed on. That was the custom.

Our house was old, two rooms were there. It was all thatched, and the floor was made out of mud. It was cool in the summer and warm in the winter because the walls were made a yard thick and that kept it air-conditioned.

I had two brothers and another sister who died at the age of infants. The mortality of the children was terrific at that time. Then I had another sister who, unfortunately, died by poisoning when she was sixteen. In the village we didn't have any doctors. We had one that used to come—the *feldsher*, something like a paramedic nowadays. Most of the time he was drunk. He used to carry the medicine in his pocket. My sister had croup, an inflammation of the throat. Since we lived quite a distance from the town and the feldsher obviously didn't know a hell of a lot, it was normal that she died. The mortality was very high. What he gave her I don't know, but she was poisoned and didn't last more than overnight.

My parents were not very religious, not fanatics. I myself was religious until the age of fourteen. I used to pray every morning. We had no synagogue at all. To pray, we used to gather together neighbors in a different village—we used to walk about five miles. On holidays we used to gather to pray. I remember I would pray very diligently. When it came Yom Kippur, there is a prayer of confessing all your sins. I didn't even know what sins were, but I more or less used to knock the hell out of myself—you beat yourself in the chest.

I followed the custom in the beginning. Later on, by reading and so on you begin to question the validity of all that and you come to some conclusion. Either you follow or you break it off. I broke it off completely. At the age of fourteen or fifteen, I started asking questions and not finding any logical answers. Then I turned away from religion completely. As a matter of fact, when my father died I was about sixteen or seventeen, and I refused to say kaddish even, because it was a question of praising God, which I didn't feel like doing. I didn't feel like following the tradition, no matter that it hurt my mother at that time. She more or less always followed the traditional religious ceremonies.

Before that, I left our home to go to town to study. Studying, as you know, is a peculiar thing in the Jewish nation. It was a necessity. Jewish people were deprived of their own land—to own land was forbidden. So no matter how hard it was for parents to send children to town and then on to bigger cities, they always tried to educate their children.

I graduated from one school, and then I went to Kremenets on the border of Austria-Hungary (later on it was Poland). But during the 1913 War the school was evacuated—it was actually closed down—and I had to look for another school. I landed all the way in a beautiful little town on the Russian steppes about ten kilometers from a radio station. It so happened that during the War we were cut off. My parents were on one side and I remained there without any kind of support. So I used to give lessons to my classmates, particularly in math, for a couple of years. When the Soviet government took over, I followed the army and I came home. That was in 1917, which was when my father died. I was about seventeen years of age.

This was a period of complete lawlessness. There was an upsurge of the Ukrainian nationalist movement, and there were a lot of periods when there was no kind of authority. Whoever wanted to exercise authority got a horse and a group of people and they were the ones that established themselves. They used to shoot a few people and instill fear. Very often we couldn't stay in our house—we used to go to the woods. We knew the woods very well, and that's where we used to spend our days. At night we used to sleep at a neighbor's. The Jews were the victims at that time, but not only the Jews, also anybody that had a few rubles, or was a little better to do.

That's the time we started to travel. We had to leave our home. We left everything there and traveled to an area that was under Poland. Somehow I found in the newspaper that an uncle I had in Camden, New Jersey, was looking for us. I got in touch with him, but it took a couple of years—until about 1920, before we came to the United States.

Bella S.

Our town was a very small town—the Jewish shtetl we used to call it. It was unfortunately divided between Gentiles and Jews. The Gentiles were on one side of the creek and the Jews were on the other side of the creek. The Jews had the commercial end of life—stores and services. The Gentiles produced products and brought them to sell to the Jews at the market. They spread their wares on the ground and the Jewish people would come out and do their purchasing. This was the relationship— the needs of the one and the services of the other. There was a close relationship between human beings, one to the other. If any friction occurred, it was in groups. Otherwise, life was quite peaceful and serene. People lived together for years and years unless they were instigated one against the other. Sometimes people were told that the Jews were the source of all evil.

We had a representative of our section in the Duma—it's equivalent to the Senate. When he came home, instead of teaching the people what's taking place in the Duma, he would instigate them against the Jews. "The fault is the Jews. You deal with them, they rob you. They don't pay you the right price for what you bring to market. They're rich. Look at the beautiful homes they have and look at the huts where you live." There was an upsurge of pogroms in Russia then. Every little town thought that they are next—a pogrom is bound to take place.

That was the time when there was organization. People would get together to organize self-defense groups at the various points in the town where people come in and go out, to see that no organized groups come into the town. A great tragedy happened then in our town. There was a Jewish doctor who was, so to say, the spiritual leader. When the danger seemed to come closer, he organized everybody to be ready to defend the town. It didn't come to it—perhaps because they were prepared. But when he was teaching one of the men to use firearms, the man was so ignorant that, the gun was loaded and he pointed it right at the doctor. There it was. He killed the doctor. That man got on a horse and he ran all through the town yelling, "People! I killed the doctor!"

At that time, there was a constant fear and my father related to us that when there was this fear that the organized groups would come in to make a pogrom, he would take me and my brother and another sister to the Gentile town to hide us there. They knew that we were very fearful and they were afraid that something might happen to us if some disturbance took place. So the relationships of the individual to the individual were very good. If my parents trusted us to the Gentile friend they had on the other side of the creek, that is an indication of the relationship.

The family in a small town was very close—close in the sense that your uncles and your cousins are there for centuries, for generations. People were born there, lived there, brought up children, the children brought up their children, without even venturing out to find out what the world outside this town is. That was due to circumstances, naturally, because transportation wasn't available, where you could just get on a bus and go to the other town. It was horse and buggy transportation.

But in those days, small town life was heaven. We were surrounded by fields, surrounded by woods. And ignorance was bliss. You didn't know to compare your ways to other ways. This was your way, this was how you lived, this was how you were brought up. Our town didn't even have as much as roads. It was all dirt roads. When it rained, you walked in the mud. In the spring the mud stayed for a long time because of the thawing out of the snow. The snow would stay there for three months, because we were in the northern part. But we didn't know the difference. When you don't know the difference, you are contented with what you have.

At a very young age, when I started to observe and see how our life is being provided by my father and by what means, I began to rebel. I began to rebel inside me that here is a man, doing nothing with his hands, not producing anything, and yet he makes a living. He was what we call here a broker. He would go to the lord of a town, let's say, and find out what he has got for sale—I mean in bulk, not for ten cents. Like a tract of wood, because there was a lot of wood being sold for burning and for cooking. He'd take that knowledge of his and he would bring it to the man that buys it. His commission was the means by which we were provided. In other words, he was a "commissioner." And I rebelled inside. It wasn't a question of discussing it and I would say, "Father, I don't like that you do this and that." I just felt, as a human being, that it is unjust and that as soon as I will be able to do something for myself, I will feel free and relieved.

Our town had no means whereby youngsters could make a living or could attain a profession. We had no schools there, none whatsoever. All our education came through tutoring. My parents paid for a tutor who would come in and teach us whatever he could teach us and whatever we needed. I remember my sister and my brother formed little groups in the evening to learn from one another. When I was beginning to grow up, I had some friends that came from wealthier parents than I had, and they had a better teacher. So we would get together and I would copy their lessons. My teacher wasn't so advanced, but we would get together and teach one another and help one another get the knowledge of the one that could attain it because of monetary stature.

When it came time for me to get a higher education, there was no way of doing it because I had to go to a different city, to a big city where they had a gymnasium. That meant that I would have to stay in that city and pay for everything—for food and room and schooling—and that was too much for my parents. They couldn't afford that. I had a brother and a sister in America already, so I thought that I would come to America and have a free education and advance myself.

The fact that my sister and brother could send home money to help out the family was already enough of an inducement for anybody to want to go to the United States. I remember there was a fellow that came back from America, and he was threatening me. "Bella, you want to go to America? Don't go." "Why?" "You'll have to sit at the machine for nine hours and you wouldn't be able to get up even. You wouldn't be able to do it. You'll get consumption. You'll get sick." He thought it was terrible. He came back with two hundred rubles—it was a lot of money—and he made himself a store. He didn't scare me. I had that feeling that I needed freedom to decide, to move, to attain.

I began to ask my sister and brother to take me to America. They asked my parents and my parents said no. My parents were reluctant to let me go because I was too young—when I came here I was fifteen. I kept on impressing my brother and sister with my reasoning and they, being free and having the opportunity to advance themselves while they were here, realized that I was right. And they sent me a ticket. I had to hide that ticket until the month I was supposed to go, so my mother shouldn't send it back. And then I came.

I wasn't of an age to get a visa myself. A group of people—a mother with some children—got passage, visas, passports. In that family there was one girl missing, so they put my name on their family's passport as this girl. She was a brunette, with dark hair, and I was light. When we came to the border to cross from Russia to Austria, the soldier that took care of that part of the border started to count the children and to look whether she is not a he or he is not a she. He took one look at me and he said, "This is your daughter? She is light and they are all dark." Right away I cried, because of the thought that they are going to separate me and send me back. But somehow or other he must have been a sensible guy and he let us pass the border. Once we passed the border, we went by train. My ticket was for Antwerp. All the other things were arranged. But this one night on the border I'll never forget—I cried so, I thought that that's the end of it.

It was both frightening and exciting. I left my sisters and brothers and mother and father. To begin with, it was my first experience to get into a train. I was never on a train. I would imagine it would be an adventure even for older people. But then I didn't have any difficulty, because there were always the agencies that transported people. The towns that we came to, where there were stops, there were always the men that took care of the people that went from place to place. When we came to the place where we had to wait for the ship, it was sort of a hotel and accommodations were wonderful—considering those days and not knowing how it was supposed to be.

Harry S.

I came from a small town which is hardly on a map. The name is Kantzuga. Originally, it belonged to Austria. Then after the First World War ended, it became Poland. Now, at this time, it belongs to the Soviet Union. It was a small, little town, with mostly Chasidic people.

I come from a very religious family. The whole city actually was an orthodox city. Mostly the Jewish people lived in the center of the city and the Gentiles lived on the outside of the city. As kids we were always afraid to go on the outside of the ghetto. It was not a closed ghetto, but when we came over to where the Gentiles used to live, naturally they always used to throw rocks at us.

The schooling system during the Austrian regime—before the War started—was compulsory. Each and every kid had to go to school. It's not like in Russia, where a lot of the Jewish kids were not allowed to go to school and they had to go to get private schooling. Here we had compulsory schooling up to sixteen years old. You had to go to school.

They had a law that you're not allowed to talk Yiddish in school. They wanted you to speak Polish. So during a recess, I was revolting and I deliberately spoke Yiddish. The kids came complaining that they heard me talk Yiddish. The teacher asked me, "Did you speak Yiddish?" I said, "Yes." I didn't deny it. She put me down and she gave me a beating with a bamboo stick. It hurt pretty hard.

This was a public school—government school. Then besides that, after that, we had to have religious school. We had religious teachers to teach us to read and write Hebrew, the Bible, and the Talmud.

To be a religious Jew you have to learn how to read the prayers and learn the blessings. I remember when I was three years old—and this is a tradition among religious Jews, Chasidic Jews—when a boy gets to be three years old, they cut off his hair but they leave his sidelocks, and then they take him to a cheder, where they have a teacher, not exactly a rabbi, but a man that teaches reading. I remember, when I was three years old—and this incident I remember like it happened yesterday—that my father carried me on his hands and he was covered up in a prayer shawl and he brought me to this cheder where they teach in Hebrew only. It's the tradition that they bring you there and they teach you the alphabet, and then there's a celebration for all the kids that are around. They gave them a cookie, and then they took me home.

After that, when you're a year older and ready to walk, you start going to cheder and they start to teach you to read, they teach you the alphabet in order you should read the prayer books yourself. I can say that among the religious Jews there is no such thing as an illiterate. Among the Jews there is a saying that the Jews are the people of the book. There was a lot of discrimination against Jews, and in order for them to be able to secure a job they had to be better than the rest of the population, and therefore they had to get themselves educated.

I was brought up practically without a father. My father died when I was ten years old. Before he died, he was sick. I remember him faintly. I remember on one occasion he took me to a dentist to another city—they had to pull some teeth. I remember that he had a nice red beard, but to remember him playing with me or taking me some-wheres, I do not remember that. I vaguely remember, because my father was a book-binder and a glazier, so when it came nights we would be in the house and he was working binding books—this I remember vaguely. As far as relationships between father and son, I didn't have any.

While I was studying the Talmud, we used to study a whole week and when it came the beginning, on Saturday, we'd get into somebody—a parent—and he would try to see how much the boy learned. Since my father was dead, I used to go to my next-door neighbor. He was a learned man, and he had a boy about the same age as I. He asked him to read one of the pages, you know, to explain to him the pages from

Talmud. He started asking questions about it, but he couldn't answer. Then he asked me the same question, and I knew it completely. I answered correctly because I did my studying pretty well. So he puts his son right alongside of me and he says, "Look at him. He knows and you don't. Look who he is and who you are." In other words, that he has got a father that is a learned man, and he expected his son to know. I came from a working class family and I am not supposed to know—in other words, he should know better. I felt very bad. At that time, actually, I started to feel a class difference. He, a businessman, a rich man, and here, we were not poor, but we struggled for a living—I come from different stock. I just felt like running out, but I kept my composure and by the time I came home I felt very bad. I didn't want to go back to that house anymore. I don't know that this was the first time that I became class conscious, but I had it on my mind. It's already a story every bit of sixty-five years, and I still have it in front of me.

The religious life was a matter of believing. You were taught to believe. In other words, it was a one-sided affair. It was not a question of reading outside books of different philosophies or different religions, or anything like this. You knew you were a Jew, you had to believe in God. This was God's commandments and you had to abide. There was never a question of doubting—you wouldn't doubt. That was a way of life.

In a sense I feel that if you believe in something, you're a happy person. We believed that everything, no matter what happens, is from God. We had faith in it, you see. But once you get older and you don't believe, then you're already not happy because you figure life wouldn't be as good as it is because if you don't believe in God you don't think God is going to help you and you don't see the outlook as any better. The time we were religious, we were happy people. I mean, it didn't help us in any way with our standard of living, but we were contented. God willed it that way, and that's the way it was. We were happy. We had no idea that somebody lives different than we do. We were contented—this was the way of life.

In my particular section where I came from, they would wear those Chasidic gowns and they had the *peyes* [sidelocks] and hats. The lifestyle was medieval, stagnant like. There was nothing to look forward to, unless somebody would get married and move to a bigger city. In a bigger city, you would have a different life. The fact is, I lived in a small town. We didn't have any electricity, no running water, no sanitary conditions. We had outhouses. And we were contented with it. You see, say, if you eat bread all your life and you haven't got anything else, the bread is wonderful. But if you start to eat white bread instead of plain bread, you say the white bread is better than the black bread, then you say you've got an improvement. Then if you get cake, you eat the cake, and it's still better than the bread. But if you have bread and you haven't got anything else, this is good, you like it, and this is it. But once you make any changes you keep on taking the better thing.

I was the oldest of three brothers. The youngest was about nine years younger than I and my other brother was two years younger. Then I had a sister who was two years older than I and I also had one sister that got killed. After my father died, my mother could not take care of the house. She had to take care of the business. While she was in the store the kid walked over from the house—she had to cross the street from the house to the store—and there was a horse and wagon with wheat that they were taking to a mill to grind into flour. The horse was galloping and she was going in the street, and it ran over and killed her. This was a tragedy on top of another tragedy.

The law there was that up to the age of seven the mother has to be in constant watch over the child—in other words, it's her responsibility if something happens. So when that girl was killed, they prosecuted my mother for neglecting the child. This was only about a year after my father died. The only reason they let her free was because the lawyers claimed that she was the father and the mother and she had to provide for the other children. On that basis, she was let free. She was not arrested, she was not put in jail, but the point is they were prosecuting her for neglect of the child.

When my father died, bookbinding was more of a skilled trade and my mother didn't know how to take care of it. So she had to stick to the glazing. It was a store and we used to sell picture frames. Especially in Europe, the Gentiles would go to church Sundays and all their holidays and they all decorated their houses with religious pictures—of the Madonna and of Christ and all that—and we would frame it for them. Then we also would sell different things, like for instance there was no electricity, so we would sell lanterns to put in candles, and we would sell glass and little mirrors. It was not so hard, you could sell something over the counter.

I had to stay in the store and help her sell, help her frame pictures. We used to get the moldings and we had a miter box and we'd make frames. Every four weeks there used to be a bazaar and all the farmers would come into the city to buy some stuff, and we were very busy. They used to come to frame those religious pictures. We knew already the sizes, and they would come in and we would frame. Later on, as we got a little bit older, I would take some glass with my older sister and we would go to the farms. We'd take a box of glass on our shoulders and putty, and look around in the houses, the richer homes. The reason we looked for the richer homes was because we didn't only want to get money for the work we were doing, we wanted to get instead of the money some products. We used to get fresh fruit or flour—there was a shortage already. The War started and there was a shortage of all these things. So we used to walk one way with the glass and return back with the products. Many a times when we'd bring it back, my mother would share it with the neighbors, with the poor people, send some bread to one or some butter.

You see, in Europe they do like this. We had enough flour to bake bread. We did not buy bread in bakeries. We used to bake it ourselves, once a week. I remember one incident—it happened to be every Friday, we used to go to the neighbors, poor people, and bring each one a loaf of bread. There was one particular party, she had her husband in the United States and at that time you couldn't hear from the United States at all, and she was too proud to accept charity. My mother wanted to help her, but she was afraid she was going to get insulted because she would be too proud to take it. I would hide the bread under my coat and go to a next-door neighbor and give it to the neighbor for the neighbor to give it to her, in order that she shouldn't feel that she's getting charity. Every Friday my mother would send me, my sister, and my younger brother to give food out.

I remember one incident. . . . I used to go to the farmers and carry glass and on the way we would meet the shepherd boys, taking care of their cows, and they would see a Jewish boy going by and they would beat you up, break the glass. But then it stopped. I came in to one farmer—I was there the week before and I took an order from him for some glass that he needed just before the wintertime, it was in the fall that we used to do that—and I was carrying the glass to him. I came over and I didn't have the glass. He said, "What happened?" I said, "The kids met me on the way and they broke the glass." He knew which way I was coming and just about when I was talking to him a kid came in for lunch. He came in with the cows. So he said, "Was he one of them?" I didn't want to squeal on him because I was afraid the next time he was going to beat me up. So I said, "No, I didn't see him, there were a lot of kids. I couldn't recognize any of them." But he knew. He told the kid, "Listen, this here Jew boy is coming to help us. I know that you were there and I know exactly who beat him up and who broke his glass. From now on," he said, "you have to watch out that nothing should happen to him. If something should happen to him I'll tell him to come and tell me, and you are going to get beaten up." Since that time, for quite a while, I was left alone. Not only that, every time I passed by, they just made a way for me.

Naturally, when you were young you did not go out of your area. As you got older you start going places, to different parts of the city, or you pass near the church—the church was near the end of the city, the synagogues were all in the vicinity of the Jewish section. When I was helping my mother and I had to go to the Gentile section to work many times I passed by and I was wearing peyes, and they would pull my peyes, and, you know, the kids would wear hats, so they would throw your hat off. We were confronted with the same in school. The Jewish kids, especially the religious kids, didn't want to go bare-headed. We would wear yarmulkes. And the Gentile kids would always harass us, throwing off the yarmulkes, pulling them off so we would be bare-headed, or pull the peyes, or something like that.

The First World War broke out in August. The Russians came in and they were there for about three or four weeks. As they came in, they started looting, and then not only did they start the looting, but the Polish people started to also loot and break windows. Then they were driven out and the German and Austrian armies came and chased them back. Then they came back for another time. About six weeks later, they came back again, and they were going toward the Carpathian Mountains. Then it became an occupation government.

During the occupation, things were normalized, but when they started already to go away, then they started to fight right over our heads. We were in a valley—on one side were mountains and on the other side were mountains. They kept on shooting across, and we were constantly living in basements. During that particular time, the Polacks would keep on robbing us—breaking windows and breaking into houses and things like that—so you felt already that you wanted to get away.

We had enough to eat and especially during the shortage we were fortunate because glass was very hard to get, especially during the War. My mother was a very liked person, even among the wholesalers. The wholesalers were not from our town— they were in a bigger city. We would hire a horse and wagon to go into the next town to bring boxes of glass and buy merchandise. My mother always got it, because they had pity on her—she was a widow with five small children. So they gave it to her. With this, we were able to manage.

Toward the end of the war things were getting bad. They started really organized pogroms. Jews would be riding on trains, they would throw them out through the windows. A Jew would walk in the street with a beard, they wouldn't cut it off with a scissor, they would cut if off with an axe. You were afraid to walk out on the street. Living was not normal. We started to get letters from the United States.

My mother had a brother in the United States. He was there a long time because my mother was in the United States when she was seven years old. She left with her family when she was twenty-one years old. She was in the United States for fourteen years. Her brother remained there because he was married, and her family—she and her brother and her father and mother—went back. That was in 1898. There was a crisis that time, a depression. The family was in the clothing business. So they went back to Europe and then my mother got married.

All of my friends received letters, their fathers were in the United States. Because most of the people that were economically badly off, the husband would go to the United States and send back money to the family, and then eventually he brought them over to the United States. Some of my friends received already from their families that they're going to go to the United States. So I said to my mother that I would like to go also. "All my friends are leaving. How about writing to my uncle to send me a visa to come to the United States?"

My mother was objecting to me going, because she went through hardship when she was here and she said it's not so good. Most of the people thought that in the United States you shovel gold in the streets. People were under that impression, but my mother was a realist, and even those people that wanted to go, she kept on telling them the bad things—that you have to work hard. An operator who worked in a shop had to bring her own machine. You walked and you carried it. She was telling us these stories. Or, she told me a story that in a shop they had the pressers pressing clothing, so in the middle of the shop there was a big oven and the irons were standing around and heating, and in that heat they had to work. She pictured a very hard picture and she said, "The mere fact that I was there is enough. You don't have to go."

But then it started already that Russia was fighting with Poland, and they were going to mobilize the people from eighteen to fifty. I was about to become eighteen years old. I was born in 1902. When she realized that I had to go to the army, instead of going to the army it was better to go away to the United States. When I applied to the United States to take out a passport I couldn't get the passport because I was so close to eighteen. So I had to take the certificate from my brother's age. My brother was two years younger. I took out the certificate on his age and I got the passport.

After I got the passport, I had to go and get the visa. For the visa, I had to go to Warsaw. That was quite a distance. It must have been about twelve hours traveling by train, and I never was outside of my hometown. I never saw a different city. I went with my sister then—my sister is two years older than I. We went to Warsaw, but when we got to Warsaw, they were fighting just near Warsaw—the Bolsheviks were fighting the Polish that time. The American consul left Warsaw on account of the fighting, so they told us that we had to go to Prague, to Czechoslovakia, in order to get the visa from the American consul in Czechoslovakia. So we left Warsaw. Then we proceeded to Prague. We got the visa. Then for the other visas—I had to get the Belgian visa—once you got the American visa, it was easy to get.

I was still religious. As a matter of fact, in Belgium we were put in one of the ship company's hotels and in that hotel they used to eat ice cream. I never saw ice cream before in my life. Next door to the hotel there was an ice cream parlor. The ice cream was something like custard. It was not the same ice cream like we have here. But I never saw it before. We didn't have it. So after every meal, we had to go and buy ice cream. But we wouldn't buy on Saturday. I would pay in advance on Friday for the ice cream so that I shouldn't make any business transaction on Saturday. I was still religious. I put on every day the tefillin. In the meantime, I had my eyes opened. I kept looking around, looking at buildings and looking at stores. I kept on walking from one place to the other, taking in the world.

There was also a boy there a few years older than I and he couldn't get a ticket. In order to get a steamship ticket, you had to go and have your eyes examined. They were very particular about trachoma—a certain disease on the eyes. He was there to be cured, and he was there already three months. So he gives me a plan that I should go—after I got already my steamship ticket—I should do him a favor and go and get my eyes examined by the doctor and give his name. I know from nothing, so I go. To do someone a favor, anytime. So, I go to the doctor to examine me, and I give his name and everything else, and I come back and give him the certificate from the doctor. They had no records. It was a big place. You don't go to the same doctor. Then he went to the steamship company and showed them that he had his eyes examined.

I asked him, "What will you do when you come to the United States, to Ellis Island, if something is wrong?" He said that when he comes to Ellis Island his relatives told him not to worry, they'll get him out of there. When we passed the English Channel from Belgium to England, as we got off the boat there is a doctor—three doctors—standing there, and they examine your eyes. They wouldn't let you into England because of the eyes. I had a plan. As you went out they put on a tag that you are OK. When I went out, he was in the back yet. After I went out, I left my satchel outside with my sister and I went back. I told them I forgot my satchel in the back. They let me back, and I gave him my ticket. Then I went out to a different doctor and I had my eyes examined. They didn't examine him because he had the ticket. So he went through. The danger of doing that—if they caught me, they could have sent me back. But the mere fact of doing somebody a favor, you forget—you don't feel any danger. You want to do it, and that's all.

When I consider a European youngster of eighteen, I figure him a man of thirty-six, not eighteen—especially what I went through. Since I was ten years old, I went through life already, like a man with responsibility. Here I envy the kids, that they didn't have to go through what we went through. All my life I hoped that my children have it better than I. I accepted no matter what—no matter how bad things were, it was better than I had before. So I accepted it. I didn't have anything good. Any hardship was better than I had. I didn't take it as anything bad. It didn't bother me. Of course, youngsters when I tell them what I went through at that particular age, they don't believe it. You have some people that are married and have two children and they don't have the responsibility that I had at the age of eighteen.

I feel I missed out, but I don't feel bad about it. For instance, I never played ball, I didn't go to any movies, I didn't go to any theater, I didn't go to the circus. I didn't have all these things, but nobody else had it. So it's not a question that I missed out on it. I missed out now that I see I didn't have it—so I can't catch a ball, or I don't know how to swim. But I don't feel bad about it. I don't begrudge the time. That was the way of life. It was a different standard than people have here. That's why a lot of people came here—because they wanted to better their condition.

Max T.

I was born in 1905, in the town of Yourovich. It was in the state of Minsk, but it was quite a distance from the city of Minsk. The nearest city to Yourovich was Mozyr, which was located on the banks of the river Pripet, which went through Yourovich down to Kiev, and on the way it fell into the river Dnieper.

Yourovich was a small town. It had a Main Street and a few little streets. At the end of the Main Street there was a road which went to a lake. We used to go swimming there in the summer time. There was also a forest where people used to spend their Saturdays. It was a resort—people used to come there for their vacations. There was no amusement park and no hotels, but they would stay in neighbors' houses. The climate was beautiful.

We were surrounded by forests and fields where the peasants grew their wheat and other grains. On the hill, we had a beautiful church that served the villages. It was a majestic Greek Orthodox church, with onion cupolas. On holidays, the Gentile people of that vicinity used to come out with their flags and their ikons, and it was really impressive. Really impressive. It was very, very interesting. We were surrounded also by peasant villages, which we used to call the *dorf*. The Jewish people did not live in the dorf.

The peasants lived a simple life at that time. Naturally, they were under the influence of the czar, and they thought that to get to the czar is like going to heaven to see God. The peasants lived a life of ignorance to the extent that they did not even know how to speak their own language. If a man from a village traveled fifty miles away and used the same language that he used in his vicinity, the other people would find it difficult to understand colloquial terms which were applicable in his vicinity but not fifty miles away.

In normal times the relationship between the Jews and the Gentiles was amicable, because one depended on the other. Most of the Jewish people in our area were artisans—shoemakers, tailors, watchmakers, storekeepers—and the peasants were forced to come and avail themselves of these services because they didn't have them in their own villages.

The Jewish people had three synagogues. They lived like in a ghetto, and one made a living out of the other. If a Jew wanted to have a pair of shoes made or repaired, he did not go anywhere except to the artisan Jew that was located in that vicinity. The shoemaker who needed leather bought it from the man that had a leather establishment there. It was like a circle. One made a little out of the other.

There was a definite separation between certain groups of Jewish people in the town. The storekeepers were the elite. Then there were the artisans. If you had a needle and an iron and a sewing machine, and you established a little factory to be able to make a pair of pants or a jacket for somebody, you were already in business. You owned the means of production. That meant you were already a boss, and you could employ a worker who could not afford to own his own means of production. He had to sell his labor. We are going into Marxism here. So there was a separation between these two Jews—the owner, the one that has, and the have nots, who are dependent upon another.

When you came to the synagogue, there was a separation there, too. There was the western part, for the less affluent Jews or the paupers, and there was the east wall, which faced Jerusalem, for those who deserved it because they were wealthy. Also, in my town, every Saturday when they read the Torah, they used to sell the privilege to come up to the rostrum and help read a certain portion. It was sold in auction. The one that could afford to buy it had the privilege of choosing the better part of that portion of the scroll. Those that could not afford it didn't get anything. Only on Simchas Torah everyone was alike. That celebrates the time when the Jews accepted the Torah from God. And on Simchas Torah the Torah was taken out of the cabinet and was handed over to the people to dance around the rostrum. It kept on changing hands, and all the Jews that wanted to had a chance to do it. This was the custom in the town where I was born.

I was never religious. When I became thirteen, my mother, being a Jewish woman, wanted me to become bar mitzvah. She was not very religious, but it's a custom. She grew up in that atmosphere from years back and she retained all that. To become bar mitzvah, you have to be in the synagogue on a Saturday morning after the prayers, and they call you over when they read the scroll, and you make a prayer. Then they pronounce you a man in your own standing. And that costs money.

At that time, my father was in America and my mother didn't have the money. So they refused to perform the ritual. My mother said, "Well, maybe you can go to the other synagogue." I went to the other synagogue, and they refused to do it also. I said, "Look, if the two synagogues said no, why the hell should I go to the third one?" I was never bar mitzvahed. I definitely was hurt because of the money aspect. There was no reason why the same kid that was there that had the money to pay for it was given all the honors and all the prayers and all that crap, but I, an innocent boy, just as innocent as the other one, should be discriminated against. There was something wrong somewhere. My mother was hurt, but if you are not politically aware of what is going on, then you don't know what to make of it. It's God's will.

In 1914 my father went to look for his fortune in the United States. My mother had a married sister in Philadelphia—she came about ten years before. So my father thought that he has a base in this country and he might be able to establish himself here. Sure enough, he did. He came and his brother-in-law gave him a very good job in a factory that he was managing, and he made a very nice living.

We struggled. My mother would buy certain things, like soap, and go out to the peasants to sell it. It wasn't a question of money, it was a question of barter—to sell it for grain, or for flour, or for potatoes. If we had a piece of bread, we were happy. That was for the whole day. If we had a potato with it, it was a holiday. As far as milk was concerned, we didn't have a cow of our own. Sometimes a neighbor of ours—a good neighbor—would send in a can of milk and then we were happy. We would divide it among ourselves and have a good time. It was a very difficult life. It was degrading, but it was not of our choosing. We just couldn't help it. This is how we lived until 1917, when the Revolution came. When the Revolution came, it was an upheaval.

I was too young to participate in making the Revolution, but I was old enough when it came time to fight to defend it. When I was fourteen years old, I joined the Komsomol and I happened to be the Secretary of the unit. I had a rifle that was twice my size, and I was afraid of it. I was in the Soviet Union when Lenin was shot. I was in the Soviet Union when the ideological conflict between Trotsky and Stalin came about. Stalin had to win. His analysis of Marxism was much better as far as building socialism in one country was concerned, because the capitalistic world didn't become capitalist all over at the same time, on the same day. In the same way, if Trotsky waited to build socialism until the world revolution, we would never have a Soviet Union now. My father knew Trotsky before the Revolution, when he lived in New York. He showed me the street and he pointed out to me the building that Trotsky lived in. Right after the Revolution, Trotsky shot back to Russia. He was a tremendous orator. A tremendous orator. And I was right there.

During the time of the Civil War, after the Revolution, I was running away from bandits. We went to the places where the Bolsheviks were in power. I didn't eat for three days at one time—there was no food, nothing. The Central Committee of the government was not organized too well and the distribution was difficult because the bandits were bombing all means of transportation and killing people. We were a group of people, and we went to a big city which was occupied by the Bolsheviks. I was walking on the street and I found a crust of bread in the gutter. I picked it up, but it was so hard, I couldn't chew on it—I couldn't even nibble a small piece of it. But I didn't throw it away. I put it in a conspicuous place because I said to myself that there may be somebody else that would be able to tackle it. The Red Army took care of the bandits eventually. That's part of history.

During the Civil War, there were nineteen countries that invaded Russia right after the Revolution—to choke it, to prevent it from coming to life. They did not succeed, but our town was one of those parts that they tried to choke off. The Polish army, well equipped, well dressed, and well fed, came in and the Jewish people there were very happy when the Bolsheviks were driven out.

The storekeepers, the artisans, and the clergy didn't want the Bolsheviks. They didn't want to have a socialist revolution. The fact is that one of the clergy said, "Now look, socialism is alright, but suppose I need something to write a scroll on. Where would I get the material? Would I go to the commissar and ask him for it when he is an atheist?" You see? Such a narrow mind. At that time they just couldn't understand how it works. They didn't realize that by supporting the allies, they were encouraging the Czarist generals to perpetuate themselves in power—the same ones who were previously making pogroms on the Jews. After the Revolution, they were also making pogroms on the Jews, claiming that if not for the Jews there would never be a Revolution.

Some of my relatives were killed then. The Jewish people at that time—the storekeepers, the bourgeois intelligentsia—were between the devil and the deep sea. They didn't know which side to turn to.

We didn't leave Yourovich until it was possible for us to reunite the family by coming to the United States. I couldn't let my mother and three sisters go by themselves. I really carried the burden. My mother and my sisters could not have made it without me. I had to be there. You couldn't do anything without an agent. We came to this country in January 1923, when I was eighteen. The year before we spent in traveling. That year I was more productive—negotiating transportation, making documents to come to this country, and all other things. You had to communicate with the United States through the consul. My mother was an illiterate person and she spoke only one language—Yiddish. I had to be the seeing-eye dog. I spoke Russian in addition to Yiddish, and I spoke Hebrew. During the time that we were in Poland, I learned to speak Polish.

When we left the Soviet Union, we had to steal across the border into Poland. We were not the only immigrants. There were transports of four or five wagons of people. We crossed the border almost without incident, although right on the borderline the Soviet patrol stopped us. But there was nothing that a bottle of vodka and some crackers couldn't patch up. We came to Poland illegally, and we had to make documents. The first stop was Revna. From Revna we went to Lemberg—which is now Lvov, in the Soviet Union. Then, from Lvov, or Lemberg, we went to Warsaw. We couldn't live in Warsaw even though we had documents already and we were legally waiting for our visas. So we lived on the outskirts of Warsaw.

The life between a socialist country just forming and an established capitalist country cannot be compared. The life that we lived in Poland was heaven. My father sent us money. We had everything we wanted. We used to buy clothes and food. My mother was very happy. She was well fed, she and her four children were taken care of, and she had the expectation that soon she would be in New York, with her husband. They loved each other very much. It was unfortunate that they had to be separated for nine years. Maybe it was a good thing, because they probably would have had another couple of children if they would have been together.

But in Poland there was always somebody that said something against the Soviet Union. I couldn't for the life of me understand that—it was like being against yourself, against your own interests. I just couldn't understand it. But, as time goes on, you become accustomed to these things. I had a little Marxist-Leninist background, and I could assess the political situation in the world.

Harry G.

I was born in 1906, in the Ukraine, in a small, little town called Balin. In the whole town there were only seventy-two families. The town was mostly Jewish— only two Gentiles. We had one synagogue and we had a bath, a very small one. Then the bath burned down, so we didn't have a bath. In summer we used to go to the lake—a small, little lake—and we used to wash ourselves there. But we couldn't swim. In winter, if you had wood, you used to make your own hot water and wash.

Naturally, we all were religious. I didn't know so much about religion, because I didn't go to school, but I used to go to shul on Saturday and we used to pray.

We didn't have any electricity, we didn't have movies, we didn't have theater. The only thing was once a year on Purim, the Jewish holiday, everybody celebrated. The town used to get together and about eight people would put up a show. That's the only show we had.

I remember when my father left for the United States in 1913. We were eight children. There were just too many children and he didn't have any work. So he just left. Before he left, he did whatever had to be done. He used to go among the peasants and buy corn or wheat and resell it. But he couldn't make a living, and that's why he left for the United States. My mother didn't do anything. She had so many children, she didn't have a chance to do any kind of work. Then one sister died, and we remained seven. Then my older brother left for Odessa. He was a revolutionist at that time.

When my father left for America in 1913, my older brother was about thirteen or fourteen. He was a revolutionist and the police were after him. My brother had a Russian education and he spoke Russian fluently. In our town not everybody could speak Russian. We understood Russian, but unless you went to school, you spoke Ukrainian. My brother spoke Russian fluently. We had one policeman in the whole town and he was looking for my brother because my brother was some kind of revolutionist. My mother had to make him a pair of boots, and he left to go to Odessa. Odessa was very far away. We never heard from him until after the Revolution. In 1919 he came to see us. He gave us a few pennies. He enlisted in the Red Army as a volunteer. They needed him because he spoke Russian and he was a very good speaker—like an orator. He never wanted to come to America and he never wanted us to send him money. In 1924 my father sent him a few dollars, and he sent it back. He never would take any money from us, and he wouldn't come to America. However bad it was in the Revolution—a lot of people ran away—my brother would never run away. Up until 1939 we used to correspond with him. Since 1939, we haven't heard from him and we can't locate him. He was in different towns and different cities, and we never could locate him.

In 1919, when I was about thirteen years old, my mother died. She died of typhus. It was a certain sickness that would go around like an epidemic. All the people that had food survived, but if you didn't have plenty of food, you died. We didn't have much food. In my town eight or ten people died of the same sickness. They didn't charge us for my mother's burial. The people who buried you usually took a few dollars from the rich people, but if you were poor, the religious people came and they buried you free. There was no charge for her burial. When my mother died, that's when the trouble started.

I was the oldest of the children then. We were four brothers and two sisters. The youngest was about five years old when my mother died. We couldn't go out to work. I used to collect old scraps, bottles—anything I could make a penny with. The only thing we could do was to help people—to bring water from the well or sometimes help a farmer in the field. We had a small house—a bedroom, a kitchen, and a little foyer. We all used to sleep in one room. There was no kerosene for light, so night time we couldn't read—we couldn't do anything. Whatever we did was until the sun went down, until it was good and dark. Especially after my mother died, we didn't have any money, we didn't have shoes or clothing or food.

In the morning, if we had sugar, we would have tea. We didn't have milk. We had milk very, very seldom. Very seldom. We were lucky if we had bread. The children always used to fight for bread. Always. We used to divide it up, and always there was grumbling—this one got a bigger piece. One sister always used to cook. She was a little one, but she used to cook—when we had food. She would make tea, make potatoes, cook corn. Sometimes the butcher would give us a little lung, or something. He used to go in the slaughterhouse to slaughter, and I used to keep the lights on for him every Saturday night, late in the evening, because he was religious. So he used to give me a piece of meat, or a piece of lung or liver or something. It was like a picnic.

Winter was very hard. Summertime wasn't so bad—somehow we had food. Summertime we used to beg from the farmers, and we used to steal potatoes from the fields. We used to steal cherries and fruit from the trees. My main thing was the cemetery. We had a Christian cemetery, and on the cemetery we had pears, cherries, and apples. We were the main customers.

We were very undernourished and we had no shoes. One of my sisters used to make us shoes from old clothing or old rugs. When the war broke out, we didn't have any clothes. We used to get bags from sugar and make pants. Sometimes we used to take two bags—you'd buy them or steal them—and give them to the tailor and he would make you a pair of pants. Or my sister used to make it. Summer it wasn't so bad. We used to go barefoot. In the winter we used to stay in the house.

At that time, in 1919, it was the Revolution. Everything was broken up. Ninety percent of our neighbors didn't have food themselves. If they had, they couldn't spare it for us.

In 1919 the Bolsheviks came in, and the Red Army established a bakery about a mile out of my town. I used to go every day to get bread and scraps. They used to give me bags from the flour and we made pants and shirts from the bags. In 1920 it was a little bit better. It was Communist then. A lot of people came in from the Soviet Union. They started to make a railroad near us. They brought in peasants to build the railroad and to build roads. There were a lot of people there, and I used to help them do anything. I used to get bread from them.

I had a lot of envy for the peasants. Somehow they were very nice to me. When I used to come into the house of a peasant and tell him I'm hungry, he used to give me a loaf of bread or a couple of pounds of apples or radishes—by us, the radishes grew very big. Sometimes I used to help them and my sister used to help them. They were very nice to us. I can't complain about the peasants.

The only time we used to have trouble was when a lot of peasants would come in to buy whiskey. Before the Revolution, in Russia, there used to be liquor stores controlled by the government. When the Revolution came in, there were no more liquor stores. You couldn't have a liquor store. So you used to have black market whiskey. Some Jewish people used to make it from wheat. So the peasants used to come in when they had money to buy liquor. They used to get drunk and sometimes they used to fight and break a window. But they were not exactly antisemites.

We had peasants that were within walking distance and peasants who were very far away. I knew which peasants were sympathetic to poor people, and they used to give us bread. Sometimes when we worked on the beets, the peasant girls used to come to work, too. For lunch, they used to bring a lot of bread with them, and cakes, hard-boiled eggs, pork, and other things. We didn't have, so they used to give us. They were very sympathetic to us.

In 1920 we got mail from my father in America. He sent us money, but it went back. In the Soviet Union, it sometimes took a year for a letter. My neighbor told me that the only way to correspond with my father was through Poland or Romania. During the Revolution, there was a lot of contraband—black market. Poland had a lot of food. Romania had food, clothing, a lot of stuff. They used to smuggle things into the towns on our side. So we'd give them a couple of pennies to take a letter to drop in the post office. From there, in two or three weeks, the mail used to go to America. My father wrote that he sent some money for us to a HIAS [Hebrew Immigrant Aid Society] in Poland. So I went there.

My town was about sixty miles from the Polish border. I went from town to town until I came there. When I started out, my neighbor gave me about five cents and a piece of bread. I walked a whole day until I came to the next town. You could have two ways to sleep—either in the synagogue or knock on a door and hope somebody would take you in. It was very difficult to knock because a lot of people were afraid. When I came to one town, a peasant asked me where I was going. I told him and he took me in his wagon—a horse and wagon. He went out of his way. I slept in his house one night and then he gave me a half a loaf of bread and some salt pork. We never ate pork. We were taught that pork is not kosher and it is the worst thing, but I had enough bread, so I went further—until I came there.

The main problem was to cross the lake at the border. The Communists—the Soviet Union—wouldn't let us cross there and the Polish wouldn't let us cross there. At night a lot of people would swim across, but I couldn't swim, so I waited. A lot of people were drowned there. In winter there were less problems—you could find out in the town how the water was frozen, and then walk over. But when I went, I had to wait. Finally, a guy took me on his shoulders and he swam over. He wanted to protect himself. Sometimes they would shoot, but if you had children with you, they were more or less skeptical to shoot.

When I came to Poland, I got the money my father sent—fifty dollars. I cashed five dollars in Poland and bought five pairs of shoes—and I still had money to come back. When I crossed the border, the Red Army that patrolled the whole thing took the shoes away from me. They gave me only one pair. I hid the money because I was afraid they would take away the money too. When I came back, I still had forty-five dollars, but we didn't have banks to cash it. I had to go about twelve miles from my town to cash the money. Right away I bought a bottle of kerosene and I bought some honey bread, because we liked it very much. When I came back, we used to exchange with the farmers—I gave them money and they gave me bread, wheat, and corn.

I kept corresponding with my father through Poland. He wanted to take us to America. He wrote that in order to make it faster, we should all cross the Romanian border, and he would send us money there. We were about seventy miles from the Romanian border. So I gave a farmer a few dollars that I had left, and he took us all to the border. When we crossed over, a man took us to Bucharest and I went to the HIAS.

The HIAS gave me the money my father sent and for five dollars a month, I got a big tremendous room—one room—out of the city, and we stayed there. We bought a wood stove—we didn't cook on gas or electric, but on wood—and we bought a lot of wood. There we had plenty of food. A lot of food. We used to buy thirty pounds of bread at one time, for two days sometimes. We used to buy a lot of herring and halvah. My sister used to get up in the morning and make a fire to put up tea. For breakfast, we had herring or halvah with bread. Nighttime, we had meat. We had meat once a day. Before we went to bed, we used to take two big round loaves of bread with halvah.

We stayed in Romania for about a year. My father sent us papers to the HIAS and he sent money to the HIAS and they bought us tickets. But they couldn't send us here because my father was not a citizen. The quota was changed then. If you weren't a citizen, your children couldn't come in. So my father had to become a citizen. It took him about a year.

I got a job during that time and my brother got a job. We worked in a big factory that made wooden crates. A man took us in there and paid us about fifteen cents a day. Then he gave us piecework, because we were very fast. It was a big factory. They used to make toilet seats and benches, but the main job was to make crates. A manufacturer would call up and say he needed twenty thousand crates that were twenty by thirty or sixty by one hundred. The manager would cut the sides and we had to put the pieces together. So we worked on piecework and with the five dollars from HIAS we had plenty of food—as much as we wanted—and we even had carfare. We used to go to see a movie (we never saw movies before) and we could change our shoes when we worked.

There was a lot of antisemitism in Romania. They used to catch Jewish people, beat them up, take them by the beard. They had trolleys with horses—like a big trailer—and people used to go in it. A Jew would be in the trolley, a man with a beard, and they used to tear his beard and do different things. But we didn't have much trouble. They didn't bother us much because we were kids.

When my father became a citizen, he took us here. We came by a freighter. The reason we came by freighter is because we stayed the extra time in Romania, and my father didn't have so much money already. Until we came here, it cost him about twenty-five hundred dollars. So we bought tickets to go by freighter.

Morris B.

I was born in an area known by all Jews throughout the world as Galicia. Galicia was a province of Austria. Austria had about eight provinces—Bosnia, Bosnia-Herzegovina, that was under the Austrian empire, Hungary was part of it, and Serbia, and also other areas which later became countries on their own. The town was Podheitze.

BESS: Weren't you born in Wisniowczik?

MORRIS: That's not even on a map. It's a little village next to it.

BESS: But that's where you said you were born.

MORRIS: All right. You want to write down the real village? Well, you'll have to write it down and I'll have to spell it for you—W-I-S-N-I-O-W-C-Z-I-K. It's about two miles from the next town, which was known as Podheitze, and that's where I really call my home town.

My mother died when I was born. I was raised by my grandmother. I didn't know the word *mother*. I could not even say the word. I used to envy kids who could come home and say "mama." To me it was so strange. I kept wishing to myself I could call my grandmother "mama," but she would not stand for it. She wanted to be known as grandmother. I did not know my father until I was eight years old.

Most Jews there were storekeepers. There were three tailors, two shoemakers.

Of course, the shoemaker always walked barefoot. The reason for it was that nobody was there to pay him for shoes or pay for repairs. The storekeepers did pretty well. Once a week there was a sort of a village fair, where a number of people from the smaller villages would bring their goods to sell on the open market. They lined up the goods and people bought. The Jews bought from the peasants who would bring in their goods. And the peasants would buy what they needed for their homes—they would buy cloth to make shirts, they would buy shoes, they would buy pants. They would buy ready-made flour and bread because there was a bakery and the Jewish bakers were very, very good. They bought necessities in the town, mostly clothing.

The town itself must have had about two hundred and fifty Jews. In the center of the town there were hardly any non-Jews. Further out, five or six blocks deep, were the non-Jewish areas. Of course, we were very close with them, the kids used to play together. We'd go down to the lake and bathe and have fun together, but the Jews kept to themselves mostly. We knew that we lived amongst the goyim—we made a living from them and they made a living from us. We lived peacefully together. We did hear that further down in Russia, which was not too far from us, occasionally there was a pogrom. We did not have any pogroms under Austria.

When we got a little older, when I was already about six, the studies we learned in the cheder in the daytime were insufficient. We had to go at night. At night meant after the evening prayers in the synagogue. The older people would go home and the younger ones would remain with the rabbi. We'd pull out the *Chumash,* or at six I already studied the *Gemara.* Gemara is Talmud. Actually it is jurisprudence. It's not easy for kids to conceive. But we studied it. To an extent we knew what it was about, even though we couldn't follow every single discussion thoroughly.

There's one thing I'll never forget. When I was a little older, my father came down to visit me—to get acquainted with his son. I was eight years old then. He did not come to my grandmother's house. He came to her brother's house, which was a bigger house. They called me in. "Your father is here." I said, "That's nice." "Go see him!" "All right, I'll go see him." I walked in to see him and I see a man with a little blonde beard, and they said, "Moishele, this is your father." I knew one thing—that you have to be very polite. When someone stretches out his hand and says hello to you, you have to respond by doing the same thing. I said, "Sholom aleichem." Those were the greetings the first time I met him. I don't remember any father hugging a kid. I couldn't say hello to my kids unless I hugged them and kissed them, but then it was a different thing.

He said hello to me, and he was talking to my grandmother's brother for a while. Then he said he would like to hear what the boy has learned. They pulled out more than the *Chumash*—the *Chumash* was the book of Moses—and the rebbe was there, the one that was teaching me—they brought him in. My father said, "How is he learning?" The rebbe said, "He's doing beautifully. He learned the Talmud. He knows what it's all about. He can read through whole pages and know exactly what goes on." He said, "I'd like to hear it." So they pulled out the Gemara and opened up a page and they told me, "Go ahead, show him what you can do." I opened up the book and I read it through with the melody as it was commonly used during the study of the Talmud. I still remember it even so many years back. It was a law in connection with if a cow has wandered into somebody else's yard and was hit by an ox and the cow has lost her unborn calf as a result of it right then, who is guilty? Somebody has to pay the damage. Who is guilty? Was it the owner of the cow who was out of luck or was it the owner of the bull who had hit the cow and made her lose the calf? Which one has to pay the damage?

Well, as kids, we didn't go into too much detail, but we knew that there was a polemic. In the Talmud generally they don't give you just the law. They give you the questions and then they give you the polemic—one rabbi says, Well, the owner of the cow is at fault. She wandered in there, it's not the guy who owned the bull's fault. He didn't bring that cow in there, she wandered into his yard and that's what happened. The other one says, No, you should have had your bull tied up. It belongs to you and you're guilty. And the polemic was going on between the two. One was Reb Yehuda and the other one was Reb Meir. Reb Yehuda says one thing and Reb Meir says another thing. So as I was reading and studying, I gave them the polemic word for word exactly as it was said there. Anyone who knows Gemara, knows Talmud, would know exactly what it was about.

But my father was one of those who was called an enlightened Jew. He didn't believe too much in having kids learn law before they know the language well, before they are old enough. And he stops me off in the middle and he says, "Wait, Moishele, 'di lernst gantz gut'—you're doing very well—but who is guilty? Who do you say is guilty?" I was struck with the question. Nobody ever asked me that. In my young head it just went through one thing—wait a minute, there are two people here, Reb Meir and Reb Yehuda, and one says one thing and one says the other. In the spirit of the second, I said, "Reb Meir." He looks at me and he says, "Reb Meir is guilty?" So I thought I fell in wrong. I said, "No, it can't be Reb Meir, it's Reb Yehuda." He said, "Reb Yehuda? What did they have to do with it? Why are they guilty?" Then who is guilty? I was stumped again. I thought, He's right, they can't be guilty, they are only giving opinions. Now who could be guilty in a thing like this? My own thinking was, at the moment, that it's an act of God. In other words, nobody is guilty there. Whatever happened, happened. It's an act of God. But instead of saying that, I was confused.

I said, "Wait a minute. It's not Reb Meir, it's not Reb Yehuda. It's . . . " And I stopped short. Why did I stop short? Because in those days, when people were young they were taught certain Jewish manners—that you're not supposed to even use the word *God* especially using it in vain, making him guilty, you can't say he's guilty. To say the name of God, you had to be pure, you had to wash your hands before you say the name of God. The earth was damp. I just bent down, put my hands against the ground and rubbed one hand against the other and made them moist—I washed my hands, to an extent. And I said, "The Holy One, blessed be he, he must be guilty." In my thinking it was perfect, but the way it came out—it was not this rabbi guilty, not that one, the Lord is guilty—that's something he didn't expect.

He stopped me right there and then. He turned around to the rabbi and said, "Stop teaching this child Gemara—the Talmud. You see that he doesn't know. It's not for him. Teach him the language and the rest of it will come later." The rabbi got very angry. He said, "That's the trouble with you 'enlightened' souls. You've become Germans almost." He said, "That child knows the Gemara, you confused him. He's going to learn the way all kids learn and in due time he'll know how to answer you so that everyone will be happy and satisfied." That was my first meeting with my father.

Within two years after my mother died he was married in the next town, which was only about two and a half towns away from there. He raised a family, he had five children. He was a youngster. He was only twenty-four when my mother died. When he married, he was twenty-six. He really was in love with my mother. My mother-in-law was one of her best friends, and they say that it was the greatest love affair that they had ever seen. But in those days, waiting two years and having a mother and a father nagging you, "It's time you got married again"—so they looked for a very pretty girl, and she was pretty. The second wife was very pretty.

He was one of the enlightened Jews. Even though he was religious, he was not a fanatic. He did not like those rabbis who supposedly showed miracles—a miracle rabbi. A woman can't become pregnant, she goes and he says a prayer and she becomes pregnant. He didn't believe in that. He showed me that there isn't one word in the entire Bible where it says believe in God. It doesn't say believe in God no place. You should know that there is a God. You should know that I am your Lord and that I brought you out of Egypt, with strong arm and with might. You should know that. Because of the fact that it was in me that I have to know and not believe, I lost a lot of the belief. I had to be convinced. And no matter what I do, until this day, I am not a follower. This doesn't sound good for an organization that used to be Followers. If I'm convinced of something, I'll fight for it. I will accept other people's opinions, I will discuss with them, and if I am convinced I will go along with them, but I have to be convinced. I'm not just a believer. I have to see things the way they are.

I was in that town, in that small little town where I was born, until I was ten years old. At that time, my grandmother died. I remained alone. My father was only about two and a half miles away with a family. My mother had another sister, my aunt Chipa, in a small town. Where would I go? I went to my aunt Chipa. She had three children and her husband had gone to America before the war to make some money to bring back.

This was an ancient custom. A lot of Jews left eastern Europe, they went to America, they worked for a couple of years and then they would come back and bring some money. Her husband was in America and she remained alone. She had a little store. She had three children and she couldn't afford four. I was the number four that came in there. So she reminded herself—he has a father, let the father worry about him.

One day, during one of those days when there was a village fair—the once-a-week fair—I was put on a horse and wagon with a peasant who had come in to bring stuff to the fair and he was asked to bring me to my father's house—to let him know that he has a child. I was put on the wagon and traveled. It was only two and a half miles, but European miles are bigger than miles are here, I guess. It took many hours to get into that town. I was put into that wagon at night, and I was brought into the town early in the morning. He dropped me off and said, "Now, you can go and look for your father." Where could I find him? I didn't know the house where he lived. I figured at that time, Where does a Jew go every morning? He goes to synagogue. So I went to the synagogue and sure enough I saw him there.

"What brought you here?" I said, "My grandmother just died." "What's with your aunt Chipa?" I said, "My aunt Chipa put me on a wagon and sent me to you." He brought me to a baker, bought a couple of rolls and he said, "Did you daven this morning?"—did you pray this morning? I don't remember whether I said yes or no, whether I davened or not—I don't remember. But I remember he asked me to wait for this particular man who was going back. He said, "He'll take you back." It seems he was afraid to bring me to his house. His wife had other children. Whether she knew that he had another son or not, I don't know. Maybe she did and maybe she didn't. Lo and behold, I was sent back to the little town, to Wisniowczik. This deal happened three times. Back and forth and back and forth.

Each time I stayed a week until the next fair. He sent me back the same day to my aunt Chipa, and I stayed a week, until the next fair. She was poor, she couldn't afford to take a regular wagon there. The last time when my aunt sent me back to my father, it was with a butcher who had come to our little town to buy geese for his butcher shop. She asked him to take me back and she told him the story.

This man happened to have been in America for several years. He had come to America and he was a nonreligious Jew, but he still had a kosher butcher shop. I remember he had one section where he had nonkosher chickens. If the rabbi said that this chicken, after they slaughtered it, was not kosher, it would go to that side—he would sell it as nonkosher. If the chicken had swallowed a nail, or something like that, it became nonkosher, and no Jew would buy it. But he would sell it there. He had lived in America and didn't believe in nonsense. He came back with his wife to the little town and he opened a butcher shop.

When he was told that story, he said, "I'm taking him back and I assure you his father will not dare to send him back again. He took me in his wagon. We were driving through the night—it was one horse and the wagon, loaded with geese. I fell asleep and sure enough early in the morning when we reached the town, he woke me up. Seven geese were dead. He, of course, was angry—not at me, he was angry at my father. He unloaded his wagon and said, now he's got geese for the *treyf* section—the stuff that was to be sold for nonkosher. But in the meantime, he said, "Come with me." He brought me into his house. In my life I never had a breakfast like I had in his house. I'm sure he made ham and eggs. I had never seen it, but he made a plate of meat and eggs and I ate galore, early in the morning—it must have been about six o'clock in the morning. He said, "Just don't worry, I'll get you there."

Instead of taking me to the synagogue, where I had met my father on the previous occasions, he took me right to his house. He got a hold of my father in his own house and shook him. He said, "Is this your son?" "Yes." He said, "If you dare to send him back once more, do you know what business I'm in?" "Yeah, you're the butcher." He said, "I'm coming back with an axe and I'll split your head in two." I was shocked.

But I knew I had to have some kind of a home someplace. My father didn't say anything. He was struck dumb. His wife was there, all the kids were there. So I stayed in the house and I got acquainted with the rest of the family.

It was not good, because actually I was the extra one—the one that was least expected. There wasn't even a bed for me. In the whole house there were five kids. There were two beds, a couple of makeshift bunks, but for me there was actually no room. In the kitchen they had a large trunk up against the wall, with a round top. Like half a barrel. That was my place to sleep—on top of that. I had to do a lot of thinking for myself. I was told I could put some rags down, or *shmates*. I went out on a day when they had the fair and when the peasants would feed their horses. They would put down a lot of straw for them. Straw was all over the place. I took a big sack and went around from one wagon to the other and picked up straw and put it in the sack. When the sack was filled, I went home, flattened it out, laid it on top of the trunk, and that was my bed. The floor was earthen, and I just would not sleep on the floor. It was damp and cold.

This was a bigger town—the town had five thousand people. It had its own courthouse, it had a jail, and a flour mill, storekeepers—no factories. Again, the town was Jewish. They also had a fair there once a week, where peasants would bring in their stuff, but there was more of everything. They had stores that had luxurious items already. There were watchmakers, jewelers—several jewelers. They had everything. They had one big shul, a synagogue—it's still in existence. At that time, that building looked like a fortress. The walls were about a yard thick, stone walls. It had a center, inside the big synagogue was side rooms. There was a room on the right which was known as the tailors' shul—the tailors' synagogue. Another one was the shoemakers' synagogue. It was amazing. All the shoemakers would get together and they had their own group and they would go davening in that shul. The others would go in the other shul. Three in one. But the major shul was the big one—that was where there were hundreds of people.

I remember that this was during the war period—1914 started the war. The Austrians and the Russians were fighting one another. The Russians were on top of the mountain. They were shooting down at the town and the Austrians were shooting back up. Jews had to go to the Austrian army and Jews had to be in the Russian army. Some had family on the other side of the river, which was Russian, and there was a fear at all times that they may kill one of their own brothers—shooting across. So Jews were praying that they would not be in that front, that they would be sent to

Italy. But they were fighting. My father was in the army at the time. They took everyone. And he was one that always had that doubt, that he would not shoot. He was taken into the general's office at that time as a bookbinder. He was a bookworm. He had a big library of his own, and he knew how to bind books, so he set him up binding documents and books. He had to find his own needle and his own thread, and that took weeks. He made his own needle out of a piece of wire, hooked up, and he made big holes in the documents.

He used to tell stories after he came home. He was in Italy, on the Italian front. They got into a town, and they set them up in people's homes, rich people's homes. And there were books standing on the floor, and they were trampling all over them. He asked them if he would be allowed to look around, to find something that he could use for his own library. And he picked up a number of books. While other soldiers were there rattling the house—some were looking for silver, others were looking for whatever they could find to sell—he went around looking for whatever books he could pick up. He came home loaded with a knapsack. He had nothing to eat on the road, but he came home with books. That was his booty—books.

In our town we were close to a borderline, and our town changed hands at least a dozen times—one day it was Russian, another day it was Austrian, and suddenly there was a Ukrainian state that came up. At that time, each group that came in gave orders that the signs on the stores must be written in their language—if there was a German sign, they had to tear it down and make a Polish sign, and three days later it was a Ukrainian sign. At that time, I was a desired guy around there, as young as I was. People took me to make signs on the other side of their signs. I knew a little bit of Polish, a little bit of Russian—enough to make signs. I would make signs on the stores in the different languages.

After the War, I stayed there for about a year. I don't remember how it came about, but I think my grandfather, my father's father, and his daughter and a son, they had fled during the war from our town. They landed all the way up in Vienna. Finally, my father said it would be all right if I went to my grandfather—they wanted me there. I said I would be very happy to go. They made me a little bundle, put me on a train, and I went from that little town to Lemberg, Lvov. There I changed the train and went to Vienna, all alone.

It was my first time on the railroad. There was a railroad in the town. I remember practically everyone on a Saturday afternoon, they used to go looking at the railroad because it was something new. They would go once a day to see the way the train comes in and the way the train leaves—it puffs, a cloud coming out of it, water on the bottom, and the train coming in would puff, puff, puff. We went to see it.

Going to Vienna on the train, it was nice. Under the benches where I was sitting, there were a couple of kids laying underneath—they didn't have tickets. They used to hide so the conductor wouldn't see them. They would ride from one town to another. Once in a while one of the kids would get caught and the family would have to pay for them. Occasionally the conductor would go in and kick under the bench—people kept bundles there—to see whether it was a bundle of somebody. There was a standard joke going around there—someone sees a kid underneath, he says, "Hey, how far are you going?" He says, "As long as my *toches* [bottom] will hold out"—because you get kicked all the time.

I was in Vienna for about three years or so when money came from America. My uncle, my father's brother, who came with us, he was a college graduate—he learned in Switzerland. He was the one who said he knows English—he knew a little bit of antiquated English. He was the master of the money that came. Tickets at that time to America were one hundred and twenty dollars a ticket. He started figuring out that there isn't enough money for eight tickets—for my grandfather, his son and daughter, my father, my stepmother, and the three of us kids—two girls and myself. Eight tickets at a hundred and twenty dollars a piece was a lot more money than he had. He had about eight hundred dollars. Therefore, he had to look for an area where he can buy tickets not for a hundred and twenty-dollars each, but for about eighty or eighty-five. He got a boat in Trieste, in Italy, and we went to Trieste. That ticket was eighty dollars, so we had enough for everybody. But that was a boat like the slow boat to China.

Instead of the normal time that it took in those days—about five, five and a half days—we traveled for twenty-two days on the ocean. My *zeyde*—my grandfather—refused to go on the boat unless they bring a Torah with them because he knew that it would take at least two weeks and the Jewish holidays would fall between. My uncle had to take from the money that was left over and buy a Torah.

It was an Italian boat, and there were mostly Italians, practically all Italians. There were exactly eleven Jews. But they made a minyan. You know what a minyan is? People to pray. One of the Jews believed very very little, and he didn't want to stay in. So he would come in, take a look where the praying took place and this guy we didn't expect him to stay too long, but the others had to stay there. Every once in a while one would go out, and when they were about to say kaddish or anything else when they needed a minyan we all would go and call him back.

On one occasion, the man who believed very little was in—so there were eleven—and my uncle walked out. He was on the end of the boat, looking at the ocean, and lo and behold I see he has a bunch of grapes and he is eating grapes. That was on Yom Kippur—we were there all through the holidays—I knew that today he was supposed to be fasting. I walked over to him and I said, "Uncle Wolf, I caught you." "Vos vilste?"—What do you want? I said, "Half-and half. If you're allowed to eat it, I'm allowed to eat it." He had no choice but to give me half of his grapes. We ate the grapes and I said, "Now we've got to go back, there's no minyan there."

Rochelle G.

I was born in 1908 in David Goroduk. Presently it's Poland, but then it was under Russian rule. It was a small town.

My father was a rabbi. He was a very prestigious man. He was a very nice kind man and very learned. He spent a lot of time studying Talmud. We had a very wonderful father—mother, too, of course, but mother you take for granted. They tend you, they take care of you, they see that you are washed, and they give you the various trainings that we get. The women were more busy with the house—taking care of it. But father was really worshipped in the house. Everybody looked up to him. We revered him because that was the atmosphere in the house. My mother instilled in the children love and respect for the father.

She was a lot younger than my father. He was married three times. He lost his first two wives—one, I think, in childbirth, and one took sick. I don't know the details. The custom of religious Jews at that time was that a man has to be married. In fact, I think after sixty days it's compulsory to be married. The Jewish law specified that a man should be married. Not a woman. Nobody specified anything about a woman. But they were treated with respect.

We had a large family. My mother had, living, eight children—five daughters and three sons. And my father had before two who lived with us, so it was ten. And they lost a few, I suppose. Our house was very large and spacious. We had domestic help to clean the house—temporary help was Gentile, but permanently that lived in the house was Jewish. Mother took care of the baking, but the kneading was done by somebody else. Mother was busy supervising closely.

My father was really outstanding. He was an outstanding personality. He was very knowledgeable, very tolerant. With all his knowledge, and with all his devotion to his faith, he had a tolerance for people who deviated in a very soft manner. At that time, there were no sermons. The rabbi didn't give sermons. His functions really were as a mediator between people, applying the Jewish laws to various disputes, and other things. Let's say if I had a dispute with somebody. Instead of going to the law we have a mediator. The two parties agree on whatever the mediator decides. It was conducted so the dispute was always settled somehow in an amicable way.

I was told a very interesting story that happened when I was a child. My father coddled me a lot because I was the youngest. I always sat on his lap. Once there was some kind of a dispute between a rich man and a poor man. They came to my father. The rich man came to the house, said hello, and sat down. I don't know if he was invited to sit down or not, but he sat down and started to present his case. The poor man was standing. So I said, "Father, they are not equal under the law. One is standing and one is sitting." That was my reaction as a child. And he patted me, and said, "You are right. Take a chair, would you please?"

In our town, I remember, people used to go out, I think on a Thursday, to make collections for poor families so they should have food for the Sabbath. We used to give them money. Some people were collecting and bringing it to them. Nobody knew really to whom and what. It was done in a very delicate manner. Jews have a great respect for the Sabbath and a great respect for the holidays, and in all parts of the Jewish culture there is a trait of sharing—it's part of the Jewish ethics and culture. So naturally in every Jewish community there was the basis of sharing to see that there would be no suffering. The Jews usually took care of their own—they didn't revert to other means of support.

My father was a rabbi, but he also used to perform certain rituals of slaughtering. He couldn't make a living as a rabbi alone because it was a small place we lived in. So he performed dual functions. To slaughter chickens, he slit their throat in a special way. It was a ritual of sacrifice. He used to make a prayer before. Jewish people still adhere to it. But I buy chickens now in the A & P.

We were considered the elite in our town. Among the Jewish people there were many strata. There was a difference in the background and that forms a barrier. We were developed. We had a very intellectual family, and it reflected in our relationship with people. I very seldom visited a worker's home—the seamstresses or other small craftsmen who used to perform certain duties. I used to go to a shoemaker he would make me a pair of shoes. But otherwise we never associated with them. It's not because we were snobbish, our mode of living was different, our intellectual quests were different.

From reading we used to get our information—not live. There was a library and our house was always full of books. From the oldest to the youngest, everybody always spent time reading—it carried you away to different countries, it acquainted you with different things, different characters, different lives. There wasn't anything else—that was the life.

I went to a very very elementary school. The emphasis was on Russian literature—learning poems, acquainting you with the poets—and more on the nationalistic side, too, anything pertaining to patriotism. I accepted it, I suppose, as a duty. It was one of those things that you had undertaken and you had to do it. Most of the Jews frequented a Jewish school, with Jewish teachers. Russian was picked up in the street. I went to a Jewish school first, and then I went to a Russian school when I grew up a little bit more.

Jews couldn't go freely to the university—there was a quota. I don't want to emphasize it, it's enough to say it was oppressive. All the laws were made in order to keep the people in line. Not to give them too much freedom—Jewish people and Gentiles. Gentiles who were peasants didn't have the aspirations for it. They didn't have the knowledge for it. The peasants, when they worked in the fields, used to get up very early and come in sunset home. Eat and go to sleep. They had no time for anything else. Although in wintertime, they had time, but I don't know what they did then. Those Gentiles who had the aspirations attained university because they were cultured—or tutored. I don't know how cultured they were. But they were educated. To have an education and to be cultured are two different things.

In later years, when my sisters grew up, they met many Gentiles—intellectuals, teachers, and other people. In fact, they came to the house to visit. Otherwise, with the muzhiks—as we called the peasants—there was hardly any association. Their interests were entirely different. No matter how poor the Jew was, he was more advanced—the mode of living, the eating, the other things. You couldn't really mingle with them. Jews are more adventurous, they have a better background than most. Learning Torah was always a prerequisite of life. That's the beginning. We have an intellectual quest for certain knowledge and that comes from the family. Even in the Jewish songs, in the lullabies, the mother sings to her children that she hopes they will become rabbis. It means education. Education was always stressed. Acquiring of wealth was not stressed so much. A Jew will never deny a child to be educated. But I don't think the Gentiles wanted to mingle either. They were very prejudiced because they thought that the Jews killed Christ.

As children, I remember we used to take a walk a little bit out of town, and the Christian kids used to run after us: "Jew, Jew, Jew, Jew, Jew." It was very humiliating. I don't think at that time we fought back. It must have been ignored. But we thought they were barbarians. I suppose if they would have attacked us physically, maybe we would have done something. We feared pogroms, but in our place we didn't have them. But we heard of it. Later on, everybody was really polarized to an extent. It was a polarized society because of lack of knowledge and lack of education and lack of mutual interest in getting together.

After the First World War, at the time of the Soviet Revolution already, there were factions. There was hope then, a ray of hope. So many events happened at that time of oppression and hatred against Jews, and we hoped that the Revolution would alleviate it. But the Revolution passed me by. The Civil War came and we were transferred to the other side. It became Polish. So I knew what was happening in the Revolution, but I was not in the center of it.

Counterrevolutionary troops passed through our town, and they were after the Jews. So, naturally, every Jewish person ran away to the fields and the forests. After they passed, my people decided to go back. Our house was broken into. We were actually wiped out. Whatever we hid in the attic—our valuables—were taken. We suspected our neighbors. We started to look in the hiding places, and everything was gone. So the local people—the people who knew—probably took things. I remember when I came from the forest, I could not find a piece of soap to wash with, and then I broke down.

Then we had to go away. We tried to get out of that town. We came to, I think, Pinsk, and tried to get in touch with my brother in America to bring us over. My brother left as a young man. I think he ran away from conscription. We didn't have any money at that time. We had nothing at all. Everything was taken away from us. I don't know how people survived. They survive somehow. My brother helped. He was a journalist. There was no problem then coming here. It was an escape. When I came they asked me what was my reaction. I said, "I don't have to look back. I don't have to look around, who's following me."

My mother and I were the only ones that left. My father died there. He died before the Revolution. One sister was here already. She came a few years before. Also, my brother took her over. I think she came about three years before me. Then he took mother and me over. There were another two sisters. We were all there together in Poland, but they couldn't get visas for America, so they went to Israel. That's why my family is there, too. That's how we were separated. But we were happy to leave because we were out of harm. We had no home, you know. We were just like refugees. Really, like refugees.

Anna T.

Before the Revolution, we lived in a very small town near Kiev. Life was very dull, particularly for young people. To us, father and mother were old people, because of the life and the way they handled themselves—father with the long beard and the long kaftan going to shul, and mother with the long dress. My mother had the Jewish kerchief and she *bentscht licht* [ritual lighting of Sabbath candles].

My mother was more religious than my father, and she believed in mitzvahs—in good deeds. She was very goodnatured. We had a very open house. Naturally, the little towns had a lot of poor people. We weren't rich, but we had food. We had milk and cheese because my father was in the dairy business, and we grew our own vegetables. All we had to buy actually was meat, and if we didn't have meat, we didn't starve either. But a lot of people had nothing, and they had two, three, four, five kids. My mother always saw to it that those people should not starve—a pot of milk, a pot of cream, a loaf of bread.

Every Friday night—you know, Saturday is a holiday, so you worked yourself to death Friday until the lighting of the candles and then you relaxed—after she got through with the day's work and she got dressed, she used to take a big empty bag and go out to the town. She went to each house to collect *challah*—white bread—for the poor people. And they knew that mama collected a bag or two so they would come and get their share. When they came, she used to tell us, "Children, you never get poor from giving."

Then we had a lot of poor people coming in, having their meals, and giving them dairy. We probably didn't want to eat it even. When we were hungry, mother said, "Take some butter, take some milk." We didn't want it, because we had too much— we wanted something else. But for other people, it was really worthwhile to eat. When we used to complain for some kind of food, my mother used to say, "Oi, kinderlach, andere kinder voltn zich gevintchen dos tzu hobn vos ir hot, und ir vilt es nit. S'iz zind nischt tzu veln esn ven andere kinder zeinen hungerik." She said, "It's a sin to refuse food that other people would be just happy to have, when you have it and don't want it." This is the case with kids, you know—when you have it, you don't appreciate it. In that respect, we grew up to share with other people that have less than us and we should see that they shouldn't be hungry either.

My mother was a soft character. My father was very quiet. He wouldn't hit you— he never hit us—but when you walked in, you shivered for no reason. Because he was so serious. He wasn't too happy of a fellow because life was hard. Life was hard. But it was a nice family life. There was a systematic routine. There was a meal and everybody had to sit at the table. Mother knew that she has to cook and we had to prepare things for the table. We always set the table. It was a nice plain life, and a harmonic life. There was no fighting, no misunderstandings. This was the life and the parents did the best they could for the children because they hadn't anything better to offer.

My father was in business and we all had to work. We used to buy dairy products from the peasants and deliver it to Kiev. We had a house and we had land and we had cows and we had horses and we had chickens and we had everything. We had our own garden where we planted corn and hay for the horses. We never had to buy any vegetables because we grew our own—we had two acres of land. We were constantly busy helping father and mother. There were cows and chicks, so we had to feed, we had to milk. Every single day was a repetitious kind of work, without any excitement.

And all of a sudden we were hit with the Revolution. I was too young then to understand the significance of the Revolution. Not only that I was too young, but I was growing up in this atmosphere of nothingness. I didn't have to work, so I didn't feel I was exploited and that the Revolution would bring me a new independence. I wasn't active anywhere yet. I wasn't at that age to realize anything. Also, I was in a small town. Who was talking revolution? Who was talking of being exploited? We weren't workers. We were in business. Maybe other people that worked for a tailor or a shoemaker and were exploited. But even then, in a small town they didn't blame him, because the little shoemaker that had a worker was exploited by himself, too. So I really couldn't assess the greatness of the Revolution. We only knew pogroms.

In the beginning the Revolution was so raw. They had to do so much to organize the people and to show them they are somebody to follow, that they couldn't take care of the little towns. The Revolution was concentrated more in the big cities. The little towns were where the peasants were and where the bandits came. The bandits looked for outlets where they wouldn't be watched and they wouldn't be punished. They roamed around and they would hide in the woods. The oats and the corn were so high. They could hide themselves. We used to hide ourselves in the corn and the oats also.

One would send a message: "We saw a couple of guys on horses, this must be this and this band." So we used to hide ourselves from them.

The revolutionary people couldn't do anything yet. There was still a war. If they captured a city, they had to see that something is done for the people to have confidence in them. So they couldn't control the little towns so much. And that's where most pogroms took place. There the bandits had a free hand to burn and kill and rob Jews.

In ordinary times we knew that the Gentiles didn't like the Jews, but I also knew the Jews didn't like the Gentiles. In general there was a very strained relation between the Jews and the Gentiles. They didn't like the Jews because the Jew was the businessman, and the Jew was the smart man, and the Jew was the manipulator. They used to work on the field and pack up big sacks of corn and other products and they would bring it to the Jewish businessman to sell it, and they felt they were robbed in weight. They could not prove it, but they felt the Jew knew how to manipulate so the weight should be less than what it is. They knew the Jew is too smart to be honest. And we weren't angels. The Jews weren't angels toward the peasants. During the pogroms, a lot of peasants that we knew did a lot of harm to us. But some of them also helped us.

My family dealt with the peasants, and their relationship to us was much better than to Jews in general. My father was a very quiet man, but he was a good person. He treated them nicely. When they came into the house, there was always a cup of tea and a white piece of bread—to a peasant, not to a Gentile in general, but to a peasant, a white piece of bread was something special. He treated them nicely and didn't rob them in prices or in weight too much. So they had respect for us. In fact, during the pogrom they took care of us. When my father was killed, they took us to their house and they were hiding us when the bandits were roaming around the peasants' territory to find out if there were any Jews hidden.

When they killed my father, he was on the way to Kiev with merchandise, and he had a few more people going with him on business there. Two escaped and one was killed with my father. We happened to pack up a lot of things, sending it with him to Kiev—if things would get worse where we are, we'd all go to Kiev because a big city was safer than the little town. But he didn't get to Kiev and we didn't see the horse and wagon because they took everything. This was done by people who knew when father was going to Kiev. We couldn't prove it, but this was the way it was.

My mother, my brother, my sister, and myself—we were the only ones left. My brother was two years older than me. He had no trade yet. I had no trade yet. And we had no way to maintain ourselves. The rest of our family was in America. I had four brothers and a sister there. My brothers escaped from the Czarist army and they were in America for years. My sister left Russia with her husband and a child in 1912 or 1914. I hardly remembered her until I came to this country. So, naturally, our brothers wanted us to come to the United States to be with them. They were here with the intention that some day we'll be here too. That was my father's and my mother's aim all the time. When things get better and my brothers make more money, they'll take us over. Our brothers used to write to us an awful lot about the American life—how people worked, how they organized. To me, it didn't make much of an impression, because I was a kid.

After my father was killed and we came back from the countryside to our town, we had nothing to do there, so we went to Kiev to make a living. Our brothers couldn't send us money at that time, and we didn't know when we would be able to come to America. We stayed in Kiev for about a year and a half. When we came to Kiev we started to deal with dairy products on the market because this was the only thing we knew. So we used to go in the morning on the market where the peasants used to bring their merchandise, cheese and milk and cream, and we bought it from them and brought it to the market to sell on a little stand.

We were very poor. We needed shoes, we needed clothes; we couldn't spare the money. But I remember within a length of time we succeeded in buying a pair of pants for my brother. So we wrote to our brothers. I wrote a letter, my brother wrote a letter, my sister wrote a letter, and my mother wrote a letter—everybody was writing about this pair of pants. My brothers thought that we were going to write to them about what is transpiring in the Soviet Union during and after the Revolution, how things are going if it is better. They were more revolutionary—they were older. So they wrote, "Is there anything else you could write to us about besides a pair of pants?" Even when we came here, they said, "That's all that impressed you about the Revolution—the pair of pants that you were able to buy? Nothing else?" We knew very little of the significance of the Revolution. We didn't understand too much.

My brothers here had a friend who was an American and he had family in Europe, too. They made an agreement for him to go to the Soviet Union to bring the families over. We knew very little how to go about it. We were too young, and mama didn't know how to go, who to see, and where to get the papers. But he was an American guy with money. Even during the Revolution, which was so young, you probably could find your way by paying. So he went to the Soviet Union. What he went through to make our papers, I really couldn't tell you, because I don't know. In the first place, we had to leave the Soviet Union illegally. During the Revolution, they didn't allow anybody to leave. He got our papers for us, and he got papers for his cousins and family, and we all came.

We went from the Soviet Union to Bessarabia, and from there, after a length of time, he made papers for us to go to Romania. To us, it was a relief. We were given a room in a hotel. The agent—we called that friend of ours "the agent"—saw that we had everything. He gave us money through our brother, and we ate and we drank and we met a lot of other foreigners coming our way. We had a good time there, not going anywhere in particular because we didn't know the language, but we visited one another and we just enjoyed ourselves that way.

We stayed there for a number of months. He couldn't arrange for us to pass the border. We had to do it very, very early in the morning or late at night. We got up a couple of times during the night and we had to come back. I guess it wasn't the proper time. We had nothing to do with it. This agent was the one who brought us to Romania, got a room in a hotel, and told us the proper time to cross the border. And then, finally, we crossed. They took us through the water on a boat.

But we couldn't come to the United States. We went to Canada. We couldn't come in with our papers. We came in January—January first, 1922—to Canada. I was then about fourteen. There, when we came, one of my brothers was already there to meet us, and he made up papers for us. We were only there a few days.

My brother made up papers, got us on the train and we came to this country illegally. We were illegal here until Congress pardoned all those who came illegally.

Jack M.

I came from a small town called Tsigovka. There were small shops—a couple of groceries, tailors, a carpenter was there, and, you know, a small working class. And then there were some people who were more well-to-do, they had big stores where you could get everything.

My father was by profession a cantor. The town paid him a certain amount of money for doing the Saturday services in the shul. In addition to that, we had about a half a dozen different things that we sold in the house. For instance, we used to make a big kettle of hot water and people used to come and buy from us a small kettle of tea, for a penny or two pennies. And then on Thursday, every two weeks on a Thursday, there was a gathering of many towns . . . they used to call it a *yarid* . . .

and they used to come together and buy and sell—horses, cows—every two weeks, on a Thursday, And my town held this kind of thing. There used to come people from many other places and they used to buy and sell—Gentiles and Jews. The Jewish people used to sell hats and pants and shoes. The Gentile people used to buy and sell horses, cows, pigs.

My mother was a housewife. She didn't do anything, but she helped to provide for the family—at that time, when the Thursdays took place, when the people from many other towns used to come into my town, my mother used to cook meals for them and they paid for the meals. And that's how it was easier for my father to go on with the family expenses.

My father was a religious man in the sense that he wouldn't do anything on a Saturday. But he wasn't a fanatic like some other people. The extreme religious orthodox people used to fast on Mondays and Thursdays—that was a religious habit for many years. And also they used to belong to certain rabbis in other countries where they used to send money, gifts, and used to go for advice. My father was not that kind of a man. He observed all the religious rules like not doing anything on Saturday, going to shul, fasting on the high holidays, you see. But he wasn't an extreme religious man like the others—he didn't belong to any other rabbi outside of my little town.

I stopped following religion when I got acquainted with a circle of boys that were progressive-minded people. We used to get together and have little meetings, and start reading radical newspapers, progressive newspapers. I wasn't antireligious, being in the house I had respect for my father, of course. I wouldn't do things that would make him sore. But outside of the house, we used to get together, we used to smoke on Saturday, and talk about helping the working people—how they are being exploited, and how the rich people are taking advantage of the poor, and how come God sees all these things and doesn't say nothing. How come my father is a religious man and goes to shul every time and he fasts on the high holidays and observes all the religious rules, whereas the very rich people we'd see they didn't observe any religious rules, they'd ride on Saturday, and everything—why are they rich and we are poor? We used to talk about all these things among ourselves, the boys, when we began to get progressive ideas.

After when we got older and we became a little bit more progressive, we saw that it's the wrong thing, the attitudes towards the girls—the parents not giving them a chance to be educated, to go to cheder, to go to shul, and even to go to gymnasium. We saw that it was wrong, and we tried to talk to the girls, you know, "Never mind what your father says or your mother says. You have to be educated, you have to know literature, you have to know what's going on in this world." We tried to talk to them, and they listened to us.

In 1917, when the Revolution broke out, I knew that the Bolsheviks are those that are fighting for the interests of the working class, whereas the others were for the rich. Lenin was one of the greatest men in those days to us. We always admired him, and we tried to get some literature of Lenin and read a little bit, and discuss. We had some circulars that we made up ourselves, you see, and we tried to give it out to the other people. They reacted very good, but of course we didn't call any strikes or stoppages or something like that because there wasn't any big factories in my town where I came from. So there wasn't in that sense a large proletariat, a large working class, where you could call a strike, or call them to a meeting sometimes. Something like that, no. But individually we did talk to them and give them circulars.

I left my little town in 1919 and I went to Odessa, because I was a grown-up boy. There was no job to be gotten in my little town. I told my father, "Look, what's the use of staying here. The family is big, we are poor, I want to go out into the world. I want to see something, I want to get a job. I want to earn some money, and maybe I'll help you too." So I went away to Odessa.

My father gave me permission and he said, "I think you're doing the right thing." I went to Odessa and I got myself a job over there. I was working in a mill where they make flour. . . . I was helping putting up the sacks, to stack up the flour, one on top of the other, one on top of the other. That was my work.

I lived with my relative. On Sunday we didn't work. We used to go out in the park and get together. Watch concerts. We used to go to a movie sometimes. Most of the time we used to go bathing—to the Black Sea. Odessa is a very big city and we used to get in contact with a lot of working people. Over there already there were meetings, there were demonstrations, there were strikes, there was everything. So naturally, it gave us a chance—everybody—to develop their mind, to participate, to take part in everything.

I would say that life became much better after the Revolution. Much better in the sense that they opened up schools, they opened up small little shops where people could get a chance to learn something and go to school and get educated.

What made me decide to leave? Because my whole family left. I had an older brother in this country that came here in 1914. Living in a small town, he couldn't find a job, he couldn't do anything. And we had relatives in Boston, Massachusetts, and they wrote a letter to him—"If you want to come out, come to us. We'll get you a job." After several years my mother and the rest of the family left. So I also left. That's why I left the Soviet Union.

I was glad to leave because, you see, not exactly a famine, but conditions were very bad and every other day the form of government used to change. When the Reds came in, they stood there a couple of days, established themselves and all of a sudden we hear that the White Guards are coming in. The Civil War affected us in the sense that you couldn't get much products. You couldn't get much bread, you couldn't get much of the other things that you wanted to have. There was a shortage of everything. The government used to change almost every week until finally the Soviet government established itself and they drove out all the counterrevolutionaries.

The reasons mostly for anybody that comes to this country is because the idea was spread throughout the world, even now, that America is the richest country throughout the world, and you can find money in the streets. In every country you'll find that the people are poor, the people can't make a living, and they have some relatives in the United States—whether it's Russia, whether it's Italy, whether it's France or any other country. Once they have relatives in this country they tell you that conditions are much better here, you've got a better chance to make a living, life is better. So naturally that's the reason why they come.

I couldn't get a visa to come straight to the United States. My mother and the rest of the family, they got visas and they went to the United States. I couldn't get a visa, somehow. I was waiting and waiting and waiting and I couldn't get it. So I went to Cuba and I lived there for fourteen months, in Havana, Cuba. In those days there was a law that if you live a year in Cuba you're automatically a Cuban citizen and the American government gives you a visa right away, permission to come into the United States. You didn't have to wait for any quotas or anything. As long as you were a Cuban citizen, you got a visa right away and you were allowed to come to the United States. That was in those days, in 1922.

From my town I went to France and over there I got the ship. It took about twelve days, and I arrived in Cuba. But being on the ship I was very seasick and I cursed my brother something terrible—why he sent me the money, why he's in the United States, why he takes me out to the United States. I was very seasick that time, those twelve days on the ship. That was the first time I was on a ship.

I liked the island very much. Cuba is a beautiful island, it's always warm. My brother from the United States, and my family which was already in the United States, they sent me a little money so I could live in Cuba. In addition to that, I used to peddle. I used to peddle stockings, ties, peddle over there in the streets. That's how I made my living.

In Cuba it was much better. I ate better, I lived better. I had better clothes. We were four, five boys living in one room—it was like a hotel, there was a shower and baths. Eating, we used to go out and eat in a restaurant.

I used to see in those very fancy and rich hotels how the American people used to come, how they were dressed so beautifully, with the beautiful cars that they used to come, and everything. So we all used to point out to each other, "See these are Americans. Look how they're dressed, look at the cars." Almost the whole world of Cuba was controlled by the United States—the telephone, telegraph. And the nightlife over there, nightclubs over there, were all controlled by the American people.

In those days, the president of Cuba was a man by the name of Machado. That guy, Machado, was before Batista. He was a thousand times worse. He was an ultra-reactionary. People wanted to organize into a union. They didn't have a chance. The sugarcane workers were treated just like slaves. Not only that, if anybody made attempts to organize the workers, they found them drowned in the ocean the next day. Every time they found another man drowned they knew that this is the work of the Machado government, not to let the people get organized.

Even there I got acquainted with some boys that were also progressive. I remember distinctly at one time a friend of mine comes over and he says, "You know, Jack"—he was a tailor—"I don't go to work myself. A soldier comes and he takes me to go to work." I said, "What? A soldier comes and takes you to work? Why?" He himself didn't understand what was going on. There was a strike over there and the boss wanted to have the people coming to work for him, but the workers were afraid to come because outside there were pickets. So for each worker he sent a soldier. It was a small shop, a small tailor shop, five or six, maybe ten people. So he used to send out five, six soldiers to pick up those people. So I said, "Look, you're actually a strikebreaker. Do you know what you're doing? You're breaking the strike. Don't go next day to work." So then he realized what was going on. He didn't realize why all of a sudden a soldier had to come to take him to work.

Harry M.

I was born in Mogilev, in Russia. It was a medium-sized city, about fifty thousand residents—about 30 percent Jewish and the rest Gentiles. The Jews and Gentiles didn't get along very well. There was always antisemitism.

The Jewish occupations in our city were mostly tailors, shoemakers, carpenters, and the rest of them were traders—small traders. I remember there were little stores like grocery stores, little yardgood sellers, shoe sellers, not big. But some of them had really big stores on the main avenue of the city, and they were the big Jews. There was no relationship between the rich and the poor Jews. They were separated by all means. Separate synagogues and even separate social events.

The rich were mostly assimilated Jews. They spoke Russian—they didn't speak Jewish. They were more cultivated. They were more assimilated. The poor Jews were more socially together. They came together to the same synagogue, they came to each other for holidays, they came to each other for weddings, bar mitzvahs. They spoke Jewish. My father knew Russian well, and my sister knew Russian well, but the Jewish tradition for my mother was that you spoke Jewish. My mother wouldn't want to speak Russian. She felt you only spoke Russian to a Gentile or if you went to a Russian school.

The rich were absolutely a group by themselves. They had a temple with a choir and a *chazzen* [cantor]. In the poor synagogue, there was regular prayers, without any choir, without any songs. The temple was entirely different for the rich Jews. A poorer person could go into a richer synagogue, but he wouldn't get a seat, because all the seats were occupied. They wouldn't come to the rich synagogue anyway, unless they were lovers of good singing and they came there to hear a tenor or a baritone.

We belonged to not the poor and not the rich. But it also wasn't a middle class. It was a little above the poor. We were mostly sympathizing with the poor, because we mixed with them in the synagogue, we mixed with them in the street, and we mixed with them playing ball and other games. My father was a Hebrew teacher and my mother had a little grocery store. We were two sisters and five brothers. My father wasn't very orthodox, but he was religious. He had to go to synagogue—he was teaching Hebrew to the children to make a living. He didn't make much, so my mother had to help him out. So we were a little above the poverty line, but actually not enough to sympathize with the affluent. And there was no middle class. The economic condition was such that either you were in business and you were rich, with a certain amount of money, or you were a clerk or a worker or a teacher, which didn't pay very well.

Our house was not bad. It had three rooms, but part of the big room was the grocery store, with a cot for sleeping. In the other room, my father and mother slept and two children were sleeping on the floor in the kitchen. I slept on a straw mattress. My sister slept on a cot also made of wood and of straw. The floor was dirt. The heating system was a brick stove with a chimney, and wood.

The town had no electricity and we had no running water. We had to go to the well to get water. A town of fifty thousand—no running water, no electricity, no telephones. Later on, in 1914 or '15, electricity came in and telephones came in and running water, but only the rich could afford it. The poor couldn't get it. In a few of the very rich houses they had central heating. But for most of the population, the heating was wood. Maybe, in the town of fifty thousand, about fifty had central heating.

If you had to make a telephone, if you had to call some official, or call the doctor, you had to go to the apothecary, and there was a phone where you called the person if he also had a phone. The only communication really was by letter. It was primitive, but they got the letters. It took a long time—a letter from America took a month.

Transportation was horse and wagon. Before the war, probably 1913 or 1912, there were three motor vehicles in our town. The whole town came out to see them. They had to restrain the horses because they were so excited that they were running away. Those motors were very primitive and they were making a lot of noise.

In our town we had a barber who was also a nurse. If you were sick, you used to call this barber and he would call the doctor if you needed certain medications. He would give you quinine for fever and castor oil for a physic. If you had a cold or pains, he used to give you cupping. This was glass cups, very small ones, and they used to put a match into it to get out the air and the glass cups would stick to your body. They were usually given on the back. They didn't know the action of it, but they used it from practical experience. They used that if you were really seriously sick or if your temperature went up, and if you had rapid pulse.

Or the barber would look at your throat and smear your throat with a silver nitrate solution. They also used mustard plaster for congestion of the chest. Mustard also brings heat. Many times your skin burned. They also used leeches. The idea was to suck out the bad blood, not the good blood.

In Europe, because of antisemitism at that time Jews had less opportunity than in America. In our town there was one Jewish doctor, but he was well-to-do, because it cost a lot of money to study, and he had to have a special permit to live in the big town where there were medical schools. Jews weren't allowed to live in the big towns, unless they were first-class merchants. A first-class merchant would pay a certain amount of money to belong to the guild, and then you were allowed to live in the town as a Jew. Jews needed special permits, they couldn't study all over.

Until I was thirteen, I went to a Jewish school. It was inferior to the public school, but we couldn't get into the government schools because there was a ratio of Jews, percentagewise, to enter into these schools. We resented this, but you couldn't help it. My older brother emigrated to America when he was about fifteen because he wanted to study and he couldn't study in Russia. Some of his friends went to America and we had some—relatives in America. They wrote him he should come. My mother was heartbroken, but the rest of the family figured he's going to come to America—the Golden Land—and he will make enough money to take us out there or come back and be a rich man and wouldn't have to be working so hard.

One of my older sisters did graduate from a government school. She got in there because she was a good student. They only picked the best out of a certain percentage. After graduation, she was teaching students privately in their homes Russian, ethics, the higher mathematics, and all the other things. The Jewish school didn't teach these things.

The antisemitism was resented. We resented to be called a Jew bastard. Although we had some Gentile friends—really good friends, just like any other, the parents of these Gentile friends resented us. They said: "Why do you play with Jews? Jews killed our God." Easter time, we once invited a friend to the house and gave him matzohs, and the parents bawled him out why he ate matzohs—"matzohs were made with the blood of Christians." But the children were still playing the same, sleigh riding in the winter together, going to the well to get water together, or going to the garden of somebody else to pick some fruit illegally.

The religious issue was the main reason for antisemitism. Other reasons were that they thought the Jews exploited them and the Jews fooled them. The whole trouble was that they thought the government, the czar, was very good to them, but that the Jews are causing all the trouble. You see, the estate owners used to go away—they were absentee owners—and in order to manage the affairs, they used to rent it to the Jews. They went away to Europe, France, Paris. Most of them didn't want to take any obligations. They had so much land and they figured the Jews could manage it better than they can, so they rented it to the Jews for a certain percentage of the products. Naturally the Gentile that was exploited saw the Jew. He didn't see the estate owner, the landowner. That was where the resentment also came in.

The Jew always thought that the peasant was very ignorant, which he was. But the average Jew sympathized with their condition and tried to treat them fairly and squarely. But some people, mostly the merchants, took advantage of their ignorance and they fooled them.

We felt that the government is misleading them and telling them lies. They wanted all the trouble to go against the Jews instead of relieving the exploitation of the people. In the wintertime, when the peasant had nothing to do in the field, he came to town, looking for work. Although we were not rich—we were poor—still we could hire a peasant for a pittance to chop our wood and put it away in a barn. I don't remember the amount of money, but usually we used to give them food, we used to give them a white challah—to them it was a delicacy. We knew that they don't make pogroms out of just their own evilness, but out of their misery, they came to make pogroms against the Jews.

In our town they organized a self-defense organization against pogroms. They had strong youngsters trying to defend each house. It just happened that in our town the peasants didn't make any pogroms. They didn't come in. But we were prepared— the Jews, the youth—with sticks and irons. Most towns had prepared self-defense.

When the World War came, the rich still lived very well. They had big contracts from the army and they supplied the officers' quarters. The town became affluent from the money from the army that was staying in the town. But for the poor Jews it was hard to get work and to get food. During the War, it was hard to get the commodities—we were short—but it wasn't starvation. We still had food.

When I was about thirteen, I didn't go to school anymore and I started working in a men's haberdashery store. I was working from eight in the morning until twelve at night. I swept the floors, I swept the counters, I unpacked the merchandise, and I ran deliveries. I was making those days about two dollars a week, and that I gave to help support my family. I was also making some tips delivering the haberdashery to rich men's estates. We had in our town about three hotels and the landowners from surrounding villages came to the town to buy. The hotels that time were walk-ups, no elevators—one hotel, a new one, did have an elevator. I had to walk up sometimes, on the fourth floor with a big, heavy package that a rich man bought and deliver it to him. And he used to give me a tip. In those days it was about two kopecks.

Before the Revolution, you had to be subservient on a job. You couldn't say nothing. You would lose the job. I remember one incident when I was sweeping the floor. There was a lot of dust during the summer, so you would sprinkle the floor. While sweeping, my head was down and I didn't look up. My boss walked in with white shoes and I swept the goddamn dirt with the water—the sprinkling—on his white shoes. He bawled me out mercilessly. He wanted to fire me. Then the manager told him that I was a newcomer, and I didn't know him. I had to apologize for dirtying his shoes. That line was continuing until the Revolution in 1917.

In 1917 the Revolution came. There was a tremendous joy and a tremendous friendship between the Gentiles and the Jews. We thought that this was like the Messiah came. "Frei geboiren." I, at that time, was fifteen years old, still working for that haberdashery store. We organized a union—a clerk's union. Naturally, the owner of the place didn't want to agree. So we called a strike. We wanted the boss to come down to the union and sign a contract. Most of the workers were old, they had slaved for so many years. They were afraid of the boss and they couldn't understand how we youngsters could oppose the boss and give the boss demands. They'd want him to give a raise on his wishes, according to how he sees fit.

About a week or two passed, and we were picketing outside. The old clerks still didn't want to get out. We had to pull them out by force. At that time, we had about thirty employees. Of the thirty, we had about twenty old-timers, some of them already in their fifties, which at that time was an old man. Some were in their forties. The union was in a storefront, with a table with a red cloth on it. We had a meeting in the union and we finally decided that the only way—if he wants to sign the agreement—is he has to come down to the union to sign. The old-timers were objecting— "How dare you? The owners, the boss, should come down to the union to sign the contract? You have to come up to his house." Eventually, on the third week, the boss gave in. He came down to the union and he signed the contract. And the old-timers sighed with relief. "My God, you guys made him do it." They couldn't believe that you could demand something and get it and not have to depend on the good will of the owner, the boss. They were even delighted. We demanded from the owner that he should give us two days off, and it was a terrific battle. Finally, he agreed to a day and a half during the week. And even with the day and a half, we still put in about sixty hours.

We youngsters got together, we had meetings, and we organized groups to visit the Council of Soviets. It was really a joy. The citizens were friendly to each other, Gentile and Jew, they went to meetings to listen to the different parties that were established—the Socialists, Socialist Mensheviks, Bolsheviks—all different parties, revolutionary parties. The youth took part in it, some of them were Mensheviks, some of them were Socialists. They organized educational classes and the owner of the shop or the factory or the store had to give every worker some nights off to go to the educational classes. We studied arithmetic, algebra, geometry, geography, and a little chemistry, and history. The equivalent of a junior high school education.

During the Revolution it was harder to get food because the peasants were hoarding the food. Instead of bringing it into town to sell it, they were hoarding it for themselves. Food was hard to get and inadequate, but it wasn't starvation. In some places people ate raw potatoes, raw cabbages. They had to go in the fields and take whatever the peasants wouldn't dig up in order to sustain themselves.

I heard about this from other towns. In our town, it wasn't bad. We were in a place where all the surrounding villages used to bring their products. It was short, but not starvation. There was no more antisemitism after the Revolution. You didn't hear anything. In fact, the Gentile was just as vehement against the old police as the Jew. They changed and disorganized the old police—some of them were put in jail. Some of them just lost their jobs. They organized new police and in our town the chief of police was a Jew. The Gentiles didn't resent it. They worked with the Jews on the new revolutionary assignment. Then the Revolution at the end of 1917 broke up in different parties. In October 1917 the Bolsheviks took over.

It was actually a honeymoon. It was more than six months, from October until April. I would say it was a honeymoon for the people. There were no fights. People used to live in peace, happy. They used to turn out to the parades, to the speeches, the meetings. Most of the meetings were made in the movie houses, because that was the only big place where you could pack in a few thousand people.

At the meetings, people would discuss—"What kind of government do you want?" Also at that time there were discussions about the question of peace. The slogan at that time, the revolutionary slogan of the Bolsheviks, was: "You don't hit a man when he's down." But it didn't work—the Germans hit them when they were down. But they would say, "Don't worry, the German brothers wouldn't hit you when you're down. When you give up the arms, you surrender, everything will be all right." And most people were for peace. We were sick and tired of war. There were shortages of food and clothing and transportation. The people figured if they'll stop the war, they'll reorganize the country and it will be all right.

Also, at that time, the French sent some troops to Odessa, to the Black Sea; the English sent some troops to the northern sea, the Archangel; and the Americans sent some troops to Siberia to support the counterrevolutionary White Guard generals. We knew then what was going on, but there were reactionaries who hoped that the French, the English and the Americans would succeed and that it would come, not the former monarchy but some kind of a constitutional monarchy, or something like that. But the majority of the people resented it. The majority of the people joined the Red Army and volunteered, actually, without conscription, to fight the counterrevolutionaries.

At that time there was truly no antisemitism. It was forgotten. We were proud, we were equal citizens, we could travel anywhere we wanted, we could get any job we wanted, we were free to live wherever we wanted. No discrimination. The Jews were very happy. Antisemitism didn't show except in reactionary circles. Those that were in the counterrevolutionary movement, they blamed everything on the Jews. It's not a question of a Russian being a Communist. Jew and Communist was synonymous, and that was their propaganda.

But Jews had their full rights, like everybody else. They were the leaders, they were the members of the soviets, they were the members of the government. The Gentiles that were with the Red Army had no opposition to it. I think there was even a law then that if you abused a Jew or used the words "dirty Jew" you were getting six months in jail.

While the Revolution was going on, the old generals—the White Guard—were still fighting the Revolution in different sections. In some towns they made pogroms and killed a lot of Jews. The Bolsheviks had to retreat, because it was actually a Civil War. When the Russians decided to stop the fighting with Germany, the Germans marched into the Ukraine and we had German troops in our town for about three months. But then the German Revolution happened and the German army withdrew. They went back to Germany as fast as possible, by any means they could. But they set up a puppet government of Ukrainian nationalists. In our town we had this counterrevolutionary government. They were against the Bolshevik Revolution.

Very quickly, the old owners got back their stores and they started firing all those people that were active in the unions, and they began taking you back to slavery. We had nothing to say. We went back to the old time, the Czarist time. The Jews then were called Communists, Bolsheviks, even though some were middle-class merchants. It was not so pleasant. They brought back the antisemitism. They blamed everything on the Jews.

That was the time that my brother from America came into contact with us to try to bring us to America. My father died in 1917, when he was fifty-three. At that time, people said, "Well, he didn't die such a young man." Fifty-three. There were very few real old-timers. Some who were in their sixties were old men. Most people died young. My father was supposed to go into the army when he was twenty-one, and he made himself sick at that time in order not to be in the army. Even in the army, they would only take a certain percentage of Jews. There was a law by the czar that if you had enough money you could buy a substitute and you would be released.

So the rich didn't go. They went to find a poor schnook willing to go for fifty rubles. But even then it was hard to find somebody.

At that time there was a certain weight you had to be to be accepted in the army. When the youngsters had to go they went on a certain diet to be underweight. They were eating pumpkin seeds, and drinking it with cold water, and this gave them diarrhea. And they didn't sleep at night, in order to emaciate themselves. Some of them recovered afterwards, but my father got his bronchial tubes affected, and the rest of his life, he was coughing. As he got older, he got colds and then caught pneumonia. As a result of this, he died.

My mother still had the grocery then, and I was working. My sister was also helping out, making a few rubles, teaching. We got along. We weren't affluent, but we got along. We didn't get new suits, we used to fix our pants with patches. Our shoes were always fixed by the shoemaker—we didn't get new shoes. Clothing was only very rarely bought new. My mother would fix things up as much as possible. And then we had our brother who used to send us money from America.

He was here working in a factory. He went to night school to get a high school education, and then he entered college. By 1918, he was drafted into the American army. He told us the story about the uncle that he came to, who was a poor peddler. They lived very poorly. In three rooms they had their own three children, my brother and another boarder. Seven people in two rooms and a kitchen. And there it was already modern. The sanitary conditions were in the hall, not in an outhouse. But it wasn't private. They had no baths, they used to wash themselves in the kitchen sink— it was not really a sink but a deep tub where you washed the laundry. To take a shower, they had to go to the public baths.

In 1918, my brother organized a group of people to come to Europe and take out some of the Jews from Russia to America. Smugglers smuggled us out of Russia into Romania and there we met my brother and started preparing to go to America.

We lived on the borderline, on a river called Dnestr. Bessarabia was formerly Russian, but during the Revolution, the Romanians occupied that part. The river, about a half mile wide, separated Romania from Russia. So a band of smugglers organized from the Romanian side and the Russian side, and they smuggled people from Russia into Romania. From Romania, you could go anywhere you wanted. Mainly Jews left, Russians didn't leave. You had to have relatives on the other side, in Romania, to accept you, to give you protection, a house to live in. The Russians didn't have it. The Russians didn't emigrate, not according to my knowledge.

I remember we went at night. They rowed you across to the other side and people met you, some relatives, and took you to their house. Other people told us stories that the smugglers robbed them of everything in their possession, under the threat that they're going to give them over to the authorities. But that didn't happen to us. We met our brother and then we stayed in Bucharest, the capital of Romania. It took a long time before you were getting a visa. You couldn't just come to the United States without a visa. Only a certain amount of immigrants were allowed. There wasn't an open door, that everybody could come in. Either you had to have a relative or you had to have somebody to vouch for you—that you're able to get a job so you should not fall on government support. So we had to wait until our visa comes and also until my brother organized the group to come to the United States.

Romania was more poverty-stricken than Russia, more dirty than Russia. It was also more antisemitic than Russia. All the laws were against the Jews. But there was terrific graft. For money, you could get anything from the lowest to the highest.

We were there, I think, about four or five weeks when one thing happened to me personally. We were going shopping—my family, friends, and I. In Bucharest the streetcars were very crowded and they had two cars—one was pulling the other like a two-car transport. At that time I was the only one from my family in one car, and my friends and my sister and brothers were in the other car. While I was standing in the car, a guy started yelling that his wallet was stolen. I couldn't understand much Romanian but I got an inkling that something was going on. He bent down and found his wallet at my feet, so he accused me that I pickpocketed the wallet. The conductor stopped the car and immediately called a cop on the corner. He put handcuffs on me and took me away to the police station.

In the police station, they started asking me questions. I couldn't get the language. I knew only a few words here and there. They gave me the third degree. I kept on saying, "No, no, no." I understood what they wanted. They wanted me to say that I stole it. I understood a few words, but not completely. And they beat me mercilessly. Then, at night, they put me into a cell, a dirty cell, on the floor, without a cot, without anything, without toilet facilities. There was an outhouse outside. The next day they woke me up in the morning and again the third degree. And again I said only "No."

On the third night, they brought in some new prisoners. They brought in a fellow, and he says to me, "Are you Russian?" I said, "Yeah." He said, "Speak to me in Russian." He says he's a long time in Romania and he admitted he's a pickpocket by profession. He asked me why I was there and I told him. He said, "Ah, don't tell me stories, you must have pickpocketed too." Finally, after the conversation, he realized that I'm telling the truth, and he says in Russian to me, "The next day they are going to take you out again. You say to everything, 'Yes, yes, yes.' Otherwise, they'll beat the hell out of you. They'll release you, but you'll be a broken person." He knew the law, he knew everything—"Say yes and the only thing is you're going to get three years and then there are amnesties for the prince's birthday, for the king's birthday, for the queen's birthday. You won't even serve a year. Then you'll come to America and you'll be all right." He said, "You're a young fellow and you can stand it."

The next day they brought me to court. In the court, they asked me, "Do you know Romanian?" I said no. They gave me a translator. He was a Jewish fellow, but he didn't know much Jewish and I knew very little Romanian. We couldn't get together. At the end of it, the guy was right. I said to everything yes and they gave me three years in jail.

Meanwhile, my family didn't know what to do. They couldn't find me. They went to the police station, but there they wouldn't tell them anything. Some correspondent that was reporting on the trial realized that I couldn't speak the language, so he printed it in the paper, and the next day my family found it and my brother came to jail to see me.

In jail was already nice. They gave you a cot and there was a chamber pot. Everybody was assigned a duty. In the morning they took you out about six o'clock and you had to build some brick walls. It wasn't bad. There was no more beating. The food was pretty rotten. There was some soup with maybe one potato in the whole bowl, and some bread and some barley. I was there a couple of days and they brought in that Russian who told me to say to everything "Yes." He said, "What did you get? I told you you would get three years." I said, "You know the law." He said, "Don't worry, you'll be out."

Meanwhile my brother came to visit me. He gave the guard money—he bribed the guard—and they treated me better. They gave me better food. Then this Russian, the pickpocket, said to my brother: "Listen, you go and see this judge, and for a thousand"—they had money which at that time was about a hundred dollars in American money—"the judge will make a special trial and release him." But, he said, "You better do it fast because that guy that accused your brother is out of town." The man was a big-shot city engineer, and there was an article in the papers about it. The pickpocket said, "When he'll come back, the judge wouldn't be able to dismiss the case. So you better go and do it today. Then you've got to get out of the country right away. Go to the other side, to Germany, because when the guy will come back they'll reopen the case and you'll be in jail for the rest of the year." So my brother listened. He gave him the name of a judge, and he gave him the name of a lawyer that could approach the judge. After a week in jail, they took me out, brought me back to court and—case dismissed!

My brother put me on a train and I went to Konigsberg, Germany. They gave me some money and I waited there about a week's time until my family came with the other group and we migrated to France, to a town on the seashore, waiting for the ship. There in France they had barracks for the refugees. The Jews of France organized the camp, supplied it with food and entertainment. It was very nice there. There was a big difference in the cleanliness. The people were friendlier, and the food was different. You didn't see such a poverty as in Russia or in Romania. It looked to us like they were better dressed and better off. But we didn't stay long. After about two weeks, we sailed to America.

Rachel S.

I was born a couple of years after my parents came back from the United States. My father, who was very, very religious, didn't like it there because it wasn't enough religious for him, and he decided to go back. They came back right after the Japanese War in 1905, and I was born after that—the end of 1907.

I was born in Minsk. It was a beautiful city, and we lived on the outskirts of the city. We didn't live in the Jewish section. The Jewish section was across the city, on the other side of us. You had to go through the whole city to get there, the cemetery was there. I remember passing by there when my grandma died and we went to the cemetery. Where we lived, there were Jews, but very, very few.

My mother was very exceptional. Maybe that's why the neighbors liked her so much. We were not religious. My father was the one that was religious and we obeyed him. He didn't allow us to read Russian books on Saturday—on *Shabbes*. Jewish books you had to read on Shabbes, that's how fanatic he was. We weren't allowed to carry money on Saturday. My mother was not religious. When my father used to go to the shul on Saturday, she used to quickly warm—you weren't allowed to warm up the food on Shabbes, Saturday, because it's a Jewish holiday. So you had to keep the food warm all the time. My mother used to make the stove and warm it up when my father was in shul.

I hardly remember my father, because when I was eight years old he went to war, and when he came back he was home four or five days and he died. He was very religious. He didn't eat anything that they served in the army. So we used to send him packages and he just ate whatever we sent him in the package, like hard salami, bread. We had a hardship when my father came from the war. He had typhus fever. We, the children, didn't stay in the house because it was very contagious. We stayed with neighbors. My mother was alone with him, and we had to get ice for him. We lived near a railway station, and on the railway station they had ice cubes because it was more modern there and they needed it for drinks. So the children used to go to the railway station and we used to beg for ice and bring it for my mother because she needed it for my father. He was sick five days and he died. He must have been in his thirties.

Then, my mother had four children and she had to struggle to make a living. She had to support four children. We were four sisters. She had a little grocery store. She had to buy things for it and she had to sell. She wasn't happy about it. She didn't care for it, but she couldn't help herself. And because of that, my uncle wrote, "Do you want to come to America?" And we said, "Why not?" America, it was a wonderful thing. I had heard all about the United States. First of all, I had relatives here, uncles. There were a lot of people, especially Jewish people, that wanted to go to a country that's free, that they can study, that they can work wherever they want.

I had my mother's brothers here—three brothers were here—that came in 1904, 1903. They heard that their sister remained with four small children and she was struggling. They wrote us letters that they wanted the two older ones to come and they'd help us. When I left I must have been fifteen years old. I was a young lady. I just finished high school. I finished in June and I left in August. It happened so fast, it was unexpected—like a surprise. We didn't expect to get the visas. We left in 1923.

It was right in the middle of the revolution. They let us out, but the reason I know they didn't like it was because they wanted young people to stay there. We were still revolutionary, although we went away from there. When we came to the United States we were very revolutionary. I figured I'd come here and make the revolution here. I wanted to go for adventures.

My mother didn't leave right away. It was just the two older ones, me and another sister. My mother was a very politically minded person. She read Russian books and she read German. She was more or less enlightened. She smoked at a very early age and women didn't smoke in Russia. She was a revolutionary in the revolution, but they wouldn't admit her because she had a store. So she had to work on a kolkhoz for two years because she was considered a kulak. Kulaks were people that did not labor. Having a little store where you were selling a little groceries was considered not labor. So she had to work for two years on the kolkhoz to buy herself out—to get herself accepted in the society. She had a good life on the kolkhoz. She used to take care of all the dairy products. You see, they put her on a job that a more educated person can do. She didn't really do hard work, because she was educated.

My uncle sent us the tickets and the money. We were two girls—I was sixteen, my sister was nineteen. We got the visas and we got our boat—a beautiful boat. It was one of the largest ships at that time, and we were very excited and very happy that we got the visas and we were going to the United States. We got on the ship and we met there a lot of friends that we met on the way—going for the visas—and we were very happy and excited. It took seven days, but there was a very, very terrible storm while we were going and the ship was delayed because of the storm.

When we came into the United States, a lot of small boats came in before us. Since they came in before, they took up the quota, and we didn't have the right to land because the quota was filled. Our ship had five thousand people coming, but because the quota was filled they didn't know what to do with us. They had to make a decision in the Congress or some other place in the government what to do with us—five thousand people. But the ship had to go back—it couldn't wait. So they put us overnight on another ship, an old dilapidated piece of junk. It was not a ship that traveled—it was a standing ship. Then the next day they put us on Ellis Island.

We were on Ellis Island two weeks, and it was a nightmare, especially for me. There was a general room for sitting during the day—men separate and women separate, but in the dining room we all ate together. Three times a day we had to go through long corridors to the dining room, the rest of the time we spent in the general room. They gave us certain things like knitting wool, or crocheting so we should be occupied. People spent their time in a lot of different ways, sitting around, laying around. There were hard benches there where you had to stay all day, and the baggage that we brought was placed on racks right on the side in the same big room.

I took sick. I don't know from what. They kept us there two weeks. Maybe from the food or whatever, I wasn't well, and I didn't want to go to the hospital. After that, we realized that if I would have gone to the hospital we would have remained in the United States because I would have been in the hospital. But I was afraid of the hospital. I was a young kid and I didn't want to go away from my sister. So I was lying down on a bench in the general room where only the women were, and all of a sudden I felt that something was crawling on me. I grabbed it on my shoulder, through my dress, and I was screaming. Everybody was running away from me. It was a horrible sensation. It was a mouse. From the baggage that was stacked on the sides, there must have been rats, mice, whatever. I was screaming maybe five or ten minutes until a brave woman came over and took it out from me. Of course, I had to get rid of the clothing because it smelled, and I couldn't eat the rest of the time I was there.

Then they made a decision to send us back. They put us on the same *Majestic* that came in, and they took us all back. Of course, they guarded us, because a lot of people wanted to jump in the sea—they didn't want to go back—so they had guards posted all over, and they didn't let us out of the cabins until the boat started out. And we went back to England.

It was very sad. We were all very disturbed. It was like a funeral. We were outraged that since we traveled all this time, since we did have the visas, they should have let us down. But they didn't. And it's no use talking about spilled milk. It seems that the steamship company was responsible for this failure of getting us on time to the United States, so we were told that we'd be housed in England and we could wait—as soon as our quotas came, we'd be sent back to the United States without any more expense. They'll house us and feed us and do whatever is necessary. So most of us agreed to stay. My mother wrote to us that we should come back, we shouldn't stay there. But, you know, forbidden fruit, just because we couldn't get in, we felt that we wanted to get in. We didn't want to go back and we decided to stick it out.

What they did was they made camps in a small village near Southampton, East-lake. They made big camps for these people, for the people that were sent back. We stayed women separate, men separate, children stayed with their mothers in tents, in tremendous barracks. It was really like barracks. They had dining rooms for us. They provided all kinds of occupations. You could go to the city, you could go wherever. We weren't detained, we were allowed to leave, because we were free people. We had soccer teams and basketball. I played soccer with girls on a team, and we had basketball games and we had teachers teaching us. Since I knew a little English—my sister and I learned English yet in Russia—I decided to look for an English teacher and improve my English. Then a lot of people approached me and they said, "You know English. Teach us whatever you know." So I did. I had eight, ten lessons, private lessons, and I was teaching those people. The money that I made on those lessons, I spent for one lesson to get a good English teacher. We had a good time. We were all youngsters. We had parties, and we had dancing, and we had singing, and we had games.

England was a beautiful country. Of course, there were a lot of rains and a lot of fogs. People were very polite. And they had certain expressions like "ta ta" when they want to say thank you. They were very nice to us, except we were very lonely. We were living by ourselves—two girls—and we were very, very lonely. We were anxious for relatives or a friend, somebody. We had nobody there, we lived by ourselves.

Finally, after two years, our quota came. We were very happy, we were delighted, and we packed in and went wherever we had to go. We went on the same ship, the *Majestic,* but it was different circumstances, because this time we knew we were getting in.

Sema O.

Sol and Bela S.

Clara and Wolf U.

Tillie C. and Sarah C.

THREE

America

Introduction

Having rejected their oppressed and restricted community in Europe, the Followers eagerly embraced the opportunity and challenge of living in a different world, still perceived by immigrants as the promised land. Although uprooted, America's freedom—compared relatively to Europe's—allowed the Followers to begin piecing together what appeared to be a new sense of community. Generally, this vision was derived from a set of reworked and adapted European values, circumstances in America, and dreams of what the new world could offer. Specifically, three factors helped shape the Followers' new sense of community—a great respect for learning, the importance of the family, and the significance of religious belief.

After arriving in New York, one of the first things each of the Followers did was enroll in night school. They did so for an obvious reason: mastering English quickly increased the possibility of their successful integration into American society. An additional explanation may be related to the reverence for learning instilled in them by their parents. The Followers were raised in a literate community that insisted on the formal religious and secular education of males and encouraged providing the basics to females. Religious education, while narrow in scope, helped cultivate disciplined minds capable of thinking analytically. Characterized by meticulous study, undertaken by devoted practitioners who were held in high esteem, religious scholarship helped foster great respect for the pursuit of knowledge and for all of those the process engrossed. In addition to religious training the Followers attended local public schools. Able to speak and read at least two and sometimes as many as five languages (Yiddish, Russian, German, Polish, Hebrew) the Followers experienced a diverse range of political and literary ideas. At a young age, they were intellectually engaged.

In America, the Followers did not limit their pursuit of knowledge to the conjugation of English verbs. The reverence for learning that the Followers developed in Europe encouraged them to challenge themselves intellectually, to push beyond established conventions and boundaries. In addition to night school, the Followers read books and newspapers at the Forty-second Street Library; they attended lectures at Cooper Union and the Ethical Culture school; on weekend evenings they went to concerts at Lewisohn Stadium and stood in the backs of crowded theaters, struggling to understand operas and plays. Their early education in America was exploratory and multifaceted. They were anxious to experience all that New York City had to offer. In effect, the respect for education that the Followers learned in Europe was applied actively after their arrival in America.

The Followers' strong devotion to family, also developed in Europe, was maintained and adapted in America. When discussing life in Europe, the Followers never fail to reveal the image of the closely knit family. Families were large; they ate together, usually worked together, often studied together, and always observed holidays together. It was not unlikely for three generations, and sometimes four, to be living under one roof. An extended family that did most things together was the standard. Divorce rates were extremely low, largely because of the shame divorce could bring to both families and, since love was not the most important criterion for a successful marriage, "falling out of love" was, perhaps, not considered the sort of tragedy that brought about separations. Marriages are depicted as working relationships designed to create and maintain family units. This can help to explain the young age at which couples married, the existence of "matchmakers," who pushed those moving too slowly into marriage and encouraged widowers to remarry after a suitable period of mourning. Religious, cultural, and economic pressure made creating and maintaining closely knit family units a priority.

Familial bonds proved even more powerful than the Followers' political commitment to the Russian Revolution. After reading the Followers' stories one wonders why it is, given their political beliefs, that those born in Russia left during the Revolution. It would seem that if one believed in communism, the Soviet Union was the place to be in 1917. Why did the Followers leave? It is important to note that most of the Followers became politically radical after leaving the Soviet Union. The majority, while still there, were remotely if at all politically conscious. They did not stay to defend the Revolution because it was only after living in America that they realized exactly what the Revolution was and why it should be defended. The few who were politically active in the Soviet Union left for the same reason as those who were politically un-aware—they had family in America. Parents and grandparents, brothers and sisters, uncles and aunts had begun emigrating to America in the early 1880s. Families that had been separated for years had always hoped and planned to be reunited. When the opportunity arose, maintaining the family proved more important than remaining in the Soviet Union, revolution or not. In addition, the Civil War that followed the Revolution increased the hardship and danger of Jewish life. Violence against Jews escalated. This increased the anxiety among families already separated and encouraged those members in the Soviet Union to come to America.

After arriving in America, the Followers moved in with immediate family, relatives, or both, recreating a variation of the European extended family. At the same time they struggled to earn enough money to send for family members still in Europe. The overriding concern was always the maintenance of close family contact. This was reinforced by the *landsmanshaft* societies, associations created to help people from the same cities and towns remain in touch after arrival in America.

In addition to maintaining and adapting their respect for learning and their concept of family, the Followers also retained and reshaped their religious roots. The Followers grew up in an environment permeated by orthodox religious faith. Born into an era that radically challenged the ideas and assumptions of traditional Europe, many of the Followers began to question all aspects of religion. Some rejected religious practice outright, considering it to be constricting and medieval. This is especially true of those who were born, were raised, or spent a significant amount of time in cities. Most of the Followers simply went through the motions, thoroughly doubtful and skeptical, as a measure of respect for their parents. A few maintained their belief, usually those who lived in small towns and villages. After only a short time in America, all of the Followers had completely abandoned religion. For those disinterested in Europe, it was a welcome, liberating development. For the few who came to America as practicing Jews, it was a more difficult experience. What seems to have been one of the most decisive factors was the strong feeling that there was too much hypocrisy involved in faithfully practicing religion in America. Plainly put, it was difficult to survive economically and not work on Saturdays; it was considered hypocritical to work Saturdays and to think of yourself as truly religious.

Also responsible for leading the Followers away from religion was their attraction to radical politics. Communism vowed to change the world with action rather than prayer. It dismissed religious belief as superstitious and backward. The Party line stressed devoting one's energy to improving this world rather than waiting for another. The Followers were particularly receptive to the promises of communism, having been oppressed as Jews in Europe and exploited as workers in America. They were reminded daily, by the unions they belonged to, the newspapers they read, by discussions at the cutting table and at the dinner table, that communism would enable them to transform their lives and the world in which they lived. Consequently, the Followers believed in communism as devoutly and passionately as their parents had believed in the Torah.

Thus, the new sense of community that the Followers created was not really new at all. The fundamental aspects on which their European community was built—great respect for learning, importance of the family, and the significance of religious belief—were all still present, only reworked and adapted to a new set of circumstances.

Ethel G. and Fanny O.

Sarah C.

Rachel S.

Harry S.

Ethel G. and Fanny O.

ETHEL: In 1907 we came. It was after the 1905 Revolution when the Jewish young men were running on the streets and trying to protect themselves. We were hidden in a cellar by a Gentile neighbor. She liked our mother and father. We were seven children. We were hidden in her basement and papa was running around on the streets and the Cossacks were running them down. My father had a nephew, a very intimate nephew of his, and it didn't take long, the nephew decided to go to America. Our father said, "If he goes, I'll also go."

My father took along two children—two girls. One was fourteen and one was twelve. The twelve-year-old they didn't want to take, but she cried, and she was the type that always had her way—she was the spoiled one in the family. So they took her along too.

The first job my father got, he shoveled snow and he got three dollars a week, and I suppose the sisters must have made a few dollars. On the three dollars, they saved up enough to send for the rest of the children and my mother. We came with mama. Four of us came with mama.

Our boat was such an old boat, the *Sarato*. It almost capsized. As a matter of fact, the second trip, it capsized. Our trip, we were sitting and having one meal—I don't remember which one it was—and the tables turned and everything filled with water. We had another sister older than us, and she was courageous—she used to go up and get food for us and everything else. She wasn't sick at all. It took thirty days on a boat like that, and we heard the next trip it made, it capsized. Thirty days on the ocean. On the sea. As a matter of fact, I think two people died and they threw them overboard. They don't bring them.

Our father came to meet us. Our sisters and brother—they must have been working, they couldn't take off, so Papa came to meet us and the sister that came with us she took care of all of us. She went with Mama, and she talked for her on Ellis Island. Our other brother had trouble with his eyes, so we were kept there for two weeks— they almost sent us back. He just must have had a cold or something. Ellis Island was a terrible scene, terrible. The crying, the lamenting of people—some were sent back, families were broken up. If you're not just right, they keep you there.

When we were there last year, it left such an impression you couldn't ever forget it. We were so excited, and when the guide took us around—some college guide—we helped him out. There was a crowd of people, and we helped him—we gave them a lot of information about it.

FANNY: People came to ask us questions about it. We knew more than the guide.

ETHEL: We enjoyed it so much. It's a wonderful trip. Did you ever go to Ellis Island? Take the boat and go down there.

When Papa took us, then it must have been the First Avenue El or the Third Avenue El—wait, let's see. It's down on South Ferry, Battery Park—so it must have been the First Avenue El. I remember, our possessions that we had—mind you, people that lived so many years in a country—the possessions that we had was a little bundle. Each one of us was carrying a little bundle. We got into the elevated, we were so excited, and we traveled. They took us to the East Side. Papa had an apartment for us on Eleventh Street. It was no windows.

FANNY: Only in the rear.

ETHEL: Two bedrooms, like a railroad flat. Do you know what a railroad flat means? They run through. The only one who has a window is, let's say, the livingroom and, in the back, the kitchen. Everything is dark. There were two rooms, dark, and we slept—three of us—in a bed.

FANNY: On the floor, too, we slept.

ETHEL: That was afterwards. Three in a bed and our brother slept in the kitchen on a little cot, and Mama and Papa, I suppose, had a little room. Things were really different then. In back of the yard, you had to walk three floors, there was a toilet—an outhouse—for everybody in the house. There were maybe four or five tenants. During the night, usually about two or three in the morning, somebody has to go—so there used to be a line-up, everybody used to line up to go.

FANNY: And there was snow and ice on the ground. And we had no electric—there was gas, with a quarter meter. That's the most important thing to say.

ETHEL: Yeah, a quarter meter. There was a meter and you threw in a quarter and you wound up the meter, for the gas. If the quarter went out—I suppose it lasted for a certain time—so you remained in the dark. No matter how many people were in the house, you remained in the dark. If you didn't have another quarter, you couldn't get any gas. There was a little stove in the kitchen, where our brother slept. And Papa used to get up at five o'clock in the morning to make the stove, so when we got up it should be a little warmer. That's how we lived. And you know how the laundries were washed? On a board, a washing board, and they were cooked in a pot, because it was licey. If you didn't bathe, your clothes had lice in it. So in order to get the clothes a little bit clean, they used to cook it on the little stove, they used to cook it for hours.

If you had white clothes—say a white sweater, a white blouse, a white something—so they used to take blue and dilute it with a little bit of warm water and put more water in it, and dip the white clothes in it so it should give it a little color.

Our father was not really religious. Mother was the one that was fanatically religious. But she was an idealist. Papa didn't care. But for her sake, he kept up. He had a beard. He used to go on the West Side, Saturday afternoons he liked to take his walk. He was a great walker—I take after him. He used to go Saturday afternoons on the West Side walking, so the kids used to pull his beard. The Irish used to live there. They attacked the Jew, that's what it was. And not only that—the Jews were so in the minority, you had to keep your mouth shut for everything. What do you think? It's like now? If you were a Jew, you amounted to nothing. So Papa one Saturday came back and he said to Mama he's not going to have his beard. He shaved his beard off. And since then, he was shaved.

When we were fourteen, fifteen, we started working. We started protesting a lot of things. We revolted against the Jewish religion. I used to argue with my mother. My mother was very fanatic. She'd say to the rabbi, "My children are not religious, but they're very, very good." She felt guilty that we didn't follow her footsteps.

FANNY: Light candles on Friday night.

ETHEL: That's the least, Fanny, lighting the candles. With my mother, I was always a rebel and I always argued. When I became older, I realized what everything is, that in the Jewish religion the woman doesn't amount to anything. You know what a minyan is? Ten is a minyan. Anyway, I always said, "Why, even if you have twenty women, you can't have a minyan." That got me revolting. Our mother was heartbroken. She was. And then when we got older and we joined Followers of the Trail, she was heartbroken. She would have liked us to follow her footsteps.

My father idolized my mother. There was really a love affair between them. We lived in a house of love. Mama loved everybody. Every landsman—you know what a landsman is?—from the same town, whoever came to America, our father wanted to show off. You know, he was rich here. In Europe I suppose he didn't have anything, so he used to invite them to the house for dinner, and Mama used to cook for everybody. Mama would prepare big tables of meals for everybody.

Not only that. Whoever came to America came to our house. Some stayed over. Mama would put them up for two weeks, for three weeks, until they could earn a little bit of money. She used to give them sandwiches to eat because they couldn't afford to buy food, and they used to sleep on the floor. Many people were in our house. They started from our home. They'd accumulate a little bit of money, and they'd send for their families.

Mama was good in everything—baking and cooking and everything. And you know where she used to bake? She'd prepare everything and run to the baker's across the way and she used to bake the food at the baker's. You used to pay him a certain amount of money and he used to bake it for you. Mama would prepare it at home, with pans, and the kids would run to the baker's and bake it.

She used to wash her hands every ten minutes. As little water as we had, Mama was so fussy—that's why maybe I'm so spotless. I'm very fussy about it. She always washed her hands, and that was her religion. You see, she handled a dairy dish, and then she had to go and handle a meat dish. She always washed her hands, so it shouldn't interfere in the religion.

FANNY: And then when you went to have your meals, you had to wash your hands.

ETHEL: She never would sit down to eat without washing her hands and saying a prayer. Today, young people go to eat, they don't know what it means to wash a hand. So although it was a religious thing, it was also a sanitary thing, you see. We had to abide. Of course, when we were young, we had to abide. In our home was always Friday night the candles lit, the house cleaned up, the table set, the *challah* at the table. Before Yom Kippur, you had to say a prayer.

FANNY: You talk about religion, give him Yom Kippur. Tell him about Yom Kippur, with the chickens.

ETHEL: You go to a shochet. He's the one that kills the chicken. He says a prayer and he cuts the throat.

FANNY: And the shower. Tell him how we used to go from school.

ETHEL: Wait, you're jumping from one thing to another.

FANNY: A few details tell him. You're not going to give him everything. It's impossible.

ETHEL: It's impossible.

FANNY: We had no baths.

ETHEL: I told you, we had no baths, no toilets, nothing. So there was a public bathing place on Eleventh Street. It was Eleventh Street, wasn't it? At that time, we lived on Eleventh and this was on Eleventh Street. A public place where people went, the children, the mothers, the fathers—certain days for women, certain days for men, and we used to go and take a shower.

FANNY: Up to three o'clock, the children were allowed free.

ETHEL: But by four o'clock, the water gets turned off, so if you're not through by four, if you have soap on your body, you have to go home with the soap on your body. They shut off the water. On Fridays, the children weren't allowed because the women went—you know, they had to live with their husbands on the weekends—so the women had to go Friday. The children were not allowed to go Friday. The important thing is no matter how much soap you had on your body, the water was shut off and you had to go home with the soap on your body. That's the way everybody went bathing, once a week.

FANNY: I'll tell you something. The American people now they can never in a thousand years live through the life that we lived through, the experience and everything. It was so unique, it was so different, you can't even imagine it. Two for a nickel in the movies you could go. Ladies used to wear feather boas. Like a roll from feathers—maybe you've seen it in movies sometimes. Like a stole, but a round one with feathers. I used to work on a comb, like, and I'd put in layers and layers of feathers. They gave you a long machine of needles, like, and lines of feathers. And I had to place them accordingly. When I took it out, it was already a feather boa. I got three-fifty a week. You could buy a lot of things with three-fifty. Do you know, when I was young I was gorgeous. I'm going to say it myself, because you wouldn't know.

ETHEL: She was, she was very, very attractive.

FANNY: I had the most beautiful face, red cheeks—

ETHEL: Purple like. Purple-red.

FANNY: Cherry lips, and big blue eyes. When I started working, I must tell you, my lunch. They used to have the big rolls—grocery rolls. Then it was a penny a roll, I think. It was very big and very cheap.

ETHEL: Maybe two cents.

FANNY: No. What are you talking about? I couldn't afford two cents. I had six rolls and strawberries. I used to wash the strawberries, put them in the rolls and make a sandwich of it. Six rolls, and a quart of milk—every day for weeks and weeks I had that for lunch.

ETHEL: I started to work when I was fourteen and a half. I started in a store—a millinery store. I came and I had the nerve to say I knew how to work. I didn't know a thing. When I looked back afterwards, the kind of work they gave me to do was for an expert—one that's been in the line for a long time. If I'd tell you, you won't understand and nobody would understand today. Like a little sailor hat—it had to be fitted out and it had a wire at the edge. It was really complicated. They don't make it today. You'd take a piece of square material and you'd pin it on with pins. You pin it with pins and you make it round all around and you cut out the head size like this. You sew into the head size first, so that the material should straighten up very smoothly, then you turned in the edges—you turned in the edges like this—and then you put pins there and we called it slip stitching. We used to make stitches right here, and the wire would sort of stand away. They don't make it today. There were no machines. We were only hand workers.

FANNY: The operators did it by machine later on.

ETHEL: Later on it was made by machine, but it was not nicely made. Then I got a job on Bond Street. I sort of always had two jobs. I worked there by night, and by day I went to Bond Street. And when I got my pay and I used to walk home, they had pushcarts all along, so whatever money I had I used to spend it to buy things. When I'd bring it home, Mama used to say to me, "Do me a favor, and don't buy anything anymore." Because I suppose she didn't like what I bought. Like ribbons, handkerchiefs, materials—buttons, notions, who knows what.

FANNY: Its trimmings, like, they call that notions.

ETHEL: I used to work on Broadway, and around there lived the real immigrants, on Orchard Street, on Cherry Street, around there. We were sort of uptown, we lived on Eleventh Street. Most of the Russian immigrants who came lived way downtown. We were considered swell, we lived uptown. Orchard Street was a different element. The Bronx wasn't then yet. There was no such thing. First they moved to Harlem, from the East Side. They were the swells—Madison Avenue, Fifth Avenue. all the Jews from downtown, from the East Side, moved to Harlem. My girlfriend moved to Harlem. Ida lived, I think, on Madison Avenue.

FANNY: From Galicia were the inferior Jews.

ETHEL: There was that animosity just the same between the Russian Jews, the Polish Jews, the German Jews. The German Jews looked down upon the Russians completely. They had no use for them. They were the aristocrats. They controlled New York. They were educated, the Germans.

FANNY: And they had no use for the Galitzianers.

ETHEL: And Jews born in America wouldn't even look at you. If you rode in a trolley car, and they knew you were a greenhorn, they wouldn't even look at you, they wouldn't talk to you, they wouldn't have anything to do with you. They had no use for you. You didn't amount to anything. Nothing at all. Not like today.

FANNY: Today you support the refugees, you do everything for them.

ETHEL: That's right. Look at the Russian refugees, we have them in Brighton. How important they feel here.

FANNY: More important than we do.

ETHEL: Sure. They called me a Communist on the Boardwalk. They said, "You're a dirty Communist." They were sitting on the same bench and we were talking. They didn't like the questions I asked them. They said, "You're a dirty Communist."

FANNY: I told her not to bother talking with them. She was curious why they came to America when Russia is a good country—all the education they had in Russia and everything else. They force you actually to go and study and study and study. When I was in Russia and I spoke to a Jewish man . . .

ETHEL: Shhh. That's being recorded, so don't talk about Russia.

Bella S.

When I came to Ellis Island, we were on one side of a fence and my sister and brother were on the other side. At first I felt, "I'm in America. It's a free country. Why is that fence there? Why can't I go over from the boat straight to my brother?" That sort of puzzled me. But naturally after that you understand that had to be because they just don't let people go in without checking them. We were examined physically and many people were kept back—particularly for glaucoma, because a lot of people had that disease. If they cured them or if they sent them back, I don't know, but they were kept back from entering the States.

It was my first venture from the town to America. You find yourself so little among such big buildings and such big things around you. I was fortunate. I didn't have the difficulties that a lot of girls had who were coming here and had nobody to guide them. My sister had been here and she had advanced herself. I didn't have to go around and look for a room like other girls would at my age at that time. My sister had a beautiful room rented from a family. There was this way of living, that if you had an extra room you had to rent it out. So if a family had two or three children and four rooms, a room was rented out. My sister always managed to live in a room in a nice house. When I came, the first house I stayed in with her was on Second Avenue between Second and Third Streets. Believe it or not, it was an elevator apartment—in those days, that was a luxury.

My sister was quite an intelligent person. She was interested in the cultural end of life here. The first thing she took me to was a concert at Carnegie Hall. That was something that I didn't dream of. She also had the same spirit of advancing in education and advancing in the material end of life. She wanted me to go to day school. I said to her, "What do you mean? You'll send me to day school? Who's going to support me?" I wanted to free myself from that. I wanted to be supporting myself. I didn't want her to work and support me. Finally, she could not fight me, so I registered in public school, evenings.

The first school I went to was on Avenue B and I graduated public school from there—whatever they teach you in the evening. Then I went to Washington Irving High School, also at night. All the education that I attained was through evening courses. I'm not particularly a linguist, but the desire was so strong to know the language, to be an American above all. The fact is that I was so enthusiastic that no sooner I stepped off from Ellis Island into New York I thought I'm an American. I didn't even think in those days I should take out the papers to become a citizen. I was an American. I'm here. What else can I be but an American?

My sister was also fortunate that she had a good trade—she was a designer. She taught me a trade in the shop. It was very interesting. At one point, while I was working, she said, "Bella, come here. There are two lines of dresses hanging, and in between you can hide yourself. Don't go out." I couldn't understand it. I said, "Why should I go there?" "I'll tell you later, just go in there." An inspector came around to look whether children were working. I was fifteen, and in those days you could get working papers then, but I looked much younger. So she explained to me that an inspector was there and we were afraid that the boss was going to have trouble, so she hid me among the dresses.

How you were treated in the shop depended on who the other workers were. If they were intelligent, understanding, sympathetic, they tried to help you instead of belittling. There were others—"A *greeneh* [greenhorn] is here. What does she know, the greeneh." But that was no problem for me. The American-born Jews had parents who were immigrants. If they were intelligent, they accepted you as one that has to take time to learn the language, and learn the way of life, and they helped you out. Those that were ignorant, if they were born in the United States or elsewhere, they were looking down at you—you're a greenhorn. After a year's time, the same people began to look up at you, because you came with an ideal, with a desire to attain education, to advance yourself. They remained where they were.

When you came into New York from anywhere in those days you came into the East Side, and it was predominantly Jewish. You didn't feel that you were a Jew, or were treated differently. It was a Jewish town. There was constant immigration from the East Side to the Bronx. The Bronx at that time was country-like. You were wealthier if you were in the Bronx. If you moved to the West Side, you were in the upper echelons.

If you had the style of life from the shtetl you lived that life unless you freed yourself, unless you yourself took America for what it was with all its opportunities. If your desire was to advance yourself, you freed yourself from that atmosphere. Others continued in that way. As a matter of fact, in the shop I used to wonder: A woman tells me she's here thirty years and she doesn't speak English. "You're here thirty years?" I couldn't conceive of that. But she stayed on the East Side. All she knew was to go home and prepare a meal and then in the morning to go back to work. There she was with her husband and relatives—they all spoke Yiddish. So you had these groups perpetuated. You find them even today.

I started to mingle with people who were more to my liking. It's interesting how you find yourself. When I think now, I could have fallen into any group. Who was there to stop me? But instinctively you are drawn to the people that you like to be with. It's interesting how we were drawn, one to the other. People that came from different parts of the world, or, let's say, just from Russia. Some came from big cities and had different understandings of life, different ways. We formed groups and from the groups I have friends now that live around my way. We are friends for sixty-five years. I was always drawn to somebody that I found to be more intelligent, that had an education. Naturally, we spoke a lot of Russian between ourselves, although we all tried to shake it off because we wanted to learn the language.

When you first come, you have your habits, your taste for food, your manners—it depends from what environment you come. I am forever thankful to my parents that they taught us to be polite, to be understanding, not to be rough, to be *balabatish*. This is a little chauvinistic, because it means a finer Jew—not the riffraff. The others are also Jews, they're also my people, but this is the background we were given, and we carried it with us. As far as the other habits, naturally you acquire the habits of the country you're in. If you can't do that, I don't know what to call you—just unable to adjust. As far as I'm concerned, I acquired the best of America and the rest is like anything else—you take it or you leave it.

When I was at the shop a couple of months, one day my sister said to me, "Bella, now we are not going to work." I said, "Why?" "We are going out on strike." By the way, my sister was a revolutionary even when she was a youngster at home. When she came here she joined the Socialist Party. There was no Communist Party in those days. From the Party, they began to organize the unions. The people that were more advanced were the ones that took the initiative to try to organize the place where they worked. So, of course, she explained to me what a strike is and what it's for, and right there and then I became a union lady.

My reaction to the first strike was of ignorance. I accepted that this is how it's supposed to be if you want to advance yourself. You get together and this is what you have to do. I wasn't put in the front, to go picket or something like that. She only told me not to go to work. That's all. Within time, I got involved in everything that took place in the union, sometimes in the leadership. But that was the beginning. That was already after the government was protecting the people—that doors should be open and there should be signs for exits. After the Triangle fire, when some 140 girls were burned to death because they were trapped by closed doors and closed windows, the government came in and had regulations that there should be fire escapes, and there should be exits.

There were thousands of incidents. I remember once we were trying to organize one shop. When the bosses knew that we were going around to organize, they closed the doors. I remember climbing through the fire escape—the window was not locked. We were three girls. We opened up the window slowly and we shouted the word "Strike!" The big guys by the presses and the cutters—you know, they were big guys—they immediately stopped working like thunder hit them. It was a beautiful reaction. Then, when they calmed down, they had their say and they had their objection. But this was the reaction. We shouted out with all our might "STRIKE!" and before you know it, everybody was dumbfounded, standing up, leaving their work.

There were a lot of people that opposed the unions. Of course, it stands to reason—the boss always tried to buy them off with little favors and he would tell them, "I'll give you the conditions, what do you want a union for? The union is going to lead your life. The union is going to take away in dues whatever you make." They had their ways of keeping them down and we had our ways of trying to organize them.

Many a time we got up six o'clock in the morning and we'd go down to the market and stay around the shops, and wouldn't let people go in. I wasn't physically strong enough to keep them back, but we tried to convince them, talked with them, we even used to go to their homes and talk to their wives. The wives didn't know—he goes to work, he brings the pay, what else do we need? We proved to them it's to their benefit that their husband stays home for a week, that in the long run they'll get the benefit of it. We had a lot of ways and methods to do it.

This condition is something that goes on even today. There are a lot of places where there are no unions and you have to go through the same procedures to talk to the people, convince them of the benefits they get by it, and so on. It isn't a thing that stopped there, there's a continuation.

We fought with all our might. When we got prices stabilized, it was because we were fighting for it. We got rent control because we fought for it. There was no such thing as rent control. There was no such thing as telling them, "Look, the price is so and so. Don't change it." We used to have groups organized. We were discontented, so we struck. We had a strike against milk, we had a strike against meat. Now you don't have it.

There is very poor leadership. No matter what your capacity is for fighting, you can't do it by yourself. You have to be organized, you have to prepare, and you have to have leadership. I give the youth today much more credit than they do yet. They have to fight against very big things. They have to fight against nuclear war. They have to fight against destruction, against poisoning in the food they eat, poisoning for their new generation, for their children. What do they do about it? They don't. Do you know why they don't? Because they are disorganized. There is no leadership. You get a thousand that come out and protest. That isn't enough. You have to protest where it hurts, and they don't do it.

Things didn't come by themselves. Everything that spelled progress, we worked for it. Anything to free a people, anything to improve a people's standard of living, in our own meager way we helped. In those days we were involved in everything. We were involved in getting work, we were involved in fighting prices, in getting a higher wage for labor—we were involved in so many things. And there was improvement.

We didn't think of a revolution in America, but we were enthusiastic about the Revolution in Russia, because we knew what the people went through under the czar— the poverty and the depression and the pogroms and what have you. Before, the peasants didn't have land. The landlord had it and he paid them a very measly wage to sustain themselves. When the Revolution came, they took that tract of land where they worked and they divided it and everyone began to have land. If that's the only thing, it was worth the effort. As a Jew in Russia, you couldn't get a higher education, you couldn't come to a city, to go into a school or to work in a factory or to do business.

You had to have your passport, and if you were not of that town, you could not do anything there. All that was thrown off and it was a great achievement. So every decent-thinking person was for it. But we didn't think of this for the United States. To begin with in the United States there was still freedom.

Practically all of us belonged ideologically to the same group. It was socialistic. After the Russian Revolution, we were not Party members, per se, but our hearts were there. Wherever there was some advancement to humanity, we were a part of it. It was something that there was no friction, no differences of opinion. We were all for the betterment of our condition—to live outdoors, to have cultural activities as much as we could under the circumstances, and politically, we followed what was progressive—what was good for the masses was always our aim.

Anna T.

I was disappointed when I first came to the United States. The picture that you had of America was that everything was so beautiful. We came into the Bronx. It wasn't so beautiful. In the first place, we weren't used to the tall buildings. In those days, there were no elevators at least in the houses that we had during our stay. Life wasn't rosy at all.

I always thought, "If I come to America, my brothers will be well-to-do, I'll go to school, and I'll go places." But my brothers worked very little and we had no trade at all. I had to start to learn a trade and my brothers had to take me downtown and bring me into a shop. I didn't know how to travel and I didn't know how to work and I didn't know the English language.

But we got a very nice apartment—a big apartment, about five rooms. We rented out one room because we needed a little help with the rent, but we had plenty of room for ourselves. Mama was a housewife. She shopped and she cooked and she cleaned. We were away looking for a job. She kept the family together. She played a very big part at that time. She worked hard, whether we worked or we didn't work. We all went all over, we came back suppertime—four, five people—we had to have food, a house where to live. She was a *baleboste* [consummate homemaker]. She knew how to keep a home. She knew how to cook, and she kept the family together.

In the house, we all spoke Yiddish because that's what we all could understand. I found it very hard to learn English. I still didn't learn it. I just got my language the way I speak—not too correctly, not phrasing my sentences the way I should.

Two of my brothers worked in embroidery. One made tassles for drapes. One was working on metal things—I don't know how to call it. But where could they send a girl without any experience to work if not to a dress shop? There are so many variations in a dress—cutting thread, which doesn't mean anything, or finishing, that's the easiest you could do—you don't have to have any knowledge or any sense. Without knowledge, without education, without experience—it's the place where you sent girls to work.

In the shop, I also spoke Yiddish. The bosses were Jewish men. They were also foreigners, but they were much longer in this country because they had enough time to work themselves up to be bosses. So they knew both languages. When you found a creature like myself that didn't know too well English, and you had to explain what to do—you spoke to me in Yiddish.

I was working in the ladies garment workers industry. I must have been already seventeen or eighteen years old. I did a nice trade. I was a draper. I don't know if you know the different sections of dresses. There's an operator, there's a finisher, there's a draper. A draper is the one that fits the dresses on the figure, makes it fit right, or trims it either with a collar or a belt or with trimmings or with a certain style, like lines of ruffles. It was an interesting trade. I liked it. I did a lot of different things that I didn't like—finishing, examining, cleaning. I don't know what made me think so, but whatever I did I thought I should do something better—not that I can but I always tried. And finally, I remained doing what I was doing, and I liked it very much. It was interesting.

Around that time, conditions weren't bad because the unions were stabilized more or less, the workers were a fighting element, and they didn't let the bosses take too much advantage over you. The bosses knew that if it's a union place, it has to more or less live up to union conditions. So I didn't have such bad experiences.

I worked in organized shops. There was no question of my joining the union, especially with my brothers around. They were fighters in the union all their lives and very active, so there was no question whether to be a union lady or not. To strive was to be a union lady, because conditions are much better. I came in 1922, and I didn't start working until 1924. About 1926, '27, I joined the union.

Only one shop where it wasn't unionized I worked. And they unionized it. I remember when the group of workers came into the place, and they said, "Stop, Strike." The door was right near a cutting table—a cutting table is long because that is where they stretch out the entire material and then they put the patterns and they cut it by electric—so it has to be long. The cutter was on one side of the table. When he saw those people coming in, he wanted to take the knife and throw it on them. He was an antiunion man and he probably wanted to show the boss that he's not one of the rabble-rousers. So they stopped him. And they stopped the shop. Of course, our girls got up right away. Then the boss saw that the majority of the people stopped, and he can't work without them. So we organized. That's what happens.

When you come in to stop a place—to organize—if the people respond, the boss can't do anything. He could tell you, "You want to go? You want a union place? I wouldn't take you back"—if it's one or two. But when the people stand up as a mass, what is he going to do? Put a sign that he wants new workers? So he gave in at that time, and they settled it. I worked at that place for three or four years. But, otherwise, all the shops I worked were union shops.

Most of the other workers in the shops were older than I. They were immigrants, but they were longer in this country than I. They were already experienced. When you came into a union shop, the people that worked there made that shop union. You have to be a little long in a place to be able to organize a shop, so they weren't my age and they weren't that short a time in this country.

I came in contact with very few American-born boys and girls. Even my neighbors were immigrants—if it wasn't the same year, it was two years earlier, five years earlier, but still immigrants, and they still spoke a broken English, if any at all. In those days, the whole country was immigrants. Even the Gentiles weren't American-born. So they really grew up among their own people. Whether the Jews with the Jews or the Gentiles with the Gentiles. They were all immigrants—from Italy, from Poland, from whatever country it was.

They understood each other very well, because they were all in the same position. None of them knew English very well. All of them had to struggle either to learn a trade or to get a job or to fight for better conditions. In the unions, naturally, you can't say that there were only Jewish workers—there were all kinds of workers, but mostly Jewish. But even the Gentiles were fighting for the same conditions. They were in the same predicament as the Jewish immigrants. So the relationship wasn't that controversial as it was later on.

I took the life in this country as a new world, a world of new adventures, of new education, of new changes, of being somebody, of seeing something, of developing yourself. But I found it very hard to achieve all that I thought would be that easy. But I knew that it was there, and the fact that we knew it was there meant we'll struggle a little more to get there—I'll get a little more education, or I'll get more interesting ways of spending time. No matter what I did, I found it more interesting than what I did in Russia—I wouldn't say in the Soviet Union because I lived so little in the period of the Revolution. I was much happier in this country, knowing that I have all the chances—even if I didn't achieve what I wanted.

Don't forget, also, we had a big help from our brothers. We had four brothers who had been here in this country for a long time. They were very, very concerned about our well-being. In fact, before we started to go to night school, they sent us to a private teacher so we could catch up the language a little better than we would have at night. They were very nice and helpful. They took us places. They took us to the movies, to concerts, to operas. They were the kind of boys that always went to something interesting for their enjoyment.

At one time, I was surprised. When I used to look for a job and come home, my brother used to ask me, "Where did you find a job?" I gave him the number—"229 Seventh Avenue." He said, "Oh, it's between Seventh and Eighth Avenues. I said to myself, "My goodness, my brother is so smart. He's sitting in the house and he knows where 229 Seventh Avenue is." How could he know? I couldn't understand it. That's how naive I was, and surprised that sitting at the table at home he knew where I was.

Once I started to work, I became an independent person. I knew a little English, and I didn't have to depend upon my brother telling me where to go or what to do. I loved New York. What shocked me was the rushing life, the buildings, the hurry-up. It was very interesting. A group of our friends that went to school together organized a club. In fact, the first meeting was in my house. We became active and we had lectures and meetings and dances Saturday night. Socially I enjoyed my life very much.

After work, I used to go a lot to concerts and a lot to operas. I went with another girl or two. Naturally, we couldn't get tickets for a seat. So we went standing—it was a dollar. We went straight from work to the opera, standing, all the way up in the old opera house. I'd call up my mother: "Mama, I'm not coming home for supper." We'd go and have a cup of coffee or whatever we had, and we went to the opera, standing. Whether I understood it well or not, I wouldn't complain. I wouldn't claim that I understood it so much, but I loved it.

The depression in those years affected us very much but, frankly, we grew up in such an economic way of life that cutting little bits didn't mean too much because we never had too much. When others say, "We haven't got it. We haven't got it," I say, "I never had it." I could always compromise, I could always economize, because that's how we grew up. We didn't grow up on luxury. The little bit we had to give up, we were used to—we always cut down, we always economized, we never had enough. I have more now than I had all my life.

Bertha S.

My uncle came to the ship and picked me up at Ellis Island. Right away, the next day or two, he took me and bought me shoes and a dress, because they didn't like the European style. It didn't make a good impression. At that time it was different than it is now.

I went to high school for awhile, and then I started to work. It wasn't my work. I learned to be a dressmaker in the old country. When I came here, I didn't have a chance for someone to take me up somewhere, so first I went to work with an aunt who worked on underwear. Only later I became a dressmaker.

My first ten dollars was sent to my mother, because I felt she should have it—I had what to eat. I lived with my uncle, my mother's brother. My first Passover here I had saved forty dollars. I came in November and in February I started to work. Passover, I wanted to buy me a suit—I was a girl, going to be seventeen. Then I thought, "I'm going to buy a suit and my mother won't have for Passover?" I went and split it. I sent her twenty dollars and kept twenty dollars and bought me a semi-suit, which I thought was logical, understanding that someone else needs it besides me. All through the years I sent my mother almost regularly, every month. When my sister was getting married, I sent her some for her dowry, then for my younger sister and my brother occasionally.

I worked in a shop with American people and they taught me the language a little bit, which I appreciated. They wanted me to teach them Jewish, but they didn't learn. I learned English really just to express myself. I don't know if I do it very well even now, but I tried. I'm always willing to learn. I went to night school, too, for a couple of seasons. And up to today, I'm willing to learn. If someone thinks I'm not expressing myself right, I appreciate their correction.

Right away I was willing to change. If I was corrected I took it into consideration. And I always observe. I observe people's habits and their mannerisms. Mannerisms are something that you adopt—you're not born with them. You are not born with anything except your flesh and blood. Some people will not change their mannerisms. They will go to a table, and they won't even know how to eat. They go to places and they see television as well as I do, but they don't observe. I saw it in a book the other day. It said: "People have eyes and they don't see. People have ears and they don't hear." Now, that's true. Those are habits and they don't want to change. I modified my habits. I don't know if I still have some old habits. This somebody else could observe, not me. But I tried my utmost.

I was willing to become Americanized. Others weren't willing. They said, "What do I need it?" But I personally felt that I want to learn the language and I want to become an American citizen. I became a citizen in 1927.

Things then were tough. Even that time, when an immigrant came, they took advantage and they didn't pay enough. When I went to work, they started me very low. I knew how to operate a machine, but I didn't know how to operate an electric. It's not hard to do—once you know how to operate it, all you have to do is take it a little bit slow until you feel that that foot works right. It's like driving. I did it finally, and I was pleased because week after week I got a raise, and I knew if I got a raise I was worth it.

When I came home and told my uncle, he said, "You're getting every week a raise—it's more than I ever did." I said, "But they started me so low." And that's how it went on. But at that time it wasn't a terrible living. We felt that we had to live with what we make, what we have. We didn't look like the youngsters today—"I want a car and I want this and I want that." Everything they want. Maybe they're entitled to it. At that time, we didn't think so.

The youth of today has it a little better. Parents of today want to give the children more than they ever had. Sometimes I feel it's wrong, because the children are spoiled. You have to make youngsters feel responsible. If you are responsible for something, you appreciate it more. Most of the children I see today do not appreciate the life of today. They didn't struggle. I was responsible for my family in Europe, but I didn't feel a burden of my responsibility. I felt it was a test that I should complete, and I appreciated whatever I had.

In the depression we had very bad times. The depression went on and on, and it affected me terribly. I was married the end of 1923 and then I had two children—one was born in '25; the other in '28. My husband didn't have a job. I took in work in the house, with two small children. I made maybe eight or ten dollars a week. At that time you were able to feed the children with a little bit. And I was on relief, believe it or not. Still it wasn't enough. We didn't have money for rent. What happened? Six months we lived without rent. The banks took over the homes—the owners of the buildings couldn't pay the mortgages, so the banks took it over. What are they going to do? Throw me out? So for six months we went without rent, and after six months, we had to go. So we went to another place, which was a little bit less rent, and it started a little bit more work, so we went on. It wasn't easy. It was very hard. But we managed. We never complained.

Feigl Y.

I traveled about eleven or twelve days on the boat, and then when I came here I went to my father's brother in Hudson, New York—a small town. I stayed there about four months, and then I came to New York, to *landsleit* [people who came from the same town in Europe]. They were people from our town, they lived next door. They knew me and they knew that I was all alone, so they kept writing that, I should come. They lived in their own house all the way up in the Bronx on 223d Street. I stayed with them a nice couple of years, and they took care of me like their own child. I had my own room, but I was very lonely.

I felt all alone in a strange country, in a strange city, without the language. I loved my little brother, and I used to cry for him every night. But I managed. I had to work. I had to support my mother and the kids in Europe. I used to travel to work from the Bronx.

My first job was with a tailor from our town who had a factory for dresses. He taught me the work and he paid me fifteen dollars a week. At that time, fifteen dollars was a lot of money. I worked and I sent every cent to my mother. When I was sick and I couldn't send any money, I used to ask the boss to give me money in advance, so my mother wouldn't know I was sick. I worked there until it got slow. In those days it was seasonal work, and it used to get very slow. But I was lucky then because I stayed with landsleit so I didn't have to worry about my food or rent. That was a great help.

I didn't go to school much because where I lived then there was no night school. It was too far. I would have to go to Harlem to a night school and come back twelve o'clock at night. Not that I was afraid—those days we weren't afraid. Harlem then was like a Jewish ghetto, especially East Harlem where the Spanish are now living. But it was too far to the schools and I was working too hard.

In the shop there were different crafts—there were operators, cutters, pressers, finishers, examiners, and others. And there was a difference between piecework and week work. When you work on piecework you have to get the price on the garment. Many times the bosses finagled the whole thing around and you never got the whole price on it. The operators worked piecework. The pressers worked piecework. The cutters worked piecework. The finishers, who sewed by hand, worked piecework. The examiners, who examined the garment, were week workers. I was working as a draper—that was week work, not piecework. As a draper, you take the dress on the figure. You see if it fits. You have to pin it and so on, and then you give it to the operator to finish it.

My shop was a union shop, so you had to be a member of the union. I was a very good union member. I was arrested many times on the picket line. In the forties there weren't so many strikes, because the union didn't believe in striking anymore. They believed we were getting along with the bosses in a nice way. But in the thirties and in the late twenties, there were tremendous strikes.

During one strike, I used to get up early in the morning to watch that the scabs shouldn't go into the building. I once was standing in the street, hiding in a building, and I saw the scabs go into a garage. The factory was on the second floor. On the roof they had a chair and they climbed in through the window. I caught them, but I was alone. So I started to yell, "Scabs! Scabs! Scabs!"

I was a chairlady in a shop for knit goods. We had a hundred girls. They knew I was militant—the workers can feel it—so I was the chairlady. If you fight for them, you fight for their rights, they can tell. As chairlady, you see that the members belong to the union, that they get better wages, shorter hours, and sanitary conditions in the shop.

At that time there were two unions. There was a left-wing union and a right-wing union. My shop wanted to take the left-wing union. So the right-wing union sent gangsters with blackjacks, and they were after me because I was the chairlady. It was a rainy day and a few girls got into a car and we were sitting there. They surrounded the car and they said, "There she is." But before they could get me, I ran out of the car through the other door. They were running after me, so I grabbed an umbrella and I hit them with the umbrella. But one girl was beaten up badly then.

From 1929 until 1934, I had it very, very bad. I lost my job in a general strike. I walked out and the rest of the workers remained working, so I lost my job. At that time, I lived on ten cents a day—a plate of soup a day. A lot of people lost money then. Even rich ones committed suicide. Oh, that was a terrible crash. Everybody lost in the banks. There was the American Bank where people lost money—their last pennies. That bank was closed.

The workers used to stay in the streets and sell apples. And there were Hoovervilles. They would get a stretch of a couple of streets and build up little huts—they used to make a roof of tin and boxes, and they used to live like that. Hoover was the President then, and he didn't do anything for the workers. The soldiers in Washington demanded that he should help them, so he sent out the militia to shoot them. Hoover was terrible. He promised a car in every garage and a chicken in every pot, but the people were starving. Actually starving. It was a terrible time.

But still the people here weren't ready for a revolution. Even with Hoover, they weren't ready for a revolution. The people who were demonstrating, demanding jobs, demanding help, those were the people that were class-conscious. They knew what they wanted and they were better dressed and better fed. They were the people who still had something. The ones that were really starving, they didn't march. They weren't ready for a revolution.

The Soviet Union was different. During the First World War, they suffered a lot, and the soldiers didn't want to go to war anymore. The revolutionary movement was working with the country for years. And then they had the opportunity—they were lucky to find that time. The First World War was terrible in Russia. America is not the country to have a revolution. If they'll see something coming, they will avoid it. They'll do something for the people. At that time, they voted for Roosevelt. When Roosevelt came in, the New Deal came. They started giving work to people and the projects started—all kinds of projects—the WPA, the Writers' Project, the Artists' Project. They didn't get much, but at least they got something. Roosevelt was elected three times because of that.

In 1934 I met my husband. We met accidentally—somebody introduced us and it clicked. We used to see each other very often, go to concerts, go to a show, to the movies, just like everybody else. We went around for about five years. We couldn't get married because times were bad. Then we decided, as bad as it is, better to be together. So we got married. First we lived downtown on the East Side for two years. Then we moved to a better place on Fourth Street and Second Avenue. We had a room and a kitchen.

We were all very poor, but we had a good time. We used to go on picnics. We used to go across the Hudson to the Palisades. We used to go to Coney Island. We used to go to concerts in the stadium at City College on 137th Street. We used to go a couple of times a week. We would come right after work, get a ticket for a quarter, and then run to a place to get a sandwich for ten cents. I used to go to concerts very, very often. Our friends were mostly immigrants. There were some Americans—they liked our bunch—that we were so jolly, having good times, going to dances, to concerts, to movies, and all that. Of course, they were all Jewish youth.

Then I remember when they announced the bombing of Pearl Harbor. I was in the shop, and I heard the news. It was a terrible thing. A terrible thing. It was so shocking. I said, "Japan dares to fight America?" It was just awful. Jewish soldiers were very enthusiastic about going to fight Hitler. People here knew what was going on in Germany, and they were trying to do everything. In fact they were trying to ask Roosevelt to bombard the camps. If they would have bombarded the camps, they could have saved a lot of Jews.

But Roosevelt at that time didn't act right. The boats were turned back. You see, you couldn't expect too much from England because she was bombarded herself. England was involved in the war. America didn't suffer except for its soldiers that were sent across, and Roosevelt could have done a lot. If they would have bombarded the camps, they would have saved tens of thousands of Jews. Rabbi Wise was pleading with him. He was sitting on the steps there in Washington and pleading with Roosevelt, "Do something! Do something!" But they didn't do anything.

The same thing was with Spain, before Hitler came to power. Everybody knew that Hitler and Mussolini are trying in Spain to see whether they can succeed in Europe. Roosevelt had the embargo that time—nonintervention. It was the same thing with France and England—nonintervention. The people that were class-conscious were trying to do something. But we couldn't do anything. What could we do? We could just help them with money, with other things, but there was an embargo. The ships couldn't go through.

Some people were very passive. When Hitler was killing the Jews, a lot of them didn't know. Those that knew were fighting. We had demonstrations all the time, but a lot of people made a lot of money at that time, and they had good times in the cabarets. They didn't care what happened to the Jews in Europe. But the ones that were interested knew what was going on. We knew, we found out. We knew exactly what was going on. We knew about the concentration camps.

I knew that my family was going to be slaughtered there. I knew it. In fact, I was on the verge of a nervous breakdown. I was very sick at that time. I once came for medicine to a druggist in my neighborhood, and I said to him, "What is this medicine for?" He said, "It's against nerves. You are very nervous. It's to calm you down." And he started talking to me, like a psychologist. He said, "They are there.

Whatever will happen, will happen. You cannot do anything. The only thing you'll do is kill yourself. You are so active now. You are doing work against Hitler. You are doing work for the American government. What will you accomplish if you kill yourself? If you will die?" I took it into my head and I said, "I think the man is talking sense." And I started to get better and better. I was very active then. I was selling bonds, I was knitting gloves and socks for the soldiers. I sold a lot of bonds for the American government. In fact, they sent me papers, commendations. I was patriotic.

Reva Y.

I came to the United States in 1923 from Russia—from the city of Odessa. The main reason we left was because my family wanted to be reunited. Our whole family was here. I was upset that we had to leave the Soviet Union, but not because of my involvement in the political movement, the Revolution at that time, but because I had a lot of friends and I didn't want to leave friends. I really didn't want to leave. I had my roots there. The heartbreaking thing was to leave friends.

But our whole family was here. As soon as we got the visas—our permission to leave the country—we came to our grandparents.

When we came to the United States we lived in very small quarters in the Bronx. It was primitive. There was no electricity, only gas. And the lifestyle was completely different. I had to go to work, and I went to school only at night. My parents worked very hard, seven days a week, in a grocery store, and my younger sister helped a little and went to school. As time went on, it improved. We did not really suffer or struggle.

I couldn't adjust myself too well to school here. The night school had grown-up people. Immigrants went to the night school. At that time, we didn't mingle with too many American-born Jews, mostly with immigrants. The language barrier was a problem but we found our own life. My girlfriends also came from Russia. We spoke the same language. I didn't know Yiddish then—I learned it here, afterward. We found some things in common. We liked concerts, so we went to Lewisohn Stadium. We found other likes—lectures. Then we got interested in Yiddish theater and we attended that. I never had the problem where I was rejected or not accepted by others. I didn't go into a circle where I wouldn't be accepted.

My job was in the millinery trade. I was just a learner in a very fancy millinery place. I was paid eight dollars a week. After awhile I left because my uncle had a dress shop and I thought I'd get into his place and advance myself. I was involved in the union then, and we went on strike. I was influential in taking my uncle's shop on strike, because I was very active at that time. I took my uncle's shop on strike. I belonged to the dressmaker's union—the ILGWU.

In 1927 I got married. . . . During the depression, my husband and I were both working. We lived according to our income. We had to deprive ourselves of certain things that we thought we could do away with. We couldn't afford to pay our whole rent, so we had a boarder. Our rent was thirty-eight dollars a month. He paid thirteen dollars and we were paying twenty-five. We had small quarters.

The priority was to culture. We didn't do away with the concerts at Lewisohn Stadium. We went all the way up to the top of the stadium for a quarter. We went to the Met. There there was a problem with the price, so we went standing—you paid two dollars and you went standing to the Metropolitan Opera. So I don't think I was deprived in any way.

At that time, I was a member of the Communist Party. I joined in 1930. I thought I belonged there. I was working in a dress shop, I was active in the union, I was active in the labor movement, and I thought that's where I belonged.

A friend of mine from the shop took me to a meeting in Union Square. To become a Party member you had to be introduced at a meeting. At the meeting, we spent a couple of hours getting acquainted, we talked about what's happening in the world, what's happening in working circles. The main concern was unionizing shops, raising wages, reducing hours. We were given assignments. Mine was to hand out papers— the *Daily Worker*. As an active member you undertake different chores, picketing, marching, handing out leaflets, selling the *Daily Worker*. We used to get a bundle and we used to give them out, saying "read the *Daily Worker*." We weren't hiding, we were open. Once you're a Party member you accept whatever you are told to do. You don't question. Once you begin to question, you drop out. Members did not question, whatever was written out we accepted. I don't know about the upper echelons, but members like us did not question. You either obey or you go. If you don't agree with policy you won't fit in, you don't belong.

I remember once we were marching on May first in 1933. It was a downpour, we were drenched, but nothing stopped us. We marched under the banner of the Communist Party. Our slogan was "Browder is our leader, we shall not be moved." Nothing stopped us. We used to stay late in Union Square Park, until two in the morning, discussing all kinds of things. We had hot discussions about Party policy and international issues.

At first we accepted everything, we didn't question. That was the way it was, that's the way it should be. Stalin was our leader. Nobody questioned, that's the theory of Marxism-Leninism and you accept it. I don't think I could have done anything else. I saw that there were a lot of injustices in America that could be changed. The first time I read the theory of Marxism-Leninism it made me want to join the Party. I don't think I could have done anything else. It wasn't a question of should I join or not, I just went in. I thought that that was my style of life. I couldn't absorb the capitalist system. Everything was the Party.

The Party came first. When it came to meetings, meetings came first. If I had to go on a picket line, or distribute the *Daily Worker*, the Party came first, everything came after. I couldn't raise a family because I couldn't stay home. I had to do Party work. Never mind supper, never mind my husband. He wasn't in the Party. He used to say one member in the house is enough. You know, we never got married. We just got a license. My grandfather died not talking to me because of that. He was upset, he was religious. I was a nonbeliever.

During the Stalin period I became disillusioned. We didn't find out all the things immediately. But after, when things began to leak out of what was happening, that was the time when we got bitter. I got terribly bitter about it. We had to give up all the ideals, all the work which we did. And I did quite a bit of work. I'm talking about going to meetings and coming home at two in the morning. Everything. The Party came first at that time. I gave the best years of my life to the Party. I was younger, I believed in the future. I believed we'll have socialism here in America. Then I began to question, I began to see things aren't right. A lot of us were hurt. It's not easy to give up something like that. You feel like you wasted the best years of your life.

A lot of my best years, I would say, I gave to the Party. We lived on Thirteenth Street in the Village at that time, and my best days I gave up to climbing up stairs to sell the *Daily Worker*. And I thought I was doing a good thing. But little by little I got disillusioned and there came a time when I just had to drop out. Actually, I dropped out when I gave birth to my son in 1945.

Harry G.

It took us thirty-one days to come to America. The boat came to Providence, Rhode Island—not to Ellis Island. My father came there, took us right off the boat, and brought us to New York.

We were very scared. Very scared. We never saw a big city like New York. Naturally, we were very impressed. When we came here, my father had four rooms for us. We were six children, my father was seven, and we had a cousin that stayed with us—my father's cousin. He had a wife and children, but somehow he didn't live with his family. He used to sleep in the synagogue and he ate in our house. We were eight people in four rooms.

My father was a presser—they called it an underpresser. He worked for twenty-eight years in one factory. The factory was for pants and kneepants—knickers. They used to press them. The cutter cuts them, the operator sews them, and they pressed them. Then they put them in boxes and sent them to the store. The boss would only take in people from the shul, and he would never take in youngsters to teach them. He wouldn't take just anybody. It wasn't like now—you must have a Negro and you must have a woman. In those days you could have anybody. This boss would only take religious people, because they wouldn't revolt so much. They were more obedient. Naturally, they were exploited.

I used to tell my father to ask for a raise. My father said . . . how would you say it in English?—"reisn shtik fun a mentschen? Er zol im gibn" a raise? "You're going to take blood from a human being? If the boss will be able, he will give me a raise." One day a man asked him for a raise. He said, "What do you think? You want to take blood from a stone? Pay a raise? Times are bad. Why doesn't that one ask for a raise?" So my father never asked him for a raise. During Prohibition, the boss used to buy a bottle of bootleg whiskey and he would make five bottles from it. He used to provide for everybody. He had a minyan in the shop and they used to have prayers in the morning—six o'clock or six thirty—and he would give them each a piece of homemade cake, so it was kosher, and then they used to work. My father worked in that place for twenty-eight years! He was a boarder nearby and he used to walk to work. He didn't have to travel. When we came, he took four rooms also not far from the shop.

My father worked, I worked, and my sister worked. I went to work right away. I got myself a job pasting in a shoe factory. The man told me he was going to give me about ten dollars a week. When it came Saturday, he wanted me to work, but my father wouldn't allow me to work on Saturday. So the boss said, "Okay, you don't want to work Saturday? You get only nine dollars." I worked there a few weeks and somehow the traveling was bad, I got confused, I didn't like the work, so I went and I quit.

Then I decided I wanted to learn a trade. I looked in the *Morning Journal* and I went to learn a trade as a furrier. I worked four weeks for nothing—not even carfare. The fourth week the boss gave me a couple of dollars and said that the next week he would take me on pay. He paid me twenty-five dollars a week. It was a lot of money in those days. So I worked a couple of weeks, and he gave me a five-dollar raise. I worked another couple of weeks, and he gave me another five dollars. After work, Saturday nights, I used to go out and sell papers.

The other kids went to school. I understood the language very well, but I couldn't express myself. Somehow, I didn't have any trouble. When I became a furrier, 90 percent of the people in the furriers were Jewish. The bosses were also Jewish. You could go on the East Side and hardly hear an English-speaking person. In Williamsburgh and in Borough Park it was the same thing. Jewish people were concentrated in ghettoes. There were very few people who weren't Jewish. A lot of European Jews came to America then. The youngsters went to school and they spoke English, but my friends spoke mostly Jewish. Night school used to be three times a week. I couldn't afford to go, so I went only for about two weeks.

Then my brother started to work—he became a delivery boy in a grocery. When he got his pay, he was a big shot already. All the money went to my father. He used to give us spending money—two dollars, five dollars, three dollars—according to how much we brought in. My father used to give us only a dime in carfare to go to Coney Island on Sunday. We had to take our own food—apples, sardines, matzohs, rolls, stale rolls, fresh rolls, pumpernickel, everything was in the house. We would pack it in a big bag, and go to Coney Island—a nickel there and a nickel back. We used to undress under the boardwalk. One day we wanted to go to Coney Island and I said to my father, "Daddy, how about another carfare to go to Coney Island?" And he said, "I never saw such children. Every week they want to go to Coney Island and every week they want dimes."

We were very happy in America, exceptionally happy, comparing it to Europe. My father used to put a quarter in the meter for gas, and we had lights. In Europe we had a kerosene lamp, but we were very poor so we didn't have kerosene. As soon as it got dark, we stayed in the dark. In America we had a toilet. As soon a we came over here, we had a toilet. In Europe we didn't have facilities. We had a lot of conveniences here. You had to bake your own bread there, and then you needed wood. In my family, if we had flour, we didn't have wood. If we had wood, we didn't have salt or matches. We used very little oil. You had to buy oil. But we used to have chicken fat or animal fat, so we used that. Everything was scarce.

There were also foods here that we never had in Russia. Bananas we never had, we never had tomatoes, we never had lettuce. We never had a lot of food. Oranges were very expensive. In our town, they had to import them. They were a luxury. If rich people would get sick, they would get an orange or two. Until I was about thirteen or fourteen, I had maybe two oranges in my life. Here my father always liked there should be a lot of food in the house.

My father used to go to a pushcart and buy anything in season. If it was a little bit not so, he would buy a bushel—a bushel of plums or a bushel of grapes or a bushel of apples or a bushel of pears. But he would never pay more than forty cents—that was the highest he would pay for a bushel. Sometimes he used to buy a bushel of pears or apples and the man used to give him a couple of pounds of grapes without money. So my sister would take the grapes with the apples or the plums or whatever it was, and she would make a soup.

My sister used to cook for us—on coal, not gas. We were six children and the cousin was seven and my father was eight. One sister went to work, the other one used to stay home and cook. My father shopped because he knew where you could buy everything cheaper. When my sister served us food, you had to eat fast. We never had enough food. All of us were very good eaters. We could swallow five rolls at a time. If you didn't eat fast, goodbye Charlie.

My sister used to serve us dinner—our main meal. Each one had one roll and then we had bread. She used to give us first a couple of herrings with onions. Sometimes potatoes with the herring. Then she used to give us soup—either with noodles, kasha, or rice. Then we used to have meat—a little bit of chicken or a big piece of meat. Chicken now is much cheaper than meat, but at that time chicken was more money than meat. And everybody got a big portion of lima beans—cooked lima beans. The only kind of vegetable we ate was lima beans. Then, when we relaxed, everybody used to have tea and a piece of cake. We had a kettle of tea—thirty cups—ready on the stove. You could have as much tea as you wanted. My father used to give everybody one piece of cake. After you ate the cake, you could eat only matzohs. My father had a friend who used to bake matzohs, so he gave him a break. My father would buy thirty pounds of matzohs for less than a dollar—thirty pounds in one box. You could eat as much matzohs as you wanted.

We had two ice boxes. One was for food and one was for different stuff. One brother had to bring the ice and take out the water. The other brother had to bring the coal. They used to alternate. Downstairs, every tenant had a shack to keep the coal—it was your coal. They used to bring a ton or a half a ton of coal—I don't remember exactly how much it was. Every day, sometimes twice a day, you had to bring up your coal from the basement. We lived on the third floor and there was no elevator. We had an old pail, a broken one, and my brother had to bring up the pail of coal—sometimes twice a day, sometimes three times a day. In winter, we didn't need much steam because there was a big stove in the kitchen and it was so hot you could get burned.

My relationship with my father was exceptionally nice. My younger brother couldn't get used to him because my father was an elderly man with a beard. But we got along exceptionally nice. My father was here so many years and he never went on vacation. He never left New York. Once, a distant cousin who had a flower business in Washington took my father to visit him for a weekend. My father liked that Friday night all the kids should be together to eat supper and he liked that they should wash their hands—religious people must have clean hands. So when my brothers would come to the table and they didn't wash their hands, my father used to yell at them: "Haven't you got respect for a father? To come to the table with these hands? You know, I was in Washington. You haven't got respect for me?" So my younger brother would say, "Did you see the president?"

He was a religious man, but not very religious. He was very religious in our little town, but when he came to America it evaporated a little. In Europe, when you went to shul, you couldn't carry anything—not even a handkerchief. Your pockets had to be empty. If you needed a handkerchief, you had to put it on your neck. You could put on a tallis, but you couldn't carry it. Here it was different. Here my father wouldn't carry money on a Saturday, but he could carry a handkerchief, he could carry a comb.

He was a very conscientious man, very devoted to the children. He never married after my mother died. He used to say, "A second marriage is like second teeth." He liked my mother very much, and he couldn't adjust himself to women in America. He never got married again. He was always devoted to us. He always saw that we had a lot of food. In the bakery my father used to buy only what was left over from yesterday—never fresh. The baker knew that if there is anything left, my father will get it. Like challahs. My father wouldn't buy challah on Friday. The baker knew that my father uses four challahs on Saturday. Four.

We were big eaters, and we had a lot of friends who used to come to the house. He would put out a challah and whiskey. This was Prohibition time. You couldn't buy whiskey in a liquor store. My father used to buy a gallon of homemade whiskey—it was like alcohol, strong like the devil—and he used to make five gallons from it. He made himself a special shelf on top of a closet, and we had five gallons of whiskey there. He used to buy it from the religious people—they needed it to make kiddush. When our friends came in, my father gave them a treat. He used to give everybody a little glass. As soon as he put out the challah, it went.

My father also had a place to buy sneakers. The boys went to school, so they wore sneakers to play ball. My father bought sneakers on a pushcart on Siegel Street in Williamsburgh. It was like Orchard Street. He knew a place for sneakers for sixty-nine cents. A pair of shoes used to be $2.90 or $3.00 in Thom McAn—a good pair of shoes—but this peddler used to sell sneakers for sixty-nine cents. My father used to pay thirty-nine cents. How did he do it? The pushcart was a big pushcart, with sticks, and the peddler used to hang up five dozen pair of sneakers on a hook. When the sun was hot, the sneakers used to get discolored from the sun. My father used to buy those sneakers for thirty-nine cents. We were four boys—he used to buy five pair. One was for a spare. What happened to those sneakers? When my brother would put on a pair of new sneakers and he would play ball in the schoolyard, the sneakers would fall apart. My father would say, "Can you imagine? Every week, I have to buy him a pair of new shoes." Then he would go in, take down the spare, and say, "Here are a pair of new sneakers."

My father was a very colorful man. A very colorful man. But he hated English. He couldn't adjust himself to English. He couldn't master it. He was a scholar—he used to read the Bible and a lot of things—but English was the worst thing for him. He didn't care for it. He went to a shul and they organized a society. They called it the Skolner Society—I don't know what it was, it wasn't landsleit. We came from a small town. Maybe there were five people in the United States from my town. Anyway, he became a member there, and they made him the secretary. Everything was done in Jewish, not in English. Somehow he couldn't master the English language.

There was a period when all the youngsters had social clubs and there were many events. There were hundreds of clubs in Williamsburgh and downtown. We used to go hiking. We used to have picnics. We used to have a lecture sometimes. We had to pay dues—I think it was about fifteen cents a month. We had these RCA Victrolas with a loud horn that came out. We would put on records and we had dancing. I used to dance the fox-trot, the waltz, and Russian dances. Then if we had a lot of money, we used to get a lecturer from a bigger club. There used to be writers' clubs and they used to come and give a lecture on literature or on this or that.

Then we became active with Sacco and Vanzetti. It was 1925 or 1926. We had a speaker speaking to us about them and about the strikes and how they were framed.

So we became active. I became very active. We used to campaign for them, we raised money to have a lawyer for them. We did a lot of work for Sacco and Vanzetti. That lasted quite a long time—until they were executed. We were very upset. Very upset.

When we belonged to the clubs, we did a lot of hiking. We used to go hiking to the Palisades from Williamsburgh. Sometimes we took the train—we used to get a nickel for carfare. Sometimes we walked. We'd take along food. We used to go to Palisades and stay until late in the evening. At that time, I was a big shot already. I always had a dollar in my pocket. You could buy a sandwich. A bottle of soda was two cents, Hershey's chocolate soda was three cents. A bigger bottle was five cents. Life was cheap at that time. Carfare was a nickel. A telephone call was a nickel. Three corn muffins were a nickel—good corn muffins, not like now.

Times change. People are now making $300 or $250 a week. To them, to pay $1.25 or $1.75 for a hamburger is nothing. Don't forget, the highest my father was paid was twenty-eight dollars a week. For him, it was bad. A nickel was a lot of money. When my brother used to help a woman carry her bundles to the fourth floor or the fifth floor, she gave him a penny. My brother would run straight downstairs and buy a glass of seltzer for the penny. For two cents, you had seltzer with a little bit of syrup—strawberry syrup, raspberry syrup. A penny meant a lot. When my father gave my younger brother a quarter, that was it. If he was short, he was short—"Go out and work, sell papers, deliver orders, do something." When my brother was already a union man, he got thirty-three dollars a week.

But some people made more. When I was a furrier, the union came into my shop and the chairman told the union that I am a good worker. The union said that I must be a union man. As a union man, I have to get at least sixty-five dollars a week. From twenty dollars to sixty-five dollars was a lot of money, but the union said we would go on strike. Finally, the union convinced the boss and they made me a union man. Then they took me off the job and I got myself a job in a union shop. I got a job for seventy dollars or seventy-five dollars a week until 1926. In 1926 we had a very big strike in the furriers. A terrific big strike. We were striking for about fifteen weeks. The union gave us from fifty cents to seventy-five cents a day in picket money, and we used to picket the shops and see that there shouldn't be any scabs.

When we found a scab, we had committees. I was very active in the committees. We had maybe three or four committees. Sometimes we used to educate them or explain it to them. Sometimes we'd find a scab who was really a scab—a strike-breaker—and we'd punish him. We'd rough him up a little bit. As far as strikebreakers who really needed the job and needed the pay for sickness or some other thing, the union gave those strikebreakers that really needed it five dollars or ten dollars a week so they should have money for food and shouldn't go to scab. When the union gave a man five or ten dollars, he had to appear every day of the week, even sometimes Saturdays, to be on the picket line or to go out and find out if there are scabs in different shops. During that period, some of the small, little shops settled—a shop with one worker, with two workers, with three workers.

When the strike was settled, I went back to work as a furrier, and I worked until 1930. I was a nailer. When you make a coat, the cutter cuts it, then the operator sews it, then the nailer puts it on a pattern and stretches it out, until it goes to the finisher. In 1930 my hands got poisoned. I got dye poisoning. My hands got swollen and I couldn't work. I got myself different jobs working here and there, but I still got industrial compensation through the shop.

Then my father became sick and couldn't work. My father got asthma, diabetes— all of a sudden he got everything. And he would never go for charity. The government then wouldn't do anything for you. There was no social security, no unemployment insurance. Nothing. You could only go to the Jewish organizations or the Catholic organizations. I kept him in the hospital a few weeks—I paid twenty-eight dollars a week—and then I took him home. A couple of weeks later, he got sick again and they took him to Kings County Hospital. In the hospital an infection developed and he died. When he died, I was the oldest in my family. I kept company with Shirley already, and I was working a little bit. I started to work in a grocery, and I used to get thirty dollars a week for five or six days a week in the grocery.

Even after I got married, I still used to contribute to the house. First we lived in a rooming house for a couple of months, and then we took an apartment in Williams- burgh. We were there, in Williamsburgh, during the depression. We went through hell. I didn't have a job. Shirley didn't have a job. There was no charity, you know. We didn't go for charity. So I used to work in a grocery sometimes and make seven dollars a day. We had a little food and we didn't have trouble with the rent.

At that time, the world went through a big revolution. Revolutions swept Europe, especially in Poland and Romania and Czechoslovakia. Roosevelt surrounded himself with people who were more or less liberal, and I think that he foresaw that with the unemployment in the United States something would have to happen. The people wouldn't stay passive and sell apples or sleep in the parks or create barracks and live in them.

So he introduced reforms. He started unemployment insurance, he gave a dole—like now they get subsidies, coupons—he gave a certain check so that poor people could buy themselves meat and groceries. There was the WPA for artists. He opened up C[ivilian] C[onservation] camps and they took all the youngsters and they built roads and parks. There were peddlers. There used to be a lot of peddlers. If you had a nickel, you'd get an apple. Sometimes we'd get two apples for a nickel, if it wasn't so *ay-yay-yay* [good]. It was tough. It was tough. But we accepted it, because after what we went through in Europe, this wasn't new to us.

Morris B.

On the twenty-second day, we came in at night and we saw in the distance what looked like electric lights. Little by little, the lights came closer and we saw the biggest and most beautiful, tallest buildings in the world. From there, we reached Hoboken—we came into Hoboken, New Jersey, but we could see New York. New York was the skyline, all the way across. It was the most miraculous thing you could see. We had to stay on the boat overnight.

I guess the customs office was closed, and everyone had to go through before they let you in, to see that you were not crippled, to see if you would be of service to America, and all that. The following morning, we each got in line, walked across with a ticket with your name and where you came from written out. We passed through and they checked everyone, whether you know how to read and write. They had a chart—a square chart of about a square yard. I saw German, Polish, Russian, Swedish, and right in the middle I saw a sentence from the Bible—in Hebrew, in large words. I laughed out loud. The guy wanted to know, "Was lachn zie?"—in German. He said, "Can you read this?" I said, "Yeah." He said read that. I read and he said, "That's enough." I still remember the words. It was part of the megillah where they describe King Ahasuerus and the outfits that they were wearing, and that they had garments made out of silver and gold threads and with purple trimming. That was the sentence—the description of the clothing that the king and guards wore. So I read it and I came to America.

That was in Ellis Island. There were inspectors and they looked you through. They did keep my grandfather. We all got off the island, and he remained there. We wanted to know why. They wanted to check him out. He had a black nail on a finger and they wanted to know what it was. They wouldn't let him off. They kept him a week. They kept him until they determined that it was just a black nail, and then they let him in after that.

My first impression—that I won't forget. When we got off the boat, and they were taking off some of the baggage and we were waiting for it, amongst the people that carried off—the longshoremen—I saw one black man. I looked at him and I studied him. He came by and I looked at him and he saw that I was studying him. He looked at me and he stretched out his hand to me. I took his hand and I noticed the inside of his hand was white and the rest of it was black, so I looked and I was just wondering, and I rubbed his hand. He laughed out loud as if to say, "What are you trying to do? Find out of it's pasted on or if the color is real?" He was eating peppermint . . . what do you call it? Round pebbles . . . lifesavers. And I looked. "Would you like one?" I didn't know what he was saying, but I thought he meant did I want one. I said yes. He gave it to me, and again I shook hands with him then and I knew that I had touched a black man. That was my first impression—I touched a black man, and I was sure there must be more. I knew there were black people in existence in Africa. In small towns, of course, nobody knew anything there. Even in the capital of Austria, in Vienna, I didn't see any black men.

Then we went to Clinton Street where my family was. That was on a Friday. And that same day I got my biggest disappointment, in meeting my boyhood chum who didn't know me and cared less—and who I parted with forever on that day. When I was eight years old in my little town, I was in the cheder and we had a bunch of chums. One of them had his father in America. His father had come home, brought some money, and took his family to America. His wife and his three sons and a daughter, they went to America. Before they left, two of us—one of them was very close to me—we practically swore, some day we would meet in America. I didn't know how, when, or whether, but some day we will.

The day that we came to America we stopped downtown on Clinton Street and Second Street. I asked whether they know the family Rubin—landsleit—where they live. They said they live somewheres Lower East. An address they didn't know, but they did know that a daughter died about a week ago, ten days ago, and there was a terrific, big-size funeral there. It was somewheres on Cannon Street or Lewis Street. I wrote the names Cannon and Lewis streets. That was on a Friday afternoon. As soon as I learned that, I left the house to look for that family.

I spent a couple of hours, walking around on the Lower East Side, this was Clinton, the corner of Second Street, I walked down one block it was Rivington Street, further down there were all pushcarts. A lot of pushcarts. I kept walking, near the pushcarts, asking if they had seen where there was a big funeral about ten days ago. No. I kept walking, Lower East. Finally I reached Cannon Street. One of the men with a pushcart said, "Oh yes, on the next block, in there, there was a big funeral." I walked to the next block—it was Lewis Street. That corner. I went down there and I asked some people where was there a big funeral about a week or two ago. "Oh, in the middle of the block, over there, on that side." "Which building?" They don't know. I started walking. I went up to the second or the third building—I went all the way to the top floor, some had five stories up, some had six stories up—I went to the top and I knocked at the door. Is there a family Rubin living here? No. No. No. No. One house. Second house. I came up and knocked on the door—"Yeah, two floors lower."

I went and knocked on the door and when the door opened . . . I still get choked up—a woman opened the door and looked at me—"Moishele." I looked at her. "Dina." I recognized her. She said, "When did you come?" Everything in Yiddish. "Ven biste gekumen?" I said, "Today." "How did you find us?" I said, "I'm glad I found you here." I said, "Is Sumeh in the house?" She said, "No, he's working." "When is he coming?" "He's coming back soon. It's Friday, he'll be home early." They kept me busy. They gave me fruit and a nice glass of soda. I hung around until the door opened and a young man walks in—about a fifteen- or sixteen-year-old boy. "Ma, I'm hungry." This was Sumeh, so I looked at him and I talked Yiddish to him. He looks at me and he answers in English. I didn't know what he was saying. "Sumeh, don't you know me?" No, he did not recognize me. He did not know me. We talked for about a half a minute—I reminded him that eight years ago we had been studying in the same cheder, we were close, we were studying from the same book. "Oh yeah, yeah, yeah." And he refused to speak Yiddish. The custom then was to become Americanized— stop talking Yiddish, talk English. So he learned English. That was the end of it. I walked out and I said I'm never going to see him again. And I didn't.

But I got acquainted with the little downtown streets. It was the first time actually that I saw the pushcarts with all the fruits on it. Amongst them what attracted my attention was something that I knew existed but I had never seen it—that was a long, yellow-colored piece of fruit, which was to my astonishment called a banana. I had at that time on the boat found a dime, believe it or not—I found an American dime. I asked how much that banana cost. It was two cents and I gave him that dime and I got change. When I began to break it in half I was told that that's not how you eat a banana. This guy showed me how to peel it. I peeled the banana. That was my first. It was good. I enjoyed it. I saw pomegranates, which I had never seen before but I knew about, and a lot of oranges. In Austria, oranges were brought down to some of the stores just before Rosh Hashanah, before New Year's, so the Jews could taste an additional fruit over which they could make a special blessing. We knew that before Rosh Hashana you could see an orange here and there, but I never ate one.

I got acquainted with the town and I inquired as to how people get to work here. I was told that there was a Jewish newspaper that was out every day except Saturday— that was the *Jewish Morning Journal—Morgn Zhurnal* in Yiddish. The *Freiheit* didn't exist then. There were several other newspapers. There was the *Tog*—the *Jewish Daily*—there was the *Tagn Blat*, which was a very religious newspaper. Even newspapers were factionalized. The *Tog* in Yiddish was a Democratic newspaper. The *Morgn Zhurnal* was a Republican newspaper. The *Tagn Blat* was a religious newspaper, ultrareligious. *Morgn Zhurnal* was also religious.

I asked where there were ads for jobs and I was told that the *Morgn Zhurnal* had most of the ads, especially on Sunday. So I waited until the following day. On Sunday morning, bright and early, I got up and left the house and went out and bought a Jewish newspaper. Jewish newspapers at that time were two cents. My Yiddish was perfect and I looked through the ads. I saw an ad which said, translated into Yiddish, "Young boy wanted to work in a crockery and gift shop." The address was given— 118 West 116th Street—that was in Harlem.

I took the paper with me and marked around with a pencil that ad. I asked people how to get to Harlem, how to get to 116th Street. I was told, there is an elevated, a train that goes all the way to 116th Street. That train ride cost five cents.

It was a shocking thing. I felt I was riding on a train, but the train goes above houses. I looked down and I see the houses and the streets on both sides, and I was walking back and forth. When I saw 116th, I got off and I began looking at the numbers. Then I looked for 118 and I reached that house and there was no crockery store there. I asked some people—and it was inhabited mostly by Jews at the time— the more affluent Jews lived in Harlem. 116th Street was a rich Jewish area. I asked for 118 and they told me there is such a thing as East and West—Fifth Avenue separates them. "This is East, you need 118 West. On the other side of Fifth Avenue it starts with One, you need 118." Sure enough, I walked into a beautiful store with all kinds of gifts—chinaware and crockery. I walked in and got the job. That was on a Sunday and they put me to work on the same day.

That first job was to help in packaging things that people bought, to put things into bags, dinnerware I had to pack in a special basket, and they showed me how and I was learning. This is where my first English education came from—from the store. The first four words that I learned in English was a word that I first thought was one word—every time a customer came in I heard the salesman talking Jewish, but I knew he wasn't. When they would walk in and ask for something he said, "Vegeforn? Vegeforn?" "Vegeforn" means "rode off" in Yiddish—*avekgeforn*. Finally, I walked over to one there—they all spoke Yiddish—and I said, "Vos meinstu vegeforn? Ver hot vegeforn?" No, it wasn't *avekgeforn*, it was "I beg your pardon." Those were the first words I had in English. Vegeforn—I beg your pardon.

I worked there some length of time. I used to work from ten o'clock in the morning until about eight o'clock in the evening. I loved the work that I did because I became one of the top salesmen there. To this very day if I pick up a piece of china, before turning it on the other side I'll tell you where it's made and which company made it. I learned from the transparency of it. I loved it very much but I did not like the hours because the more I perfected myself in the work, in the selling and taking care of the store, the longer hours I had to work. I had to work until ten, eleven o'clock at night.

Then I figured out that this is no life for me, because I had to find a place where I could go to night school. I had to study. Then I found out that where we lived downtown there was a school—a night school. From there I went to the Educational Alliance. The Educational Alliance had a special school for grown-up immigrants. That's where I studied, and later in prep school, which was also right there. I don't hesitate to say that within one year my English was the same as it is today. I was very young and absorbent—I took in everything.

The little that I knew of the English language I acquired the first year when I came to this country. By sheer stubbornness I had certain principles and lived by them, and if I have to fight the whole world I'll fight the world about them—I had made up my mind that I must learn English fast. Any word that I heard in English I had it translated to me, and immediately I used it in a sentence, even if my sentence was cockeyed, until my language became the American English language. That's how I learned my language. Life was not too easy in those days. Those days we would just as soon try to forget, but you don't forget. It stays with you.

After I quit the job in the shop, I found a job in a paperbox factory, feeding a machine. I worked there for some length of time and I thought that I was doing very nicely. Instead of making twenty-some-odd dollars a week, I made thirty dollars, I worked less hours. One day I went visiting someone I knew who was related to the family and had opened up a fur shop. The fur industry actually consisted in the beginning of all Jewish people. It was started by German Jews. They were the first immigrants and they brought the trade with them. Later, the European Jews got into it. When I was in it there were practically all Jews, very few non-Jews. I remember one in particular—Paul, redheaded, non-Jewish. He knew Jewish as well as the other Jews in the shop. He used to talk Jewish because he always worked with Jewish guys. There were very few of them who were not Jewish.

The fur shop I went in in 1924. I must have been about twenty or twenty-one.

The guy had just started in business, with a partner. The partner was a cutter and he was an operator, and the partner took a liking to me. "Morris, why do you have to work in paper boxes? I'll make a cutter out of you in no time." Here I was already making thirty dollars a week, and that was not easy. He said, "Believe me, you'll make more here." I said, "Can I get thirty dollars now? Then I'll start Monday." He said, "No. But if you start tomorrow, not Monday, you'll start with twenty-eight dollars—two dollars less than what you are getting. I guarantee you'll make quite a bit more." I said, "OK, it's a deal."

The system in the fur trades used to be that every time someone wanted to learn the trade, they had to go in and first work on the floor, be a floor boy, handing things to the cutter, to the operator, taking away things. When you work with fur, with garments, you have to wet the skins, straighten them out, all kinds of things. When this fellow told me he'll make a cutter out of me in no time, I saw a boy who was wetting skins and doing those things. I said, "Yes, but I don't want to do this. Can I be put to the table immediately without going through that?" He said, "Yes, you have my word for it. Come in the following day."

I didn't want to wet the skins because it was dirty filthy work. You had to take skins, a bundle of skins, take them apart and one by one put them in front of a table with a round, big *shisl* around it.

BESS: He doesn't know what a *shisl* is.

MORRIS: Well, like a big baking pan, but the size of a table. You'd lay the skin in there, take with a wet brush, and rub the skin with water to make it wet. Take it away, put another skin down, make it wet. You'd make wet a whole bundle and then you'd give it to the cutter, because when the cutter has to start working on it it has to be soft so he can stretch it. That's the floor boy's work. I didn't want to do that work. I wanted to be a cutter. And he promised. He said, "Yes, you come in tomorrow morning and I'll put you straight to the table." That's the most unusual thing, to come into the industry and go straight to the table. You had to work for nothing or next to nothing before they ever put you there.

The fur manufacturing industry consisted of five crafts. The top craft was the cutter. The cutter did the cutting of the garment, did the matching of the skins, and even in Persians where it was not too easy to match the curls, we had to cut out the bad and set in another piece to match it in so perfect that you would never know that it was a strange piece put in, and put together the garment. It was laying flat on the table, and then the cutter had to put together the skins next to one another, row by row, pick up the whole bundle, which was already a whole garment, layer by layer, and then the whole was put together in one bundle and given for the next operation to the operator. An operator was one who sat at the machine. The fur cutter had to use a knife—a steel knife shaped in a certain manner, a pointy knife, very very sharp. You could hold a piece of paper against it and just slice through and it would cut. It was very sharp. That was the cutters.

The operator who got the garment put together by the cutter, had to sew piece by piece, not to make any errors with lines or with skins. When he sewed it together it became a garment, but much smaller than what the cutter did. Seams took in to an extent, skins shrank a little, but he was in charge of sewing up the entire garment. The third operation was another mechanic known as the nailer. His job was to take the garment after the cutter and operator were through with it, lay it on a flat, long, wide table, mark out with chalk the pattern of the garment and the size that it has to be—mark it out with chalk—take the pattern off and leave the table only with the chalk where the garment should be placed. Then he had to wet the entire garment by using a brush over it. Even though the skins had been wetted before, he would have to rewet the entire skin on the left side of it, on the skin side, and begin nailing it to the shape which was marked out by chalk on the board, making sure that it reaches the full size of the garment. That is, the nailer actually had to make the garment into a garment—take what was sewn together and make it into the shape of a garment.

Then this was put into a drying room, a hot room, with the board that it was nailed on—they would stand up the board and shove it into that room, take another garment and do likewise, and during the day he may have had about eight or ten garments on boards, put fifteen into that room. They would leave them overnight and the following morning they would come in and pull out the boards. After the cutting, operating, and the nailing was done, the next process was called squaring. Squaring meant a cutter—less experienced, less skilled—his job was to go with a knife around the edges of the garment which was nailed and cut off what was beyond the original marking that was on that board—making it smooth all around, without raw edges where the nails were. When he was through with it, there were no more nail markings. That was the squarer's job. He was sort of a second-class cutter.

After that was the closing job. Closing was given back to another operator who did nothing else but closing the garment to sew up the sleeves. Then the completion of the garment was to be done. Completion meant putting in a lining. The finisher would have to cut in the lining according to the shape of the garment, which was also by pattern. When that was done, the floor worker would come into play. That's the one that I did not want to be. He had the original job of getting the skins wet for the cutter. In the industry they had a nickname for him. They didn't call him the floor worker, they called him the *machnass*. *Machnass* is a composition of two Jewish words—*mach nass*, "make wet." Make it wet. That was his job, to make it wet. He would pick up the garment, put tags on it, marking the size. If the nailer was not too perfect and he could not bring up the garment to the full size, then a smaller pattern had to be put on it, and cut around for the next size. The garment was hung up on a hanger and the salesman was ready to sell or make deliveries. Deliveries, by the way, were also made by the floor workers.

I wanted the top mechanical job for the garment. Anything that happens to a garment, no matter what it looks like in the very end, is generally considered either the please of the cutter or the fault of the cutter. The cutter had to take responsibility for the garment. He had to keep an eye and make sure that the operator sews it right, that the squarer does the job correctly, and keep an eye on the finisher to see that he does his job.

A mink garment may take as long as a week to make, or there are some lower-grade garments that can take two in a week. A Persian garment can be made one a day, a cheaper-grade can be made two a day. Then there were seals. A seal actually was a product that looked very smooth, dyed black—and it would take about a day to make. Then there were imitation seals, which were made from rabbits. They used to cut them just as long as the seal, skin and dye them the same color. Then there were rabbits without being dyed—rabbit skins were the cheapest. So how long it would take a garment to be made depended on the type of garment you were working with, if it was the better line or the cheaper line or the medium line.

The cutter had to work at his own speed. There was no such thing as beating another man. There couldn't be competition. There was no such thing. The union didn't allow competition. If a man was naturally a fast cutter, he would base his price on the basis of the average production of the shop. If he produced two garments a day and somebody else produced one and a half garments, he would get the equivalent of about twenty-five percent of his wages more than the other guy. Speeding was prohibited by the union. Occasionally it would happen that some guy would come up and he would want to get the job and he would sweat, but we would call these speed-up artists and the workers would push him out of the job. He wouldn't stay there.

I was initiated into the fur industry little by little, it did not take too long. I began working as a cutter with the partner of the firm showing me what to do and how to do it. Within one week after I started at twenty-eight dollars a week, I already earned thirty-five. I worked for the next five weeks at the same price—thirty-five dollars a week, which was then not considered bad for a beginner, taking into consideration that those who learned the industry and wanted to become cutters in most cases had to spend a year or two until they perfected themselves and they could go out and get a job in a different shop, where they had not learned.

The system was that no matter where you learned you cannot make above a certain amount of money, because the boss always felt that he's got to get the benefit out of you. So if you're worth sixty dollars and he can get you for thirty-five, he'll keep you there a whole season, which meant a year. In those days the industry was mostly a summertime industry, working about five, five and a half months—the summer months—with a little bit in the winter for the spring line, February, March, but the basic part of the industry was the summer industry.

At one particular point, after working about six weeks in that shop, making thirty-five dollars a week, which was not bad for a beginner—I had forgotten all about the paper box factory and I now was a furrier meeting with other people who worked in shops—I learned that there is such a section called the fur market. The fur market was at that time concentrated on Seventh Avenue between Twenty-seventh and Thirtieth streets. Those were a number of big, tall buildings, where every single compartment, every single floor, had a fur shop—some small, some big. People used to go out during lunch hour and be on the sidewalks. They'd get an hour for lunch, but probably eat for ten minutes and then be out conversing with other people in the industry. People learned about different jobs, what this one does, what that one does. That was called the fur market.

My initial job was also on Seventh Avenue, but it was a little bit of a shop on Twenty-third Street, between Twenty-fourth and Twenty-third. One day the firm needed an additional operator, and a man came up—someone they picked up in the market. This fellow worked for about a week or two and got to know me and he told me about the fur market. I took a walk, during lunch hour with him, and I met other people, and from that day on, there wasn't a day when my lunch took more than fifteen minutes. The rest of the time I was in that market talking to other people.

Sure enough one man meets me who happened to know me. He said, "Morris, what are you doing here?" I said, "What am I doing here? The same as anyone else. I'm a furrier." "Oh, you're a furrier? Who are you working for?" I said, "What difference does it make?" He said, "Well, I'm in business with a partner and I can use a cutter. Are you a cutter?" I said, "Yes, I'm a cutter." "What are you working at?" I told him the line of work that I had done. He said, "Just come on and work for me." I said, "No, you're not going to pay me what I'm worth." "What do you think you're worth?" "I won't leave my job unless I get sixty dollars a week." I at that time learned that most cutters get up to sixty dollars a week. He said, "Come up, let me try you out." I said, "All right, I'll be up there tomorrow." Several days elapsed and I did not go up.

In the meantime, a union delegate came up to the shop where I had worked and announced himself as a union delegate. This was not a union shop. He came in and said, "This is the union and we are organizing the shop. Which one of you are workers here? Three people got up—myself, another fellow, and a nailer. He said, "OK, this is a strike." So I walked over to this man. "What is it you want and why is the shop on strike?" "This will have to be a union shop?" "So why does it have to be on strike? Can't we go down and register for the union and come back and you can negotiate whatever you have to?" "OK, we'll have it your way, but you've got to come down to the union." I said, "All right." One of the other fellows did not want to go down there, but I had a little talk with him and convinced him that from what I know about unions it's worthwhile—"Let's go down and let's listen to them."

Finally, we did all go down. We came down and that time Ben Gold, who later became the president of the entire international, was just about getting ready to run for office as the manager of the local furriers in New York. They brought me into his office. I talked to him very simply. He asked me my name. I told him. "What do you do in the shop?" I told him. "How much do you earn?" I told him—thirty-five dollars a week. "Don't you think you're worth more?" I said, "Yes. I know that I'm worth more, but I'm also told that you can't get more. I don't need much money, but other people doing the same work get so much more, practically twice as much, there's no reason why I shouldn't." He said, "You know young man, you I like. You stay here. You don't go back to the shop. Our business agent will go up to the shop, talk to your boss and try to unionize the shop. In the meantime, you're staying out until this thing happens."

This business agent it seems was not too smart, and he began yelling, screaming— "I had to spit blood to get these fellows out." I stopped him right there. "Wait a minute. Didn't you come in and wasn't I the first one who approached you and I told the boys to go down and we went down within five minutes after you came? You did not have to say a word. We all walked down." Hearing this, Ben Gold turned around and told him to go into another room. Later I heard that he gave him the devil for doing that, for saying that. Of course, the fellow wanted to make it sound like it was a hard job getting the shop down.

In the meantime I was told not to go up for one week, and to see if I could get a job in the market. After you get a job in the market and you see what you're worth and you want to go back to the shop, they will have to give you what you're earning in another shop and perhaps even better.

I went to the market and met that man that asked me to work in his shop. He said, "Didn't I talk to you several days ago and you told me you would come up to see me?" I said, "Yes, but I wasn't ready." "Can you come up tomorrow?" I said yes. I already knew that I wasn't going to work the following day. I came up and he put me to work. I worked with him—he was a cutter as well. I had what was known in the trade as a very smooth cut. If I sound as if I am boasting, I am, because I was really fast in those days. I was a youngster, and I made two garments to one that the boss made. I was supposedly excellent there. He said, "You have a job. You're getting sixty dollars a week and if you continue working the way you do, you'll make a lot more." I said, "OK, I'm working here."

One day later, my old boss—the one where I learned the trade—came up and looked at me, watched me work and said, "Morris, what are you doing here?" I said, "Well, I was told by Mr. Gold, the manager of the union, to stay out one week. I understand that they're having a board meeting on Thursday, when new applications will be taken up for membership, and I was told to wait until the board meets. When they do, I'll have to go for my union book." "Well, maybe you'll work for us." It turned out that this firm where I had gotten the new job was dependent on my other boss for credit at some of the fur skin dealers, and he was scared. He was afraid the other guy would hurt his credit. "Aren't you coming back?" I said, "I'm here, I'm a furrier now. I appreciate what you've done for me. You've taught me."

That same evening, the new boss came over to me, "Morris, I like your work, you're excellent. I want you to work for me, but I have problems and I'm afraid I'll have to let you go. Go back to your other boss." I said okay. The following morning, I walked into the other shop and the boss who had come up to the place said, "Why don't you take off your coat, put on your apron?" I said, "No, we have to discuss this." "What is it you want?" I said, "You know, I'm getting sixty-five dollars a week. Of course, you came up to the shop. I don't know whether you threatened the man or he took it as a threat, but he told me I couldn't work for him—he's a friend of yours, tied up with you in business, and he doesn't want to hurt you." I told him, "I wasn't going to work for him, but that doesn't mean that I have to work for you at the same thirty-five dollars a week. If not that man, I can get a dozen others. I know where the market is, there is a demand for cutters, so let's be friends and let's forget about it." "Oh, we were planning to give you this coming week forty-five dollars, and a week or two later you'll get fifty-five dollars." I said, "Well, that still doesn't make it—forty-five, then maybe fifty-five. Why should I wait? Those number of weeks that I will be working elsewhere, people watch me work and I'll be worth much more than the sixty dollars I was originally offered. So you're not doing much for me."

Well, the guy was arguing, and finally he came up to the fifty-five dollars. He said, "Look, isn't it worth it to you, this season, to lose five dollars on the wages—I know the man offered you sixty dollars and you can get much more—isn't it worth five dollars to you to know that we enjoy your working with us and that you'll be working for five dollars less?" I said, "Well, I don't know. I'll come in Monday." "What's with Thursday and Friday—there are two more days?" I said, I want to become acquainted with people in the market. "Don't go to that market, they are a bunch of Communists there." I said, "What's Communist?" "They are out to ruin every boss." I said, "Well, it seems to be that the whole world is Communist because everybody works for bosses. If that's communism, I must be a Communist too, but I'm not coming back until Monday."

When it reached Monday, I did come in, but in the meantime I got to know more people. When I came before the executive board, the manager of the union took an interest. There must have been about a dozen and a half people waiting for their union books. He called me in first and he said, "This young man"—he made actually an appeal to the board, he didn't need it—"this young man has helped us organize a shop. I can foresee good things for him. I want him to get his book and let him go home. Don't make him hang around and wait." I was immediately called in and a decision was made. I received my union book the following day. A book at that time was I think sixty-seven dollars and twenty-five cents. A union book is allowing you as a union worker to work in a shop. In every shop there are people working and one of them is the chairman to look after the union business, to see that there are no violations. He asked for the union book. If you have no union book, he sends you to the union. So when you come up you have to be able to show a book. The following day, I came in, got my union book and paid for it, and out.

Our union was known as one of the left-wing unions. Since I had learned that the union people were the ones that were really getting better conditions in the shop, I felt that I ought to take an interest. Anytime there was a meeting, I was there—local meetings, other meetings. I would occasionally ask for the floor, be given the floor, and give my opinion. It seemed that they took my opinions well, and then I was urged to run for the executive board of the local. At that time I told people that I was not ready yet. I was still young. In 1925 I was twenty-two years old. I let it slide and I worked in the industry until the early 1930s, without being part of the union board or anything else—just what was known then as a good union man.

There was such a thing as a left-winger and a right-winger, and I asked people in the market, in the fur market, "what is the difference between a right-winger and a left-winger?" I didn't know what it meant. "Well, the right-wingers are ready to sell everything to the boss. They don't care for the workers, they're just interested in working a lot of overtime, no matter how little or how much they get in the shop. They're not interested in having the union come in and sort of dictate to you what you're supposed to do." I said to them, "What is a left-winger?" "Well, a left-winger is more for the workers than the others. They are interested in building unions and becoming leaders of the union, not to allow the old-time leaders to maintain superiority forever." I said, "Well, that means I'm a left-winger." That's how I named myself a left-winger, and I stuck with that all these years. For years I followed not just the Socialist Party line, I followed the Communist Party line. From each according to his ability, to each according to his need. Integration. Everything. We all followed the line.

In 1926 was the strike known as the greatest and longest general strike the fur union had ever had. That strike lasted for seventeen weeks. Of course, the strike resulted from demands that were put out by the union which the bosses refused, but at that time the leadership in the union, the left-wing leadership in the union, had just been about one year old. It took over the leadership of the union in the local area by 1925. They put up the kind of demands that the bosses were not so ready to give.

The first demand that was made in the entire labor movement in those years was for a forty-hour week. Prior to that, it was forty-eight. And Saturday was compulsory—you had to work four hours on a Saturday, whether you liked it or not. The demand was put up for a forty-hour five-day week. Of course, the bosses would not give in too easily, and the international union—which was the body above the Furriers Union local in New York, that was the international of all the fur locals throughout the country—they came in and they began negotiating with the manufacturers.

When they started negotiating with the manufacturers, they tried to finish it fast. They called a meeting that they had made a settlement. What did the settlement consist of? Among a number of other things, a forty-two-and-a-half-hour week instead of a forty-four-hour week. A meeting was held in the Hippodrome—at that time there was a big hall known as the Hippodrome—they used to have the Barnum and Bailey circus there, plays, and everything. Later it was removed and I don't remember what became of that, whether it was the Manhattan Opera House, or something like that. But the Hippodrome lasted for many years. That was where the meeting took place. When people began flocking to the meeting, there were some people from the international put at the gates, at the door, and others from the right-wing part of the union, and those that were opposing the Gold administration were pointing out to them which ones were the left-wingers, "Don't let them in, they'll create trouble." They discriminated. They didn't allow too many people to get into that building that were known as left-wingers, and the hall was packed with the other furriers. But when the conditions were made known, that the settlement was made, the few left-wingers that did get in there, those of us who were there, began to yell, "We want Gold." They did not allow Gold in. The hall resounded with that "We want Gold" to such an extent it was impossible. They tried to say a few words, and nothing was permitted. Nothing. The meeting lasted for about an hour and a half, with the outcry of "We want Gold."

That was the end of that meeting and the strike was taken over again by the Gold forces. It came up at the end of the seventeenth week, the bosses realized they had to settle with the administration that's in power, and they gave in to a forty-hour week. That was the first industry in the entire international union movement—I don't know about international, the entire union movement in America—that had a forty-hour week. The start was made. Later we organized more shops and the international sort of took a back seat. The Gold administration lasted for many, many years, more than thirty years.

During those seventeen weeks, we went through hardships, because actually at that time I had not accumulated too much money from my work. I must have had at that time an accumulation of about two hundred dollars, or something like that, and every week I had to use part of that money to live on.

I had a function in the strike hall as part of the machinery that kept records— records of where the various groups were sent out for picketing duty, how long they were there, when they came back, and if a fellow did not show up for any reason or length of time, to find out where they were. It was necessary to put a tail on them to find out if he doesn't go scabbing. We had a group that did just that type of work, and I was part of that machinery. They got a third-degree questioning. If we found out that they did it again, in some cases, they were sent to a committee which handled them—in some cases physically handled—and made certain that if they ever go again they won't anymore. Some of them were cured in that manner, but there were scabs in every strike. The scabs were not so many—there were many more union people than scabs.

The scab would sneak into a shop when no one would see and the boss would bring him food. Some of them would sleep in the shops—we had some of those as well. I remember one of the provisions in the agreement when we finally settled, was something that the bosses insisted on, that those who were caught working—and they weren't called scabs but "those who were caught working"—at any time during those seventeen weeks that they be permitted to go back to work. Some compromise was reached. They would be permitted to go to work, but not in the shop where they were scabbing, and of course they had to pay heavy penalties.

The strike lasted for seventeen weeks, but I was in trouble for longer than that. As soon as the strike was settled, my shop—which at that time was a trimming shop that only made collars and cuffs and muffs, not full garments—was very slow, because the cloak trade had not picked up, and that depended on the cloak trade. When they got busy, we got busy. For twelve weeks after the strike I did not work. And that was a great hardship. The strike was really something that was a memorable thing.

I worked in the industry about five more years—until 1931 or '32, I thing it was 1932—when the trade became so bad that there was no work at all. I know the depression started in 1929, but until it reached the fur industry, it was in 1931, 1932.

There was a certain period when Ben Gold went to Moscow and he stayed there for a while. It seemed that he had his differences with the Lovestone movement, and he was inclined to go along with them, and there were others who felt that he ought to be straightened out. He took a trip to Moscow and he stayed there some length of time and then he came back.

During that period, the industry was very, very bad. There was no work at all. The few dollars we had left we used up. It was really cold and we had no heat. For a couple of days I was pushing a cart, selling knishes. Even that people didn't have a nickel to buy, and one day I got so disgusted that I decided to hell with it, I had enough. I thought to myself, "Well, if anybody is hungry, let him come and eat knishes." I walked off and left it in the street.

Then I got a letter from my father-in-law, who was in Boston—my Bess was born in Boston. We were married in 1928. This was four years later. I was told in that letter, "We know that you're not working right now and you're now a married man. If you come to Boston right now there is something ready for you that you can't get in a thousand years. Someone is ready to give up a fruit route—he had a truck selling fruit and vegetables off a truck. A New York boy, he built up the business and he's giving it up. You can get it for next to nothing. For two hundred dollars you can buy the whole thing." I picked myself up and I went to Boston. I got a Dodge 1929 truck for two hundred dollars. And then I started the fruit business. This lasted for about a year and a half. Suddenly I got a call from New York that the industry has picked up and I could come back now. So I gave up the whole business, got rid of the truck, came back to New York and I started working again.

It was during that period, after I came back, that I found out there was a workers' club not far from where we lived. We obtained an apartment on 170th Street and Boston Road and there was the Prospect Workers' Center. Mainly it was where people got together for enjoyment, spending their time. Some carried out some political activities, et cetera. It was boys and girls, and some even met one another and got married through the club. It was nice while it lasted. We ran concerts. I remember one concert in particular, we had about eight hundred people there. It was terrific. Saturday night concerts.

Most of the people had become Americanized. All the business was conducted in English. But there were not too many American boys there, mostly European stock. Frankly, the circles that we were into were all Jewish groups. There was not too much of coming in with the average American youngster. We were all very active, running affairs, raising money, and quite a number of our people from the clubs joined the Spanish volunteers, the Lincoln Brigade—some never came back. We knew that this is where the big powers are trying out their hardware. We knew at that time that the Italian government was helping the Spanish Fascist government of Franco. The Loyalists did not have too much help. They had the American brigade and they also had a German brigade there, and they really could not win that war. They lost it.

During the McCarthy period—I don't know if I ought to go into it, because it was really a deal that no matter where you start, you can't finish. There was too much for the average worker to take. We had it to such an extent that to the union they would send down FBI people to check on who was a Communist and who's not. I was called in, and they told me, "We know you're not a Communist." I knew that they had a little recorder under their coats, taking in every word that you said. They would say for the record, so people would talk to them, "We know you're not a Communist, but who are the Communists here? Give us their names." On public record, in the union, we had one who identified himself as a Communist and that was Irving Potash, who was the manager of the union at the time. So we all told them the same thing— "We only know one who was identified as a Communist and that's Mr. Potash." I think during that period he was already in jail and up for deportation and all that. "He identified himself as a Communist, and he's the only one—there are no others here."

The fur union was actually the bulwark of the left-wing union movement. It culminated in a number of unions that considered themselves left-wing unions, and they called themselves the Needletrade Workers Industrial Union, that was in competition with the fur union, which was then taken over for a period by the so-called right-wing elements in the union. There was a split between left and right, left-wing unions was one and right-wing unions was another, and for a period of almost ten years we had two unions in the industry—a left-wing union led by Ben Gold and others, and a right-wing union led by Kaufman, Stutsky, Silverstein, and a number of others. That was a right-wing union and a left-wing union. The New York City fur industry was basically run by the left-wing union until there was a movement that began to unite the unions into one. Little by little, some unions united with others and of course the left-wing union was out of the American Federation of Labor, the others were in the Federation of Labor. Then when the CIO came up, the left-wing union did join the CIO, but the others were in the American Federation of Labor. When the CIO later joined the American Federation of Labor and they went in completely to make one unified labor movement, the fur union as well as other unions began looking towards amalgamating both unions together.

In 1935 there was a merger—the left-wing union and the right-wing union merged. The leadership actually, slowly, was taken over by the left-wing elements— the entire international union. It took a few years, but we were in control of it until 1954. In 1954 a merger was made between the fur union as one union and the Amalgamated Meat Cutters and Butcher Union, which was an AFL union. In that manner it took it back to the AFL. The AFL had refused to accept the furriers, especially because there was the left-wing element in it. A merger was made between the fur union and the Amalgamated Meat Cutters, which at that time felt that they would take in the furriers as part of their union, but the furriers would have to make great sacrifices. The idea was to merge that phase of American industry together. After some lengthy discussions, the fur union had agreed that the only way to get back into the AFL and to have one strong union—the union was faced with the Taft-Hartley law, it was hard to organize, people had to sign non-Communist affidavits at the time, and some were not inclined to do so—that in order to get back into the AFL, sacrifices would have to be made and they would have to come back into another AFL union.

So then the merger between the two—the fur and leather, not just the furriers here but the fur and leather union, and the Amalgamated Meat Cutters and Butcher Workmen—took place in 1954 at a sacrifice. The sacrifice was that all the leaders of the fur union would have to resign. The designations were later narrowed to not all, but the most important ones would have to resign. Ben Gold would have to resign, and especially the New York fur union leaders, of whom eight were labeled undesirable by the AFL. They had no proof that these people were Communists, but the meat cutters at that time said that they could not come to the AFL to approve the merger unless they show that they have eliminated those who the AFL considered more than just left-wingers, they considered them Communists. They decided on eight, that these eight would have to go. The manager, the assistant manager, and some of the business agents who were more active than others and more known than others—they would have to resign.

I was one of those who was designated to resign. I never considered myself a top leader of the union, but at that time I was already a business agent, with a lot of years, and I felt that the sacrifice was necessary. I did not worry about making a living. I knew that I was a cutter and I could go back to the trade. Of the eight who resigned,

Ben Gold was the first one to resign. I resigned from leadership of the union as a business agent, and I went back to a shop to work.

Max T.

We came to the United States on the Red Star line. It took about twelve days to get here. There were a lot of people on that boat. Crooks, too. There were people who made voyages especially among the immigrants, to steal their possessions. They know that an immigrant that comes to this country brings watches, necklaces, rings. We didn't have any experience with them because somehow they always picked on the ones that were more conspicuous than we were.

When the boat came into New York harbor and I saw the skyline, somehow it didn't impress me. I lived in Donyetsk, where they had buildings of four, five, or six stories, and I was in Kiev for a certain period of time, where there were taller buildings than that. But one thing did strike me. My father didn't have a car—he didn't know how to drive (and neither do I, to this day)—so we went to his house by subway. To take a cab would have been too expensive. When I went down in the subway station at Bowling Green, I saw a black man sweeping the floor. I didn't like it. I said to myself, "This reminds me of *Uncle Tom's Cabin*."—I had read it so many years before in Russian. "Is this the kind of job that is allotted to a black person? To sweep the floor?" I thought there was something wrong.

I wasn't impressed at all by the United States when I first got here. If I would have come to the United States to a father who was well-to-do and didn't have to work hard for a living, things might have been different. But I saw the way things are and I said to myself that there is no purpose to this life here. I was not impressed.

I wanted to go back after a year. But then, you know, you become swallowed up in the mainstream and you remain. A youngish person's mind can very easily be molded to acquiesce—if I'm using the right word—to certain situations. Then when you become older, and you start to look back, you see that it's not a question of a mistake but perhaps it would have been better to remain there. My major reason for leaving the Soviet Union was that it was nonsensical to have my father come back to Russia, especially during the turmoil, the instability. I couldn't let my mother and three sisters go by themselves. So I had to do it. But I was always looking for something to compensate for something I was missing in life, and I didn't know what I was missing. I couldn't find myself.

My father prepared an apartment for us when we came. We lived in a nice neighborhood on Prospect Avenue and 160th Street in the Bronx. I got my first job in a place somewheres on St. Marks Place making sweatbands for hats. I got a job there and the boss showed me how to work on the machine. I was a young boy and I was shooting hundreds of pieces—it didn't mean anything to me. He liked me because I was productive. I was the only one there. The boss had a man coming in to cut these pieces from larger pieces, and he was suspicious that the man was using the telephone. So he used to tell me, "You see that man? When I am going out, if that guy is using the telephone, tell me when I come back."

Once he called me into the stockroom and showed me that he had three walls covered with packages—let's say a hundred pieces tied up with a string—one on top of the other, one on top of the other. I looked at it and started to laugh. I said, "Can you imagine what would happen if this whole thing collapses and falls apart—what kind of a job you would have to sort it?" He said, "Well, we make money out of this." I made nine dollars a week there.

I used to give the money to my mother. I concentrated on my education. I didn't know what I was looking for. I wanted to become an actor, so I attended an actor's school. I was studying drama with some of the cream of the Jewish theater and I participated in quite a number of plays. But then I saw that there is no future in it. When you have a job, it's only a temporary one, and when you have no job, you're a bum. I figured I have to make a living. So I chose a trade.

I started to learn the shoe trade. It so happened that I learned the trade very well. I became an expert on it. I worked a good part of my industrial career in the shoe line. I did everything. There's fancy stitching, ornamental stitching, and also putting the upper part together—it's being done by machine. From there, I went to work on lady's handbags, and I retired from there. In between I was a mechanical draftsman. I finished with a high mark, the only problem was I couldn't get a job because of my background as an industrial worker and also because of unemployment in the industry. Naturally they hired the experienced people instead of those that just finished their courses.

I did a lot of things, but I didn't sell newspapers. Maybe that was my biggest trouble—if I had sold newspapers, I could have been president of the United States—that's how they all started out, selling newspapers. My main aim when I was still in the Soviet Union was to become an engineer. Had I not left the Soviet Union I would have gone to Moscow to study engineering—they wanted to send me to Moscow.

When you live in New York, your environment is mostly Jewish. You do encounter some Gentiles on the way. If you have discrimination among your own Jews, you're bound to be discriminated against by different denominations. The American-born Jew was looking down on the immigrants for a number of years. It was quite visible in the factories. No matter how good a mechanic you were, when you came to this country and applied for a job, at least in those years, you were not able to get the same compensation for the work as a person who has been here for many years. I don't know if you call that discrimination, but it was taking advantage of the fact that you lacked the language and you lacked the experience. The language is a big factor. A big factor. My father and mother always spoke Yiddish. They assimilated a little bit due to necessity, but not in order to jump into the melting pot. They kept strictly to the old ways of life. They didn't deviate.

When I first came to this country, I wanted to know a lot of things, and I wanted to see a lot of things. By nature, I was a very curious person. I wanted to know how other people live. I once walked with a group of youngsters to an Orthodox church and spent a couple of hours there to see some of the people that were instrumental in making pogroms against the Jews, and to see how they behaved in this country after running away from the Revolution. I succeeded in doing that by attending certain functions in various places. At that time on Lenox Avenue in Harlem there were a lot of Russian eating places and nightclubs. Once we were sitting at the table—a group of about twenty of us—and somebody yells out, "His Royal Highness!" It was General So-and-so, so everybody got up. The guy comes in and goes straight to the kitchen. He was washing dishes there. That gave me a sense of satisfaction, you see, to draw the analogy between my life in this country and his life in this country.

Then there were a lot of things that I was too young for when I was in Russia, or I had no access to it. I made up for that in a short time in this country. We went to movies. The Capital Theater at that time was the main movie house. And we went to plays. We did not go much to the ballet or the opera—that came years after. Museums came years after. Mostly what I did then was read. Between the time that I was born and the time that I came to this country in 1923, I had very little to acquaint myself with world literature. So I read Turgenev, I read Tolstoi, I read Chekhov, I read Dostoevski, a few plays of Shakespeare, and some French authors—Maupassant, Dumas. I also read a lot of books in Hebrew, because I studied that language when I was in Russia. And then the main thing—Marx and Lenin.

Harry M.

We came at night. The lights were shimmering over New York. This we never saw in Europe, never saw in Russia. All the big buildings—tremendous. It was a beautiful sight. The boats, the buildings, the lights. Then when we stepped off the boat the next day, we stopped in the immigration center on Ellis Island. My brother took us off the boat and he took us to my uncle on Essex Street.

We were there—my two brothers, my sister, my mother, my uncle and his three children, and a boarder they had besides—all together in three rooms. They had a coal stove for cooking and heating. The toilet was out in the hall, one for ladies and one for men. Every floor had about ten tenants, and there were only two toilets. You had to get up early in the morning to get in first. And then you had to rush to work. It was a hard battle with sanitary conditions. The bathing facilities were in public baths, not far from my house.

I spent a couple of days with my uncle and then we went to look for jobs. I didn't know English, so I picked up the Jewish paper and found a job on Prince Street, chopping felt soles for slippers. The job at that time was six days, eight hours a day—forty-eight hours. It was very good. I chopped. I was a chopper on a big, heavy machine. They laid out felt materials to a height of probably about five, six feet, and you pressed down your foot and the machine chopped out soles—different sizes. You had dies—different sizes, different dies. So you took the die, put it on the felt, and the machine pressed it down and chopped it out. The conditions were very noisy. All the machines were making a lot of noise, metal against metal, chopping out with the dies. You couldn't hear yourself talk. And everybody was busy.

We couldn't wait until twelve o'clock. Most of us ran out in the street then to get some fresh air, or we had our lunch out in the street. Naturally, we took lunch along—usually a sandwich and some dessert or fruit—because we usually couldn't afford to go to the restaurants. At five o'clock, we came home to eat supper.

After we were about a month's time in my uncle's, we tried to get our own apartment. Finally, we landed uptown in the Bronx, in a fifth-floor walk-up. We had our own toilets. We got three rooms, and we were very glad because before there were three rooms also, but we had so many people. The East Siders felt that the Bronx was a luxury. It was. In the Bronx it was more modern. The house was more modern. We had steam heat, there were baths, and we had a telephone. Downtown you had to go to public baths for sanitation. You didn't have your own toilet—you had to go and wait for your next—there were only two toilets on the entire floor. Sanitation was better, the apartment was more comfortable, roomier, and it wasn't as noisy as downtown on Essex Street. That was a section where most immigrants came first to settle. Up in the Bronx it was a luxury.

Then we started to go to night school, from seven until nine, to learn the language and to learn other subjects like mathematics and history. After working in the slipper place for about six months, the place slowed down—there was no business—and he laid us off. I had to look for another job. The next job, I went to a place and there were about twenty people ahead of me. The foreman comes out and he looks you over—how strong you are, how tall you are. Finally, he picked me because I was tall and hefty. This job was a soldering place for kitchen utensils. We made soap dishes, strainers, graters, pot holders, and other things. My job was soldering these things together, all made from iron. This place was very hot, because you had to keep the fire all the time to have the iron soldering. After a week working there, I couldn't take it anymore. I burned my fingers, burned my hands, and I quit. The foreman gave me a bawling out, because, he said, "After all, out of twenty people, I picked you and now you quit." I didn't like the job.

The next job I went in is to a place where you collect old carpets, you tear them up, and make them into new ones. My job was to take the carpets, put them in a machine with teeth, and tear them up. That place was so dusty—from the old carpets—that you couldn't see yourself. And there were no masks. But it paid very well—about $20 a week, which was a lot of money. But you became so dirty that it took about an hour when you came home to make yourself clean. Your skin, your clothes—everything was black. I worked there for about four weeks, and I started coughing, so I had to give it up.

The next job I found was in a suitcase and valises factory. I was the paster, pasting in the lining into the suitcases, which also was near a hot stove, to keep the glue liquid. You had to dip it in with a brush, smear the cases, and put in the lining. I worked there during the summer. It was very hot, but still I needed the job. I worked there until September.

In September I quit the public school and I went to private preparatory school to make up the equivalent to high school. The preparatory school was at night. During the day, I had a job. It was always my idea that I would go one day to college. So you had to work during the day and go to school at night. The only day of rest we had was Sunday. Sunday we used to go to the park, take a ride to the Statue of Liberty, or go to open park concerts that used to be free. Monday I went back to work.

After I quit the pasting the valises job, I went into a wholesale drug company to get some acquaintance with drugs. My brother was a pharmacist and he wanted me to be a pharmacist too. This job was a nice, clean job. There was no dirt. I was usually handling pick-up drugs and itemizing on the shelf whatever the order called for. You put it in a box, and you packed it. The main thing for me was to acquaint myself with the names and the uses of certain drugs.

In 1925, after going two years to preparatory school, I went to take the Regents. I passed the Regents and I applied for the School of Pharmacy at Fordham University. And they accepted me. The tuition fee was $300—a hundred dollars each term. School was only three days, so the rest of the time I was able to work to make up for the tuition. The three days I worked were from 9:00 to 12:00 in a drugstore, and it took me an hour to travel home and an hour to travel to the place. The time it took me to travel, I studied. Otherwise, I would have no time. Three days I had school, at night I worked from 6:00 to 12:00, and days I worked from 8:00 to 12:00. So the only chance I had to study was on Sunday and part-time during the time I traveled to work and back from work.

Most of the college students were immigrants, about 60 percent, and 40 percent were native boys. Some people in a joke would call you "greenhorn," but that's all. There was no discrimination. The disadvantage for us was that we were older boys. The natives were youngsters. When I was in college, I was twenty-five. So it was hard to compete with the youngsters, but we made it. In 1927 I graduated.

I became a citizen in 1926, five years after I came. That was the law. In order to become a citizen, you have to wait five years. Some people could not adjust themselves. The main reason was that they came from a better life in Russia. It was not the poor ones that complained, it was mostly the affluent, or the intellectuals who could not adjust themselves to work here in a factory. They wanted to achieve their goals in their professions, but they didn't have any money. They were told that the United States was an easy country to get money, so most of them were disappointed. But I never felt like going back. I adjusted myself in this country. When I went to become a citizen, they gave you an oral test. They asked who was the president at this and this time, and they asked about the Civil War and they asked questions about life in America. Very, very few questions were asked.

After I got through with college, I got a good job. The hours were long, but the pay was good. I worked in a store for about two years. At that time, my younger brother also went to college, my sister went to work. My older brother already had his own drugstore. My mother was doing the shopping, cooking, the cleaning. She liked the United States very much. She was happy with her children. The only trouble that she had was that one of my sisters—the younger sister and her husband, with a child—remained in Europe. So her duty was to work and get them over to the United States. She succeeded in about 1926. That time we were getting crowded—three more people in the same apartment. But my mother didn't complain. She was a hardworking woman. Although she was in her sixties, she still carried all her shopping up to the fifth floor, heavy bundles, and at that time there was no delivery. She used to go herself, bring it up, still make meals for everybody, and keep the house in good shape.

In 1928, some fellows I worked for took me in in partnership in a store. We opened up a drugstore. I didn't have much money—I saved up maybe five hundred dollars the two years I was working, because I had to help out my family. But they gave me a break and the store was very successful for the first two years, until the depression hit. When the depression hit, wages went down for a pharmacist from sixty-five dollars to twenty-five dollars. A porter was getting about eight dollars a week, a junior clerk, an assistant, was getting about twelve dollars a week. It was pretty tough. We struggled. But we had jobs, because we were self-employed, so we managed.

Other people in the depression time were standing in bread lines, they were thrown out of work. At that time, there was no unemployment insurance, no social security. Things were so bad that at night people would stand near the restaurants when they threw out the garbage and pick over the barrels to see if they could salvage some food. A lot of people were dispossessed from their houses, because they couldn't afford to pay the rent. Hoover was the president then. People were actually going out onto the street selling apples. They probably made a few cents a day. There was no Medicare. Either you had money to go to a private doctor, or, if you didn't have money, you went to a clinic—a hospital clinic—and there weren't many either. People who were sick would stand in the hospital all day because they couldn't afford a private doctor. That lasted from 1931 to 1935. Then in 1935, President Roosevelt inaugurated NRA, National Relief Association, WPA, Public Works, and they put people to work improving the parks or painting over places. They gave them some means of sustaining life, but with very little pay.

In 1931, I met a young lady. She was working at a restaurant as a cashier. She came for advice to the drugstore. I courted her for about a year's time, taking her out to places, to parks, for boat rides, movies, sometimes just going for coffee and dessert in a restaurant—we never went in for regular meals. And then we got married. My wife also came over here from Russia, but she came as a youngster. After we were married, we moved to a one-bedroom apartment, on the East Side, near my store. Then a couple of years later, my wife gave birth to a child—a girl—and then she stopped working, to take care of the child.

Wolf U.

We came on a boat. The ocean was very rough, I remember. But I made it. I came here. One fellow, a friend of mine—a Gentile—even after I left he used to write to me that I must return, that I have no business to leave the Soviet Union because things were being done to build up the country—that I have to come back. It wasn't so easy for me to do it. I had my mother and my sister. There was no question of going back. We had to make a living here and stay here. About this there was no doubt. I remained here.

In the beginning I went to Camden, New Jersey. The ship landed in New York, but then I went to Camden, which is just across from Philadelphia. RCA had its main plant there at the time. I used to work for them. I had different jobs. A thousand and one jobs I had. In the beginning I was mostly a laborer. I worked loading ships on the Delaware River in Philadelphia. Eight, ten hours a day, loading about a hundred pounds on a chain, going one after another one. The temperature must have been about a hundred inside. I came home nearly exhausted.

My sister worked, I worked, and my mother worked. And we could hardly pay the rent. When we came here there was not any kind of an assistance from anybody. There was no organization, like nowadays for all those people that come from many countries—they assist and they do some kind of a medical help. In those days there wasn't anything. My mother worked at home—she used to get home work. That was a terrible exploitation. She used to make curtains. It required a lot of concentration and long hours. At the end of the week she used to get four or five dollars. She used to sit up until late, eleven or twelve o'clock. We used to help her.

After I worked at loading ships, I worked at making writing pens on steel rolls— I forgot how you call it. I was cheated out by my fellow worker there, I remember. I didn't write down what I did, and he used to write what I did for what he did. They used to pay me about half the salary that this fellow used to get. Eventually they saw that I didn't produce anything. In another place I used to work at setting brushes in tar. This is a little bit hazardous work because once you get the boiling tar on your hands, the skin comes off. My hands were always raw. I found out that another fellow used to get about sixteen dollars and I used to get nine dollars. I asked the boss why. "I do the same work as the other fellow does, why do you discriminate against me?" Of course, I could hardly speak English then. The boss said, "If you don't like it, you can go home." That was his answer.

Then I worked for RCA on cabinet work. Something got into my eye there. I got an ulcer and went to the hospital. They tried to burn off the ulcer with electricity, but they didn't know how much to use. I heard them say, "We tried to do it, but it didn't work out." I actually became blind on one eye. I asked the doctor why he did it. The answer was "Two eyes are a luxury. One is sufficient."

We acclimatized ourselves here. Those days the surroundings were more for people that came here to the United States like us. So it was customary to meet with people. I belonged to a club, attended lectures, and all that kind of activity.

I had a friend in New York who was taking up pharmacy and he said, "Why don't you do it?" So I applied and I was accepted at Fordham. I had graduated high school in Russia already, so it was a question here of passing the English examination and then I was accepted to school. I attended school for a couple of years. I made it with coffee and apple pie—that was my energy. I managed somehow to make it. It's not important. A couple of years later, I graduated—that was about 1927.

We were a group of about a half-dozen people, and we had an idea of trying to form a union. An effort was made in 1919 or 1920 to build a union of pharmacists. I believe they called a strike at that time, but it was not successful. So we tried again. We walked from store to store, spoke to students, and little by little, a union was born. It officially was crowned the Pharmacists' Union in 1932.

As far as getting a job, for people that had even the slightest accent, it was difficult. Even in the field of pharmacy, any kind of an accent or foreign name was against you, but somehow we managed. When it was a question of organizing a certain place, this was my first task. The job used to come later.

The question of picketing in those days was very audacious work because we used to be threatened by gangsters on the picket line. In those days a picket line was not popular. It was not popular at all. I remember—as a matter of fact not only in this field but in the field of art—at that time Diego Rivera made the mural in Rockefeller Center, and they were destroyed overnight, because he put in a head of Lenin there. We picketed there too—because of the destruction of the mural. That was in the thirties.

We picketed, we had strikes. Until 1955 I was a member of the union. As a matter of fact, I have a withdrawal card. I am a senior. I'm still a member of the union, of 1199. It became 1199 after we joined the AFL-CIO group. I was active in the union activity—that was my main social work, union activity.

During the time of the WPA and unemployment, I was working for the WPA in the mural project. When I was still at home, in Europe, I remember there was a refugee from Germany there. One day he was sitting on our porch and he was painting a sunset. I was fascinated at that time by what colors can do. And that remained with me. I started to draw, and little by little I took a liking to it. I saw that I got some results. In 1928 and '29, I used to attend the Educational Alliance on East Broadway. We had an instructor there, but mostly we learned from our fellow students. Sometimes we used to get a live model. And that's how I started to paint.

After the WPA folded up, it was a problem what to do, whether to do artwork or to go to work as a pharmacist. I was registered to be a pharmacist. I went to work in Mount Sinai Hospital, Lenox Hill Hospital. It wasn't sufficient for me so I used to work besides—moonlighting. I used to work at night. So my hours were started at seven o'clock in the morning and lasted almost until twelve. Very long hours. But the only work that I enjoyed was painting because that's a process of constant discovery—searching and discovery. That's the only work that gives me satisfaction. In the beginning I used to paint mostly proletarian themes, but now I go more for abstract.

Harry S.

When we came here there was no quotas. If you had twenty-five dollars on you, then they let you go. If you didn't, somebody had to come and claim you. Coming here, my uncle sent me money—enough to get up to Antwerp, and in Antwerp I sent a telegram he should send me some extra—fifty or a hundred dollars extra than the price of the tickets. I was always under the impression, although he never asked me, that I'm going to give him back the money, because my mother explained to me that people are working people, you've got to work for a living—it's not rich people. I bought myself a nice suit and shirt. I was dressed, when I came here. I didn't look like a foreigner just coming from the other side, because I was dressed like a real American. In Antwerp I bought everything—a spring coat, and some shoes, and a suit and shirts and ties. And I came dressed like a real American.

We came here exactly on Columbus Day, on October twelfth. It was a holiday and we had to stay a day over on the ship, and then on the thirteenth we came down.

When I came to Ellis Island, they asked me if I had any money. I had twenty-five or fifty dollars, so they let us out. We were dressed like rich Americans. A woman gave us an apple to eat. I took out my penknife, cut off a quarter, peeled it, took out the core, and put a slice in my mouth. Then my uncle comes and sees us, and he says, "These are the greenhorns. An American doesn't eat an apple like that. He bites into it." That's how he recognized us. We didn't know him.

Then he took us—we walked to his house. On the way, going on the East Side at that time, we were walking over there and I saw that it was filthy. So I said to my uncle, "This is America? This is New York?" He got peeved. He said, "What do you mean?" I said, "It's so dirty, filthy." I told him, "If this would be in our hometown, we had health inspections every week. They go around and see if anything is dirty—right away you get a summons. And here in New York, it's dirty." He didn't say anything to me, but later on he told me, "Listen, I am here. I'm a captain in the Democratic Party. I'm a president of a shul, and a president of a society. I brought up five children and here you come, a greenhorn, and you tell me that it's dirty?" I said, "It was dirty. I can't help it." I saw he was angry.

Finally, we got into his house. He lived way down on the East Side, on the fourth floor, in a four-room apartment. The toilets were in the hall, no bathrooms were there. Coming from the ship, the first thing you do is you've got to go and take a bath. So they took us to a bath somewheres maybe ten blocks away. His wife took my sister, he took me—to a public bath. That's how they were living. And I was supposed to stay there.

He had there a girl, one daughter, and three sons, and he and his wife. They lived in a kitchen and three more rooms—one room was a dining room and the other one was for beds. The girl was on a little folding bed and the three boys were in one room and he and his wife were in another room. He wanted me to sleep in the same room with the boys. The room maybe was eight by ten. I figured, "This is the man that sent money?" He looked to me so poor. When I saw that I said, "The first wages that I'm going to make I've got to give him back whatever he spent on me—not only for the steamship ticket but he also used to send money before.

I was there for about three days. But I was very uncomfortable. On Sunday, I had another uncle from the Bronx—my father's uncle—he came to see us, and he took us over to the Bronx. He was also on the top floor, the fifth floor, but it was a steam-heated apartment, a bathroom and a shower, tremendous rooms. He wanted me to stay with him. I felt the other uncle is going to be angry—he brought me here, I should stay with him.

Before I came here, my mother gave me certain pointers. "When you come to the United States," she said, "don't live with your family. Don't live with your relatives. Don't work for your relatives. And don't remain working in the place where you first started as a greenhorn. Don't remain working there because you'll always be a greenhorn. After you start working, get yourself a job somewhere else." I always had that in mind.

I stayed with that uncle that brought me here. He was a religious man. I used to go to shul with him on Saturday. He had a landsman of his who was a glazier. He takes me over to this landsman, and he wasn't there but his wife was there. I came in there, and she told him, "Such a nice boy, why do you want to make a glazier out of him?" She talked him out of it—I shouldn't be a glazier. This was a line that I knew, but I was too delicate of a boy to be a glazier. A glazier in the United States was rough work. So he met his friend in shul who had a grocery store, and he asked him to give me a job. So he said, "All right, come in to work." I came in to work, and he told me I've got to work from six o'clock in the morning until seven o'clock at night. Why six o'clock in the morning? In those days, you used to deliver rolls and milk to the houses, to the customer. There was no bottled milk in those days. You used to get a can of milk and then the women would come in in the afternoon, they would bring the can and you would fill it up with a quart, two quarts of milk. In the morning, six o'clock in the morning, you had to deliver them, because the husband had to go to work seven o'clock in the morning. I got seven dollars a week. Seven dollars a week because you're not working on Saturday.

Here, already, my religion was fading because I see the hypocrisy in it. People are supposed to be religious and they're not. To me, it was either-or. If you're religious, you're religious. For instance, you're not allowed to work on Saturday. By us, on Saturday you're not allowed to do anything. So here he wouldn't work on Saturday, but he'll go to the theater on Saturday, he'll buy things. You were not allowed to do it. To me, it was not a question of deviations.

I worked one week. I worked two weeks. Then I happened to be passing by another store, and a guy sees the way I was running so fast, delivering orders. So he asked me where I was working. I told him I was working on this and this job. So he says, "You come to work for me and I'll give you fifteen dollars a week." I said,

"Saturday?" He said, "You'll have to work on Saturday. You're off Sunday, but not Saturday." He said, "I'm sorry. You want to work? You look like a nice boy, come to work for me." So I go back to the place I'm working and I said, "You know Mr. G. from Prospect Avenue stopped me and he told me he's going to pay me fifteen dollars a week, and you're paying me only seven." I said, "I'm going to work for him." "But," he said, "you have to work Saturday. Your uncle wouldn't like it." I said, "I know, but I have to support myself. I've got a mother in Europe where I've got to send money and I've got to pay my uncle back money. I can't work for seven dollars a week." I told him I quit and I went to work for that Mr. G. I came back to him and I told him I want to work.

I worked there two days, and after two days working they came around from the union—they were organizing the grocery clerk's union. I should become a union man. I didn't know the first thing what it means a union. So the man told me, "You've got to go out on strike." Then they tell me a story that I've got to pay two dollars for the union book. Alright, I take out two dollars and give him two dollars for the union book. Then he tells me the conditions. "You have to work ten hours a day, six days a week, and the pay is twenty-five dollars a week." So I tell him, "Give me the job, I'll start working today for you." He says, "Come in tomorrow." I figured that they're going to give me a job. So I come the next day and there is another guy and he doesn't speak Yiddish—he speaks English only—he doesn't understand Jewish. They gave him two picket signs, and they sent me over I should go with him. I figured I would go with him, I'd get a job. I didn't know. They took me somewheres to 225th Street and Broadway to a store and put me down to picket. The guy is going, so I'm going. I come back the next day—I figured they are going to pay me for it. No, they don't pay. The next day I came back and he tells me the same thing. I said, "I'm sorry. I can't do it." First of all, I was ashamed to walk in the street. Somebody may see me. I told him, "I have to get a job. I can't work without pay because I have to support myself." Although I was still staying with my uncle and he didn't charge me, I can't be like this. He says, "Well, I'm sorry." Then I wanted to get the two dollars back. He says, "From the cemetery there is no returns." These are the words he told me. In other words, you can't get the two dollars. I said, "I've got to look for something different."

I went to look for a glazier with my uncle. We passed by a store. It so happened it was the time of year around October, November, December—before the winter there is work. My uncle said, "Can you use a boy? Break him in?" The guy took pity on me, so he took me to work as a glazier. He was a Jewish man. A nice man. He took me in. I knew how to cut glass, but it's a different system entirely. The glass cutters are different. In Europe they used diamonds, a diamond cutter. Here they used steel. Then you have to sit out on the window. In Europe you don't sit out on the window. You took the window on a table, you put in the glass, and you put it in. So he takes me on a job to putty windows, and here I have to sit out on a window and to putty them. He was standing inside, holding my feet and I'm shivering, but I got used to it. I was working for him for a couple of months. He paid me something like fifteen dollars a week, and fifteen dollars a week was already good. The work was hard, but I didn't mind it.

I got already a room for myself—as a boarder. It was a nice family. It was nearer to the place where I was working. It was on the first floor, near a cousin of mine. The cousin told me anytime to come in for supper. But I didn't want to. I used to go to restaurants to eat. When I started I was getting fifteen dollars a week, I paid five dollars a month for the room. Then I would send five dollars to my mother and then I would give five dollars to my uncle to pay off. I used to go Sunday to my uncle, and pay him every week five dollars.

I was working there for a couple of months. I liked it and he liked me. It was very nice. Then he told me, "It's slow, but come in anytime if we'll have some work." I didn't know about slow seasons, so every day I would come in. "Any work?" "There's no work." He was sitting around doing nothing himself. One day, he told me, "Boichikl"—you know, kid—"don't worry so much. Work and trouble you'll have plenty of through your life. Don't worry." Then I said, "This is no good—I can't work at something that I can't be working on slow seasons."

I got the newspapers for ads and I started to look. Somebody advertised for a delicatessen store. I figured, it's a food store and it's steady, so I went to look for that job. At that time already it was a little bit the depression and there were a lot of people out of work—a lot of people out of work. I came over in the morning, Sunday morning for the job—and this was near Columbia University—and the man comes in and there are a lot of people. The man didn't open up the store until about nine o'clock and I came there about six, seven o'clock and there were a whole bunch of kids standing there and each one was saying that he was working in this place and that place and they were all talking about how they know the business. I don't know the first thing.

I was working as a glazier and I was working two weeks in a grocery store. The boss comes in and it was a slow Sunday morning and everyone is running after him, he's running from one person to the other. I was standing on the side, like an observer.

After everybody was all through, he said, "What do you want?" He asked me in English. I knew already a little because I went to night school. Every public school had night schools—because at that time there was a lot of immigration. He started talking and I explained to him that I came about the job. The job was advertised in the Jewish paper. He started talking Jewish to me and he explained to me the job. It paid fifteen dollars a week and you have to work also from seven in the morning until seven at night, and you have to wash the dishes, sweep the floor, clean up, and all this stuff. Then he tells me to call him. I called him up and he tells me to come over and see him in the afternoon. He'll give me the job but he wants to talk to me about it. I came over four o'clock and he explained me again the details and he interviewed me, and he told me to come in next morning to work. I worked there for a week and by the time the week was over he gave me seventeen instead of fifteen. Then I asked him, after a while when I was there, "How come there were so many boys applying for the job, and they all knew how to work and you took me." So he tells me like this: "You know, you're the only one who was honest." I told him I worked for a grocery store. I told him exactly what happened. Then I worked for a glazier. And I told him the story. He said, "Whatever they knew, I know they didn't know anything. They were all bluffing. I want to get a man and break him in my way. Since you don't know anything, I want to break you in."

I worked for this man for seven years. I worked myself up to the highest paid in that particular line. And I never asked him for a raise. He always gave me every time. Once I found five dollars more in the pay envelope. I went back and said, "I think you made a mistake." He said, "No I gave you a raise." He didn't even tell me.

Working there, I came in contact with a lot of Gentile people. I didn't find any antisemitism from them, and I didn't find any animosity against me. They considered me just working. It didn't make any difference. Among the Jewish-American students, for instance, I could speak English, but my accent was bad. They were curious—they wanted to find out where I came from. I come from Galicia, and among the Russians they say that the Galitzianers are like people with horns. They asked me where I came from, what part. I'd tell them Galicia. They'd say, "Oh, you look like a regular human being." They had a picture that these people were different.

Religious life I gave up. Once I lived for myself, I stopped putting on the tefillin, the only thing I observed is I used to go for the high holidays to shul. I used to come to my uncle, to my relatives, and naturally I would observe their customs—for instance, I wouldn't eat without a hat. I would come into the house with a hat on. They knew that I was working on Saturday.

When I was here the first couple of years, my mother asked me whether I was still religious. I wouldn't tell my mother. I didn't answer her on the letters. She kept on repeating, sending a letter again—"Are you religious?" I sat down and wrote her a letter about how the Jewish people live and I described to her how they bought churches and made synagogues out of them, and when it comes to the high holidays not only are the synagogues packed but they are renting theaters and movies and they turn them into synagogues and people are paying ten and twenty dollars for a ticket to go in to hear the cantor, and all that stuff. Of course, I said, they don't wear anymore the peyes and beard, people are clean shaven. *Fartik* [finished, over, done with]. She writes me back a letter, "It's very nice how you describe the Jewish life, how the people are going and all that, but are you still putting on tefillin?" I didn't want to tell her, and I didn't tell her, but then when she came here she found out. When she was here I just put them on for her sake, in order not to hurt her feelings.

After I was here for three years, I made enough money to bring my mother over with the kids—I had two more brothers there. By 1923, I had enough money. It takes time. I sent applications for visas and passports and then I rented an apartment and bought furniture for four rooms. Even at that time there was a shortage of apartments to rent. I had to go look for an apartment because she was coming. In the beginning I was working in the store from seven in the morning until seven at night. Then I started to work nights. I worked from twelve in the morning until twelve at night. The lunch hour, the students would come out—it was a student trade. I used to come in at eleven, actually, instead of twelve. I used to work on Amsterdam Avenue, so I would take the subway down to Ninety-sixth Street and from Ninety-sixth Street to the Bronx. Many a time instead of a Bronx train I took a Broadway train and I would fall asleep and go to the last stop and then go back. I would come home sometimes two o'clock, but when I used to come home I used to go around the streets and look where there is a To Let, and mark down where there is a To Let for rooms. Then the next morning I would get up early and I would look.

Finally, I found an apartment—it was a corner apartment and it was available. The super was a Polish woman and she said to come tomorrow to see the landlord. The landlord happened to be an ex-judge. While he was there, I asked, since it was a corner room, where is there a line to hang the clothing. The super said, "You have to go on the roof." I said, "The roof? This is on the second floor." She said, "You can pull a line from one window—from the kitchen window to the dining room window—it's a big stretch, but you can put it there." The landlord tells her to give me the apartment. She said, "But he wouldn't be responsible. Such a young fellow." He said, "If a young fellow had in mind to worry about where to hang the line he'll have the responsibility to pay the rent." So I got the apartment just because I asked about the line. Then I bought furniture.

In 1923 I was twenty-one years old. I had the responsibility of bringing over the family from Europe, renting an apartment, furnishing the house, and supporting them. Whatever money I made, I gave it to my mother. My sister also started working, but she didn't make much. I was actually supporting them. The rent in those days wasn't much. I think it was something like twenty-three dollars a month. The rent was cheap, and food was cheap. My mother was very economical. My mother kept on urging me, "Why don't you give up the job?" My younger brother started to work already and he was bringing in some money so they didn't have to depend on me only, and she urged me to give up the job and get a job doing work like every human being. It so happened that I had a fight with my boss, and I quit the job.

My mother was very happy that I quit. She wasn't afraid, because the kids were already self-supporting. The family was not like here, everybody draws their own. The children were working and they brought the money into the house. I had it in mind that I wanted to be a printer. I went into a school for linotyping. They had at that time a course for two hundred and fifty dollars. I was about ready to pay the money in order to learn the trade. But then I met a fellow that I knew. He was a compositor and I told him I was over at the Empire School to take up linotyping, he started to talk to me and he explained to me that you cannot get a job unless you are a union man and the printers union you can't get into. I said, "They promise you a job." He said, "Yes, they promise you a job. Maybe they'll send you somewheres out of town for a job. Then you'll have to come back and you'll have a hard job getting into the union." He himself wanted to get into the union as a compositor. And he couldn't get in. So I gave that up.

I figured I would go back to glazing. What I liked about it was that it was outdoors—you didn't have to be cooped up in a store. That was also the season and somebody advertised for a job as a glazier. They advertised a job paying eighteen dollars a week. I quit a job where I was getting sixty-five dollars a week, and at that time sixty-five dollars a week was a lot of money. I was hesitant to take it. Then I came home and discussed it with my mother and she said, "Don't worry about the money. The main thing is you should be happy with what you're doing." I said, "All right, I'm going to try."

I called up the next day and he told me to come in. When I worked in the delicatessen I used to wear a white coat. Here I put on a pair of dirty overalls and I walked in the street and felt I was the happiest man alive. At that time, they played a movie, *Seventh Heaven*, where a guy is working in the sewer and he is promoted as a street cleaner—how happy he is that he is promoted to a street cleaner. I felt exactly that way. They were selling tangerines, a dozen tangerines for ten cents, and I was walking from one job to the other, walking and eating tangerines. I came home and I was a new man.

I liked the work I was doing. He told me he'll give me eighteen dollars. The next week I got twenty-five dollars. Then I was raised up to thirty-eight dollars. Then he didn't have any work. It became slow, but he didn't want to let me go. He had a friend, a Hungarian, that was in Manhattan, working on Seventy-seventh Street and First Avenue. He said, "You work for me three days, I'll give you nineteen dollars, and you work for my friend for nineteen dollars the rest of the week"—in order not to let me go. So I worked for the two of them. They were very nice people. Then I didn't want to work for the two of them because after I used to work for one on Monday, Tuesday, and Wednesday, when I came back next Monday anything that was left over from Wednesday was still waiting for me. I figured I was doing a whole week's work in three days. Why should I do it? I said I didn't want to work there.

From there, I went to work for another guy, also not far from where I lived. This was right on Southern Boulevard, on 163d Street. He was doing window shades and glass. He did some fancy work. He worked mostly Park Avenue and Madison Avenue, in those fancy houses. He was also hanging awnings. One day, around Decoration Day, he sends me on the fourteenth floor to hang up some awnings. I said, "I'm not hanging awnings." I didn't want to do that type of work. You had to hang out through the window, and I said I'm not doing it. It was not only that I was afraid, but I figured once I start to show him that I do it, he'll make me do it all the time. He tells me, "If you don't want to hang the awnings, you can quit." It was ten o'clock in the morning. I take off my overalls, take together my tools, and I quit. He comes over and says, "What are you doing?" I said, "You told me to quit. I quit." "I meant you should wait until you get through. You wait until five o'clock." I said, "You want me to wait until five o'clock to quit, you should have told me five o'clock. Don't tell me at ten o'clock in the morning." "If you quit, I'm not going to pay you for yesterday." I said, "I'm not concerned whether you pay me or not. You told me to quit, I quit."

Then I figured I'd open a store. The same kind of business that I did. I couldn't get a job because I couldn't get into the union. It was too much money for initiation. The union wanted seven hundred and fifty dollars. I figured it would cost me only about two hundred and fifty dollars to open a store. There were plenty of vacant stores in those years—it was the depression years. I invested two hundred and fifty dollars, and I rented a store for thirty-five dollars a month. I bought about ten boxes of glass and some shade cloth, and then I started to fix up the inside with some shelves and some bins where to put the glass and the material. I built myself a table and I was in business.

At first, the business did not go so good. As a matter of fact, at one time I wanted to quit and give up the store and go to work. My mother told me at that time, "It's easy to run a business when business is good. Any damn fool can run a business when business is good. The thing is to hold on in bad times and wait for the better times"— which I did. Many times I spent a whole day in the store and maybe two or three dollars worth of work would come by.

But after all, it turned out. I picked up more business and I made a living. I never wanted to get rich. If I wanted to get rich probably I would work a little bit harder. We made enough for a living and that's all there is to it. I never drew wages. I lived very primitively. I took from the business whatever I needed. I paid my rent in the house. If we needed to buy clothing, whatever, I took from the business. If I would draw wages and say it's coming to me so much and so much I would have closed up right after a year. But I figured I'd keep on drawing from the business and when it comes the end of the year, I'll check up. If I see I live and I pay my expenses and I didn't lose any money, okay. If I lose money, I'll close up. But always we managed that every year I had enough. We lived through.

I just worked at alterations and I worked for private people—window shades— and when venetian blinds came into style, I sold venetian blinds. I didn't have anybody working. I worked with my wife. We had a kitchen, and we ate down there. We enjoyed it. From the minute we closed the business and ate, we right away had our activities, whether it was a concert or a lecture or some activity in the club.

While I was working as a glazier, I joined a workers' club, the Prospect Workers' Club. We used to have dances every Saturday night. I met Rae there at a dance. She was interesting. She was a pretty fair talker and we had interesting conversations. We made a date and started going out. I remember the first time I took her to an opera. She used to go to lighter things. I was more serious. I took her to a concert, to a lecture, to an opera. Our ideas were the same. We decided to get married. Her brother-in-law didn't approve because I was a Galitzianer. It seems that he went out once with a Galitzianer girl and he couldn't get the best of her, so he was against all Galitzianers. He only wanted her to marry a Russian. But she has got a mind of her own—she didn't ask anybody. My mother probably would have wanted me to marry more of a religious person, but she didn't object in any way.

It seems that when people come over from the other side, they group among their own people. There was such a thing as landsmanshaft, of people that come from the same city. Actually, you formed your own ghetto. It was not forced upon you. But somehow you wanted to live among your own people. The club I belonged to was mostly Europeans. We attracted a number of American-born youngsters, because we had dances. We found that the American youngsters, all they wanted was baseball and all these sports. We stressed more serious things. We'd go to concerts, to museums. We used to go to demonstrations concerned with improving conditions. For instance, during the depression there were a lot of rent strikes, and we would participate. People were put out of their houses and their furniture would be put out in the street. We would mobilize groups and go over to the street and take the furniture from the street and bring it back up to the houses. This was the kind of work that we were doing.

We didn't do things because somebody forced us to do it. We did it on our own. There is a certain satisfaction. If you help to bring up furniture from the ground floor to the fifth floor, it was hard work, but we enjoyed it. We felt the woman and children would stay there for another three months until they will dispossess her again, and then we'll come around and put her in again. From these things there was satisfaction. I don't regret what I did.

I became very active with the ILD—which was the International Labor Defense, fighting for workers' rights and helping imprisoned workers. At that time it was Tom Mooney and Warren Billings, and then it was the question of the Scottsboro Boys and Sacco and Vanzetti. We used to go around collecting money. I used to stand in the street with boxes to collect money for the defense of political prisoners. Many times, I used to take off from work a half a day. There were demonstrations and I used to participate in the demonstrations.

This organization was backed by the Communist Party, and I used to go to the headquarters during the day. I would go to the headquarters of the Communist Party and I would get literature to distribute and boxes to collect money. They all thought I was a Party member. One time, they asked me whether I was over at a unit meeting—they kept meeting on certain nights. I told them no. They said, "Why? It was a very important meeting." I said I didn't know anything about it. They were shocked when I told them I'm not a Party member. They were really flabbergasted. They said, "Here you are a man that does more work than ten Party members put together." I said, "I want to do things on my own, whatever I feel like doing. I don't want to be dictated—you got to do this or you got to do that." I didn't want to join. I never joined the Party.

During the war I had a big sign in the store that I was collecting for the Russian War Relief. I was branded in the neighborhood by some reactionaries as a Communist. Of course, I know that a lot of people did not come into the store because they were quite reactionary. Despite the fact that we were all working to defeat Hitler, they hated Communists and since Russia was connected with Communists I was a Communist—that's what they branded me, but I never belonged to any party officially. Once a woman came into the store. She was a customer of mine. She asked me, "Tell me the truth, are you a Communist?" I said, "My political beliefs are private. I'm not asking you your beliefs. I'm not asking you whether you go to synagogue or if you fast on Yom Kippur. This is up to you and you can do whatever you want. I'm not going to tell you my political views. I'm not going to deny anything." I said, "I don't believe as a principle you have the right to ask me this question." I said, "I'm not asking you your private business either." So she said, "Well, I know you're an honest man, you're a nice fellow."

The ideas of communism attracted me first of all because I had a worker's background and I felt that the worker was being exploited. I felt that the worker should be compensated for the work that he is doing. The main attraction was the idea of the equality of people—that everyone is alike, Jews, black people, Indians—there is one human being. This was the main attraction. I remembered as a boy I was pointed out as a Jew, that the Jew was different. So this was what attracted me. That also made me work. Especially I worked among the black people. There were the Jim Crow laws and I would come and talk to them, and fight against the Jim Crow laws.

At that time, they published the *Liberator*, a progressive Negro paper. I would travel to Brooklyn—I lived in the Bronx, but I would travel to Brooklyn, where a lot of Negro people were concentrated—and I would distribute this paper and the *Daily*

Worker to show them the light, that we were helping them, we are with them, we are not discriminating against them. I was very much accepted among them when I spoke because I had a very nice approach. I would go over there on a Sunday morning and try to make them read this paper and show them that this paper is fighting their cause.

Once I went in with another man. He knocks at the door and when the man comes, he shows him the *Daily Worker* and says, "This paper is fighting against lynching." The approach was like hitting somebody over the head. Here the man is in the North and he wants to forget about the lynching that is going on. He wanted to throw him down the stairs. I didn't get scared. I went over and said, "Listen, the man just opened his mouth. He doesn't know what he's talking about." I started talking nicely to him. He invited me into his house and I sat with him for about half an hour and explained to him what the paper is for, what the idea is—that they're trying to have jobs for everybody, give each one the same amount of money. In other words, you as a black worker shouldn't be exploited and get less money than a white worker, you should have the same rights like any other person, you should feel like a regular human being. He listened to me, and then I gave him the paper to read. I didn't want to take any money from him. I concentrated on him. I came back the next week and I gave him again a paper. After a couple of weeks, I got from him a subscription for three months, a subscription to the *Daily Worker*. You see, it's a matter of using tact.

Many people felt that we should not give out the papers free—we should get paid for them. At that time there was unemployment—it was 1931, '32—and for people even five cents was a lot of money to give out, especially for something that they don't want. My idea was, and I urged the committee, that they should pay for the paper and we should give it out free to the people. One was very much objecting and he says, "I'll go out and I'll show you. I'll go out with you and I can collect all the money for the paper." I went with him on a Sunday morning. He knocked at the door and he said, "Help an unemployed worker and buy a paper." So naturally they gave, like charity—"Here's five cents." Probably they took the paper and threw it out.

I went back to the board and made a monkey out of him. I said, "What do you mean? You're not out to sell the paper. You could stand in the street and put your palm out and probably they'll give you money." The main thing was to propagandize and make them read and explain what this cause is for. I won my way, and then they allotted money and they used to give out the papers for a couple of weeks to the people, and then concentrate on the same people—explain to them what they read in the article. I would explain to them that it is fighting for the workers' cause.

At that time, don't forget, we didn't have unemployment insurance, we didn't have social security, and the main fight—the slogan—was for bread and jobs. We used to call for demonstrations, we used to come around and tell them, "Here you're unemployed and other people are getting rich. You're unemployed, you haven't got a job, you're not working. We fight for equality, we fight for jobs, we fight for social security, we fight for unemployment insurance." And we used to give them leaflets for demonstrations for unemployment insurance.

Once, I think it was March sixth, 1931, there was a big demonstration—about a hundred thousand people were at Union Square—and then the police came like Cossacks with horses and they destroyed us and chopped heads. We marched to City Hall to fight for unemployment insurance, and finally it was won, but it didn't come easy. These groups were in the foreground. There were the workers' clubs, and the workers clubs were not actually affiliated with the Communist Party, but they were backed—they supported some of their ideas. I felt it was right.

At that time, especially among the religious people and among the bosses, they said that the Communists are Godless people. Many times I used to come to my mother and, since my mother was very religious, she felt very much hurt that I followed this. So I sat down and talked to her and she listened. I said, "I just am doing exactly what you've been teaching me all the time. You taught me to help people and be good to people. I knew cases where she would pay their rent in order they shouldn't evict them, throw them out. I said, "I'm doing exactly what you're doing. It's the same thing." She said, "The only thing is if they would only believe in God." She was very religious. I said, "I respect people that are religious. I'm not against anyone that is religious. They want to foreclose a synagogue because the mortgage isn't paid, they come around to me to give them a dollar, I give them a dollar. I try to help people that are in need." Of course, it didn't always click, but it pacified her a little bit.

As a matter of fact, there were once two Jewish men going around collecting for a yeshiva—this is a Jewish religious school. One of them wants to go in to my store and the other one said, "Oh, he's a Communist. He's not going to give money for a yeshiva." The other man tells him, "But he's a very nice man, let's go in." I was standing outside in the back. They didn't see me, but I heard their conversation. They come in, they say they have a raffle—the raffle is a dollar. Instead of a dollar I give them two dollars. They walked out and the man said, "You see, I told you he's a nice man." I always respected anyone's beliefs, but the man was actually shocked because he expected that he would be able to tell the other one, "You see? The man wouldn't give anything because it's a religious thing and he wouldn't do it."

My mother could not make peace with the idea that I was not religious. Naturally, I had influence on the other two brothers, and she was afraid that they would not be religious on account of me. This was the only thing that hurt her. She was not against me doing the things that I was doing. The only thing was that she wanted me to be religious. When I came into the house, I respected her views. I never argued with her about religion, despite the fact that my ideas about religion had changed completely.

At that time the slogan was that religion was opium to the people. This was one of the slogans. I felt that people are being exploited, that workers are being exploited on account of religion because there was a certain feeling of contentment. In other words, if you worked for a religious Jew, he'll tell you this is God's will—he has to be rich, and you've got to be poor. That's supposed to be God's will, and I couldn't see any justification in that. I changed completely. When I was in Europe, I saw only one side of it. Here I was able to read different books about discussions between atheists and religious guys, and you see their views.

My mother was fanatic religious. She had one belief—that when her husband died, and she remained by herself with five children, God helped her and she was able to raise the children nicely. She was never being helped by anybody and she was on her own. In other words, God helped with all these things. She brought up her children nicely, they had a nice education, they were always dressed like the rich people and nobody had any pity on them. So she felt that God helped her and that kept her belief. In other cases, some people start to feel—God punished me, he took away my husband and right after that a child is getting killed. That person would come against it. She, on the other hand, after things turned out and everything went smoothly, she believed in God and she kept on believing it.

She was very much religious when she was in this country. As a matter of fact, when my mother died, the funeral was in the house. She died in the house and she never was taken to a funeral parlor. Around the corner from here there were two synagogues. The coffin was taken to the steps of both synagogues and the rabbis came out and made a eulogy at each one. Practically the whole street was closed, all the businesses were closed. There was a procession. I'll never forget that.

Rachel S.

We were very avid readers, and we read about all those skyscrapers and buildings, so when we came here and we saw it, we took it for granted. We took it very natural—we weren't shocked. It wasn't like somebody who never heard of it, they come and see those tremendous buildings and the beautiful sights. First of all, we came from a large city, and second of all, we read a lot about it. So we knew all about the life in the United States and the buildings, the streets, the thoroughfares.

The uncle that sent for us was a very rich man. He was the president of a rubber company. He lived in College Point, Long Island. He had a private home, he had a boat, he played golf. His wife died a few months before we came. He had three children. He had a maid and a cook and a gardener and a chauffeur. When we came here, he fixed us up an apartment on the third floor of his private house. He bought new furniture and he put us in. Two lonesome girls that spent almost two years alone without a father or a mother. He put us in the apartment and he said, "Don't do anything. Have a good time." He was very nice to us, but he was a very busy man. We never saw him. We only saw him when he came from the office to change into knickers to play golf or change to go on the boat. We wanted to go to school. School was far, you needed a car to travel to school. And we wanted to go to work to send our sisters and our mother money.

I had here another uncle—my father's brother. This uncle lived in Brooklyn. He had a candy store. In the back of the candy store he had two rooms. He lived in the two rooms with two children. His wife was a very hospitable woman, a very warm person. We went to visit this poor uncle and when we came there his wife was like a mother to us. She gave us so much love and warmth that we decided that we didn't want to stay with our rich uncle. So this uncle who had the two rooms in the back of the candy store said, "Why don't you come and live with me?" We came back to the rich uncle. We packed in our belongings, and we left. That was the end of our riches.

After moving in with the poor uncle, my sister and I got a job in a factory. This was a factory for infants' wear, small little dresses for infants and party dresses for children up to six. He gave us a job for my sister and for me, and we were sitting there and trimming. The owner of the factory realized that we could do more than that, so he started teaching us different machines. We were week-workers, and he figured he could gain more from us. You know, we were two intelligent girls, except that we came from Europe. We knew the language a little bit. I knew more than my sister, my sister didn't take much to it. So he started teaching us every time a different machine, and we worked a very short time trimming.

After that, the two of us started working on machines and little by little I learned how to work all the machines in the factory. I used to work with the designer. I used to make samples for the sample maker. After a little while, I was a bona fide machine worker, a sample hand, a big chief. This particular line of business, infants' wear, needed a different sort of machine. They didn't sew on one machine everything. There was section work. They had buttonhole machines and button machines and overlock machines and Singer machines and tucking machines and pleating machines and ruffle machines—and a number of other machines. And each machine you had to know how to work. The tucking machines had six, eight needles because they made tucks and at the same time all the tucks came out. If one needle broke, if one thread broke, you had to redo it. I knew how to work on all the machines. The only tool we used to have that was our own in the factory was the scissors—everyone had his own scissor.

The owner knew and the foreman knew—every time they got a new machine they used to come over to me. Nobody in the factory knew how to work the new machine, they used to come over to me, "Rae, you know how to work that machine?" And I used to say, "Sure." I went over and I fooled around a few minutes with it, and I learned. The boss knew, I learned from that—he knew I didn't know how to work that machine. So whenever it was sometimes slow—there were seasons and then there were slow times and in the slow times they laid off a lot of workers—I was never laid off, because when they were slow, the designer was working and I was making samples for her.

When you make a sample, you have to go from one machine to the other one, because each part of the dress has to be done on a different machine. And I did that. I was never laid off. I always worked. If he didn't have work on one machine, I worked on another machine. If not, I worked with the designer, making new designs, new dresses, new styles. I had a busy life there, and I carried on there, too. My sister, although she was older three years than I, was a very quiet, fine girl. They all liked her. The boss liked her.

I always had fights with them—with the foreman. If I saw any kind of injustice or something, I didn't want to tolerate it. So I had fights with them. I was very important in the factory, because he used me for different machines and I knew it. So I took advantage. Every time I had a fight with them, I used to quit the job. I'd say,

"I'm quitting." When I quit, I used to come over to my sister and I would say, "Rose, let's go." She said, "What? When?" I said, "We're quitting." We used to go to the elevator and the boss used to run after us and he used to say, "Why are you going away? Why?" And then he used to beg us to come back. Once he didn't beg us. And we walked out and we looked for another job, but we couldn't find it. So we came back to the factory, and we came back to work.

We went to public school at night. We used to start working at eight o'clock and we worked until five. School started at eight o'clock. We rushed home and ate supper and we rushed to school. We had to take the bus to school. In evening high school most of the students were older people. There were no youngsters there. Mostly immigrants. There were some American older people there that decided to go to high school. But we mingled with people that were our own kind. We met people like we were, immigrants, that spoke our language, that knew our habits, that knew our culture. We were very studious. I didn't go out with boys for a long time because I had no time. Weekends, I had to do homework. I really refused a lot of dates. I turned them down because I had no time and education was very important to me.

Until 1930 I lived with my uncle. My sister was married from there, and then I met Harry. My uncle moved away to Newburgh, New York. He opened a little store. My aunt's whole family was in a certain business that was very profitable. They used to sell yardgoods and remnants. All those stores were in cities where there was a lot of Polish population and Russian population that did a lot of their own sewing. My aunt's family decided to fix up a store for my uncle in Newburgh, New York. They did, and they moved away there. Naturally, I remained, but I already was going out with Harry, so he went and found a room for me to board with somebody. I lived almost a year with a woman that I boarded with. It was very sad to board with somebody. But I couldn't help it because my sister had a very small apartment, and I couldn't stay with her. I really didn't mind it, because I didn't spend too much time in the room. I was all the time either working or going to school or going out with Harry.

We were introduced at a dance. He wasn't too much of a dancer and I was a terrific dancer. I was dancing and I said hello to him. We spoke a while, and then I went home and he went home. Then one day I was riding on the bus, and I was sitting down—who comes in? Harry comes in. And he's passing me by. I said, "That isn't good." I stuck my foot out and he fell over. He tripped. He looked up and he recognized me. Then he already took me home, he walked down from the bus where I had to get off, and he took me home, and after that we started going out.

I didn't want to go out with him. He asked me to go out but he looked very young. I was a serious girl—I was already in my twenties—and I didn't want to fool around with kids. He looked like a kid of eighteen. I said, "No, I'm sorry. I don't rob the cradle." He showed me his driving license. He was twenty-eight. I was so shocked, and of course I started going out with him, because he was much older than I. He was very serious. He quit his job for some reason or another just when we started going out. So he didn't have a job. He didn't want to get married because he hasn't got a steady job. But I said, "I don't want to wait." And I forced him. We married a year after.

We were supposed to get married in a rabbi's house because his mother was very, very religious. She was wearing a wig—you know, real religious from Europe. To us, we were not religuous, and it didn't matter. But he respected his mother a lot, and I respected his wishes. So we decided to get married in a rabbi's house and that's all. What happened was his mother took sick—she had pneumonia and she was in bed. We brought the rabbi to her bed and we married in front of her bed. It was some wedding.

We got our own apartment right away, because he went into business. He couldn't get a job. The work he was doing, he decided he could do it himself. We rented a little store and his sister helped him out. She stayed in the store. He bought some merchandise for about a hundred dollars—we didn't have to invest much in the business—and he went looking for business.

I was still working at the factory. I worked about a year after at the factory, because it took some time until he got into it. You have to get customers. It wasn't a business where people came in and bought something. It was a landlord trade. We were doing window shades. He was a glazier. He was installing glass in windows. So he had to get landlords to give him work. He had to go canvassing from house to house to get jobs, and it was very hard. His mother helped him out a lot in encouraging him. She was telling him that anybody could make a success if it's handed over to you, but you have to go after it and try to do it on your own. And he did. We struggled. And I was working, so I was bringing in money. And his sister was helping him out. Then his sister gave birth to a baby, so she couldn't help him anymore, so I gave up my job and I had to stay in the store.

My boss was upset. The boss offered me I should be a forelady. I should train the people, the girls, to work as fast as I worked because I had certain systems of working. I was a very fast worker. So he gave me a proposition I should become the forelady, and I should show the girls the way that I'm working—my system. I didn't want to be a forelady. I turned down the job.

We were in the store forty years. It meant day and night together except for the few hours he went out to make some jobs. I was doing manual work. I had to answer the telephone when orders came in, or people complained about something. But most of the time I was sitting by the machine working. He was preparing the shades and I was sewing the shades. I learned how to finish them. I learned how to take them on. I was doing a lot of manual work there.

And I learned how to make very good fish. We had a kitchen in the back of the store. I was supposed to have boiled fish and while working inside the store I forgot about it. White fish has a lot of fat. The water boiled out and it became real crunchy and delicious. He said I'll never be able to duplicate it. When I used to cook eggs, they used to bounce up to the ceiling because I forgot. You know, I was inside the store sewing or doing some other work, and I would forget about the kitchen. We ate in the store during the week. After we finished eating supper—we had a frigidaire and we had a stove there—we used to rush upstairs—each one at a different time—and take showers and go to the club, or go to a lecture, or go to a concert. We had a very busy life. But weekends we used to eat in the house.

We belonged to the Prospect Workers' Club, which had a thousand members. We did a lot of things. First of all, it was a social club, and a workers' club. It was a big organization of a thousand members. We participated in all kinds of demonstrations— May first demonstrations, and when there were picket lines, we were participating in strikes. It was made up of mainly immigrants. There were very few Americans, if there were any. There was a lot of things doing there. There was a chorus and all kinds of other groups. We were all young, and we used to have picnics, and we used to go swimming together—big crowds—and we used to do a lot of singing. We had a very nice time. We even used to charter a boat, and go for a whole day on a boat. We used to charter the whole boat, just for our group—a thousand people.

We raised money from dues, and we used to have concerts. Every Friday there was a lecture, every Saturday there was a concert, every Sunday there was dancing. And we had a committee that ran it. We used to sell tickets, and we had money. We were to the left. We raised a lot of money for different organizations. When they had strikes, we supported them. We used to give money to the *Daily Worker.*

HARRY: To the *Freiheit,* to the Communist Party.

RACHEL: To the left-wing organizations. We had a lot of fun. We had a wonderful time.

HARRY: That's why we never got rich.

RACHEL: Yeah, we used to lock up when everybody was open. The stores used to be open and ours used to be locked—we went to a meeting, we went to a lecture, we went to a concert, we enjoyed life. All my life I really didn't go for money. Money didn't matter to me so much. I like to go out to concerts, to read good books, to see good plays. This mattered to me more than furs.

One time we had some old shades that Harry piled up in the basement. There was a man that came to buy old shades. They used to make rags for washing cars— they used to wash the shades and the shades were made of a material that used to become soft, soft rags. Those rags were used for washing cars and cleaning windows. So he bought them from us. We accumulated so many old shades in the basement, the man paid us five hundred dollars. Harry took the five hundred dollars and said to me, "Go buy a fur coat." I said, "Why do I need a fur coat? I don't want a fur coat." I didn't need it.

I always tried he should work less. Everybody used to be open until ten, eleven o'clock. We closed up five-thirty, six. We went to eat supper, we went out to visit friends or something. Saturday we started closing up twelve o'clock to come to the country. Then a year or two later, I said, "Why do we have to come in for half a day? Let's close up Friday." And we went away Friday. Money didn't matter so much to me. If we'd be open, we'd make more money. But I didn't care for it. I wanted to enjoy while we can. Some people drop dead before they enjoy life a little bit. So I'm enjoying a little bit. I do what I like.

We had a good time. And we did worthwhile things that give you satisfaction, and I'm not ashamed of anything we did. Of course, we changed now. As you grow older, you get more sophisticated.

Jack M.

When I came here, looking at those skyscrapers and everything, I was wondering whether all the United States looks like this or only New York is like that.

We lived in Brownsville, Christopher Street—a cold flat. It cost about twenty-four dollars a month. We were six—my mother and five children. We had four rooms—a railroad flat—three bedrooms, a living room and a kitchen. It wasn't bad. We kind of liked it. Of course, there were some hardships, like buying coal and buying a piece of ice.

When I came to this country looking for a job—how do the Jewish boys look for jobs? There was a newspaper by the name of the *Morning Journal* and there they had Help Wanted, where they advertise for jobs. I saw that they wanted to have a boy in a doll factory. So I took down the address and I went down there. The boss comes over and he says to me, "Where do you come from?" I said, "Originally I'm born in Russia, but I come from Cuba." He said to me, "Cuba? Maybe you know a fellow by the name of Hymie Meisl?" I said, "He's a very good friend of mine." He said, "Oh, if you know my brother, I'm going to give you the job."

He told me, "Look, the beginners I pay only twelve dollars a week. But because you know my brother and you give me regards from my brother, I'll give you fifteen dollars a week." So that's what he gave me, fifteen dollars a week.

My factory was on Greene Street, downtown. We were working fifty hours a week, nine hours every day and five hours on Saturday. But then when the NRA came in they slashed down ten hours right away—it came down from fifty to forty. Of course, the bosses didn't like it. They said, "We wouldn't exist long. We can't afford it." So we were working only forty hours—eight hours a day, no Saturdays any more.

After the NRA, we organized a union also—the Doll and Toy Workers Union. They called meetings of every shop and they told the people to pay in a dollar to go on with the organizing—it costs money. You take a hall for a meeting, it costs money. You've got to print leaflets, you've got to take down the workers—if some of them don't want to come, you've got to threaten they should go down on strike. And that's how the union was organized—the Doll and Toy Workers Union of America, they called it.

I used to come to work with a book called *The ABCs of Communism*, written by Bukharin. In Jewish. I used to take that book every day, sitting in the subway reading it. One time one of the bosses noticed the book. He used to read the *Forvertz* and the *Forvertz* in those days was still a Socialist paper, a good Socialist paper. Although they disagreed with the Communists, it still was a good Socialist paper. And he used to read the *Forvertz*. So when he saw my book, *The ABCs of Communism*, he said, "Oh, what are you, a Communist?" So I said, "Well you're not far from being a

Communist either. You're a Socialist. You read the *Forvertz*." So that shut him up. He couldn't argue with me any more.

I mostly used to talk with Jewish workers over there. The language was free. I could express myself better, convince them better that they should read the *Freiheit*, read the Jewish literature pertaining to the movement. In English it was hard for me to express myself the first couple of years. I had some who were Zionists, you see. I told them, "What difference does it make to me whether I'm being exploited by a Jewish boss in the United States or I'm being exploited by a Jewish boss in Israel. It's the same thing. I don't want to be exploited. I want to better my condition."

When I came here as a young fellow, I was right away interested in many things, many more useful things than some of the American boys were interested in. For instance, I couldn't understand somehow why young people are so crazy about certain things, which to me didn't look interesting at all. I was very much puzzled why I can't see many young fellows at a concert when a symphony was playing, or at a good literary play on Broadway. They would rather go and see a ball game. To them, a ball game was more important than to see a good literary play on Broadway. Somehow, I couldn't grasp it. I couldn't see the reason for it. European youngsters are more down to earth. They are more class-conscious, they are more serious. I ride on the train, for instance, I can see many people holding newspapers in their hands. You'll find among the young people maybe one out of twenty reading a *New York Times*, the rest of them read the *Daily News*.

I was a great admirer of the Soviet Union. I used to go to all the meetings. I used to subscribe to the working-class periodicals and newspapers. I used to go listening to some speakers talking about the Russian Revolution—the differences between the Czarist government and the Russian Revolution. I was a great admirer—I supported it a hundred percent.

At the beginning I wanted so much to go back to the Soviet Union. But I didn't have the money to go, and I got married—you raise a family. I didn't want to leave my mother. Now I would like to go. Very much so. Although I still don't agree with everything that's going on in the Soviet Union, nevertheless I still would like to see it.

At first, not only I but to people who were in high positions of the working class and high positions of the Communist Party, Stalin was like a God to everybody. Some people used to say, "How could Stalin be wrong? How could the Soviet Union be wrong?" Then we saw how Lenin also disagreed with Trotsky but still and all he didn't put him to the wall to shoot. And he got rid of all the Central Committee of the Communist Party over there in the Soviet Union, and then more and more killings and killings and purges and purges and killings until the whole thing came out in the open and we saw he is no good—that's all.

I was never a Trotskyite. I never agreed with Trotsky, because I followed the official line of the Communist Party. Stalin was against Trotsky, so naturally the Communist Party was against Trotsky and the membership was against Trotsky. I think that socialism in one country is better than having a world revolution. Because I would say every country has got differences on how to raise the consciousness of the working class—there are different conditions, different economic conditions, different cultural conditions. Everything is different and you cannot just make a world revolution. You cannot copy a revolution from one country to another. Every country has got to work out its own ideas, its own working-class consciousness, and I don't think that Trotsky was right.

The Communist Party here followed the line of Stalin. They justified everything that Stalin did.

FLORENCE: Since the holocaust, we changed our views. We were internationalists before. But since the holocaust, since six million Jews were slaughtered just because they are Jews, I personally changed my attitude. I think he also did.

JACK: I wouldn't say that I'm not an internationalist anymore. I'm still sticking with the working class throughout the world regardless of nationality, but because of the holocaust, the national feelings—feelings of being a Jew—got a little stronger now, because of the six million Jews that perished. Somehow I became more Jewish conscious, more national conscious.

FLORENCE: In the Soviet Union they don't preach what they practice and you see that after sixty-five years of the Revolution people still have nothing there.

JACK: I wouldn't say that they have nothing. They have much much more than they had under the czar. Historically speaking, the Soviet Union made great great advances.

FLORENCE: I don't want to compare it with the czar. Sixty years.

JACK: Historically speaking, I say the Soviet Union made great great advances, you see? Culturally, technologically.

FLORENCE: That's it, that's right. That's all, nothing else. Nothing for the people.

JACK: I won't say nothing for the people. Nothing over there for the people? For the Russian people?

FLORENCE: I say we haven't got communism over here, but the working class here has more than any of them ever had in Russia, and they . . .

JACK: Listen, never compare two countries. Historically, . . .

FLORENCE: I am comparing. This is a capitalist country . . .

JACK: Historically, the background of this country and the background of the Soviet Union are completely different.

FLORENCE: It should have been after sixty years . . .

JACK: The Revolution that took place in Russia took over a country with . . . with . . .

FLORENCE: Sixty years! Sixty years, Jasha. And they're so rich in natural resources, they haven't got no bread, they haven't got nothing there. You fail to understand . . .

JACK: They haven't got no bread?

FLORENCE: No. They buy bread from here.

JACK: It's not because they've got no bread. They buy grains and there is an exchange of other things.

FLORENCE: They should have had plenty of everything—an abundance of everything.

JACK: Sometimes there's a shortage of grain through certain natural conditions.

FLORENCE: They achieved on the cultural front, yes. On the technological . . . that they did. But for the people there, very little. For their personal consumption, for the personal needs, very little, no homes or nothing.

JACK: I feel different. I feel first of all that Russia went through two or three wars. The last war that Hitler was there it will take them many, many years to build up the country and to have the things that they had before—what Hitler destroyed. So never compare this country to Russia. For the time that we are here this country had wars you know where? On other territories, but not on this territory. So this country never suffered with the exception that American boys were killed. Where Russia had wars on their territory, and every time war took place, just imagine what was destroyed over there.

FLORENCE: And now that they calmed down a little bit, they're making war elsewhere.

JACK: OK. We're not talking about that. We're not going into that.

FLORENCE: OK. I want nothing to do with them anymore.

JACK: You won't like to see it?

FLORENCE: I'd like to see what it is, but . . .

JACK: That's all that it is. I didn't say I would like to live there. No. I wouldn't like to live there.

In this country I had a better chance to go to school and learn and go to meetings and go to lectures. It was entirely different. I found in this country a better chance to get educated and to mingle with a lot of people which I could learn something from them. Better opportunities, naturally, than in a small town in Russia. New York, I don't have to tell you, is a big city, with a lot of movement. It was alive, so naturally I was active—I used to go all over, take part in everything.

In Russia, the cultural activities were very limited, very much limited. Limited in the sense that there wasn't enough literature, there wasn't enough speakers, there wasn't enough people to enlighten these certain things. In this country I could afford to have all these things that I wanted to have—more knowledge, more education, more meetings, and more activities. Economic conditions were better in this country than on the other side—we ate better, we got dressed better, we used to go to concerts, to opera, to ballet, which we never saw and never dreamt of in a small town in Russia.

I became active in the movement. I used to read every day a newspaper. Over here I could afford to go to libraries and get all kinds of books—Russian, Yiddish, and then English. I used to get together in houses and have house parties, used to go to all kinds of affairs of the radical movement, the progressive movement—memorial meetings, a Lenin memorial was here, and the American-Russian friendship societies, meetings of the Young Communist League, the Communist Party. Even though I wasn't a member, there were open meetings, and then open-air meetings in the streets—especially before elections when the Communist Party used to put out their candidates, we always had open-air meetings in the streets and we would have a crowd of maybe five or six hundred people listening to the speakers, which was very interesting. You could learn a great deal. I felt that it's a beautiful country but something's got to be done about the conditions of the workers. And I became active.

It's not a question whether you think to be a Communist or not, if you are taught that you are . . . if you are educated enough, if you read enough, if you realize, if you understand—if somebody is leading you and gives you to understand—the Communist Party must be the leading force in this country to educate the workers in this country, they would realize maybe a revolution is possible some day in this country. But it seems to me that, I don't know—I'm not much of a theoretician—but it seems to me that the Communist Party is not shaping the policy correctly.

You haven't got the conditions ripe for a revolution in this country. First of all the most powerful leading organization to lead the working class in this country should be the Communist Party, but the Communist Party is very weak. As a matter of fact, you have a hundred million wage earners in this country, a hundred million workers, and you haven't got one representative from the Communist Party—not in Congress, not in the Senate, no place.

Second, this is the richest country in the world. That's why the workers are better off over here. The bourgeois class is very clever. They're very smart. They know how to throw a bone—a little bone—to the working class to keep them quiet, they shouldn't demand certain things. But there are certain conditions, natural contradictions, within the capitalist system—like a depression. It's a natural contradiction within the capitalist society—it comes and you can't help it and that's all. All of a sudden ten million workers, eighteen million workers, twenty million workers are being thrown out of work and they don't know what to do with them. Robbery, killings, rapings, prostitution are products of the capitalist system. It's true to a certain degree some are lazy, some don't want to work, and some are naturally bad, but still most of the faults I would pin on the capitalist system. Capitalism has got so many natural contradictions that in years to come the capitalist society will be abolished. It will be abolished altogether.

Sarah C.

Charlie S.

Ethel G.

Bela S.

FOUR

A Shtetl on a Hill

Introduction

Camp Followers of the Trail was designed to provide rest and relaxation for politically radical thinkers and activists, especially those of the working class. Anyone who believed in the cause of internationalism was welcome. From the camp's inception, however, members and visitors were predominantly eastern European, more specifically Russian Jewish immigrants, who felt most comfortable speaking and reading Yiddish and Russian. Despite the Followers' professed cosmopolitanism, the camp that they established resembled the European shtetls in which so many of them were born and raised. Its isolated physical location, its less than friendly relationship with the surrounding Gentile community, the Followers' emphasis upon the pursuit of knowledge through lectures, readings, and discussions, their portrayal of relationships within the camp as similar in intimacy and importance to relationships within a family, and their devoted belief in a system of thought all suggest affinities with the European community of their youth.

As the Followers grew older, they moved to the middle of the progressive political spectrum. Increasingly disillusioned with communism's promises and with the Soviet Union's antisemitism, the Followers describe themselves as having become "Jewish-conscious." In effect, they came full circle, performing a secular twist along the way. Journeying from the strictly religious ethnic identification of their parents, they arrived in America and attempted to balance political internationalism with a secular concept of ethnic identity and wound up Jewish-conscious—a secular form of ethnic identification without the radical political edge.

The name that the Followers chose for their camp is perhaps more revealing than they intended. Not only were they hikers following the physical trail of nature, or politically committed Party members and fellow travelers following the ideological trail of communism, they were also eastern European Jewish immigrants following a trail of values established by their ancestors. The camp's continued vitality after over sixty years of existence may reveal the value of these trails, as well as the character of those who followed them.

Singing

Harry G. and Harry M.

Shuffleboard

At the pool

Bella S.

In 1920 there was a man named Macfadden who wrote in the newspaper *The World*. His idea was that we have to live outdoors, that we are too much confined to the inside—we live in the shop or the office or the factory. When you have free time, he said, be outdoors. This appealed to us a great deal. So we organized a group and we started to go hiking. Hiking at that time was very popular. We used to go hiking every Sunday—rain or shine we'd go hiking.

We called ourselves the Followers of the Trail. Once we were a group, we organized ourselves into a club—a social recreation club. We'd go away early in the morning, stop in the woods and the fields, spend the day outdoors, and come back at night. Even in the wintertime, we hiked. We had a fellow near the reservoir that used to prepare our meal for us. We hiked all morning, came to a nice warm house, had a meal, and then we'd start hiking again. It went on quite a while.

Then we decided, it's good hiking, but it would be good to have a place to stay for the summer. So we got places from people. Lewisohn, who had the Lewisohn Stadium in City College, had an estate around Ardsley. A group of us elected a committee to go to Lewisohn and ask him to give us the privilege to camp for a summer on his grounds. They weren't occupied by anybody. He had grounds all over and this was a part of it. He liked the idea, and the manager gave us permission. In order to feel that it isn't a bunch of hoodlums but an organized body, we paid him, I remember, seventy-five dollars a summer. He was enthusiastic about the idea of having a group of young people behaving so nicely and living so beautifully together. We all pitched our tents there. Everyone had a tent. Down below was a running brook and that was our bathing place. We made ourselves a baseball field and a volleyball field. When the end of the summer came, we would pull up the tents. They saw we are such a decent bunch of people, so they said, "Look, we'll allow you to store your tents in our barn." So we stayed for quite a while.

Then all of a sudden we got notice that a road has to go through this property where we were and we will have to vacate. That was the time we started to look for a permanent home. We were already imbued with the idea that this is it—we have to have a place to come and spend the summer with our tents, but it should be permanent, we should not have to pack away our things. We started to look around. We looked for a place where it would be accessible to the main highway. What was the reason? We were hikers. We would hitchhike. If you are far from the highway, you can't hitchhike. We didn't have another means of transportation. If you go by train, it costs fare, and it's away from the station. We were looking at different beautiful places, but they were too far from the highways.

When we found this place in Peekskill, we thought, "This is it." It was right on the Albany highway. On Sundays, couples would station themselves in different spots—it shouldn't be a mass, and that was the way of transportation. We hitchhiked back and forth to camp. In Ardsley we had a kitchen. It was a big tent, and this is how we conducted our life there. The kitchen was portable, you could take it apart. We even brought that kitchen here—that was our first kitchen. There was no light, only kerosene lamps. There was no running water. We had to start from scratch. The first thing we built was a diningroom. We didn't have regular toilet facilities. We still had outhouses. But gradually the idea caught fire. People began to flock to us. We immediately established it as a place where we'll be able to charge people outside of the membership, to feed them. And that is how it started.

In the beginning, when we came up here, we all were workers and all our camp business was conducted on weekends. When we came up here on the weekends, it was beautiful, it was perfume. We didn't know that there was a factory down the road that produces oilcloth and that they don't give a continental for what the fumes are going to do to the people. We would come up sometimes during the week and find a cloud of thick fumes. We encountered that, but we couldn't do anything about it. When we complained, they said, "You came here and you found it. Why did you buy? The factory was here before you. And, besides, our population doesn't complain. They make a living from it." This was their bread and butter.

When we bought the place, we needed money. We had to put down a thousand dollars as a deposit. Each person paid in fifty dollars for membership, and that covered the first payment. Then, as I said, there were people who were not members but wanted to come to us to be outdoors and have a meal at the same time. So we organized it into a business, accommodating friends and charging them so much per weekend. The price was very nominal. We charged just to cover the advances to build, to do things. Everybody that came to us became the builders. They were imbued with the idea that we have to work together, whether we're members or outsiders. That's how it worked. Gradually, we built up the buildings. We didn't build it all up at the same time. That required a lot of money. First two bungalows, then another two bungalows. The second years, we built the casino, we put in electricity, we put in facilities—and it all came from the people who came to us for vacation, to spend the time with us.

As soon as we decided to buy, we formed an organization, legally. We had a president, a vice president, a secretary, a board of directors. We still proceed in the same manner.

When it was a camp, every member as well as the guests registered in the office. If I came up for a weekend, I went to the office, registered, got my ticket, paid my fee, and that's how it worked. On this basis, we ran the business. We had an office, we had a bookkeeper. It didn't happen just when we came, but gradually. Most of the population were members. But then came people called "privileged campers." We rented them a tent or a bungalow for the season, and that gave them the privilege to be charged for food the same rate as members. Many members were at first privileged campers.

At the beginning, there were regulations for choosing members—no employers, only workers. Employers were taboo. Of course, we didn't have any, but that was the idea. Otherwise, there were no restrictions, black or white or anything.

Then again, the element we were, we attracted similar people. People with different ideas, like religious people, they wouldn't come to us. Gradually we attained a very good following. There was a lot of work going on here. A lot of work.

During the Spanish Civil War, we were for helping the people that carried on. Our place was very active in a small way—we managed to raise money to send an ambulance. Anywhere we could get a dollar, everything went for the ambulance. If one had a car and he took you home, pay a dollar, pay fifty cents—it goes for the ambulance. That was the goal. It was a big undertaking. I have a picture of the ambulance—it says Followers of the Trail on the side, and there are the children selling raffles.

The Second World War was a different approach, a different ideology. It was not a war from an idealistic point of view, like the Civil War in Spain, between the right and the left. This was a war against humanity. Every sane person should have been against it. It goes without saying that we were very much involved. To our great sorrow, our great Roosevelt didn't prove to be the great Roosevelt. When it came to the Jews, there was no humanism in him. But we did all we could. There were a lot of organizations working for war relief. Russia lost almost a country—fifteen million people. We had an organization known as the Russian War Relief, that later worked against Nazism. But our hands were tied. We couldn't do anything. What's more, to our great sorrow, the American people didn't know much about it.

When the Paul Robeson concert came about, we were also quite involved. We had a new car then, and our son went back and forth—we kept sandwiches and drinks for the concert. When he was coming home, he wanted to come back a safe way, because he knew every corner around here. But the police said, "Oh no, you go there," where the line of hoodlums were standing. And they smashed the car. They organized so that they could hurt everybody that was involved, and they saw that there were a lot of people from our camp involved. When we went to fix up the cars, they said, "Oh, you were one of those that were there?" You had to lie, to tell stories. But we were labeled even before that.

The town around here is very conservative. They're all Republicans. When we came here we brought in something new—we went around in halters and shorts. So the first thing was they marked us as a nudist colony. We're nudists! Once you are a nudist, you can't be a Republican. You won't be a Republican, if you are a nudist. Then we were everything. If you're a nudist, you must be a Communist. Then, in the beginning, we were active in the town. We had a lot of teachers and other professionals who utilized this place as an outlet for Party work—they used to go to the station and distribute leaflets. There were CC camps nearby and we had the boys from there come to us. The people in the town put two and two together. The very fact that a group exists here, and we have nothing to do with the authorities, so they thought we must be some sort of anarchists. But we never had any relationship with them. We were up here and we led our lives in our manner. They were conservatives and to them, it was queer. If it was queer, it must mean something not kosher, you know. We were entirely separate from the townspeople. But they were always wondering, "What is up there? What else do they do except go around naked?" The worst thing they could call anybody was a Communist, so naturally they called us Communists.

Later on, with McCarthy, people became fearful. The following that used to come to us in great numbers dwindled down to very few. The people like teachers and professionals stopped coming. It was interesting. They were the ones that carried on, they were enthusiastic—we have to do for the people, we have to propagandize, and this and the other thing. But when it came actually that it might threaten them, they were afraid of their bread and butter. And we didn't blame them. But we already had an establishment that required a lot of money. We had to have a cook and a manager and a bookkeeper and waiters. We were confronted with a situation where the membership had to put up money to carry it on.

Now there were no more ideals. In the beginning our purpose was an ideal purpose. Once it got to be from the point of view of dollars and cents, it didn't pay. We didn't have the income we needed. There also were other elements involved. As people got older, the diet has to change, you can't eat communally, you have to have so much at this time, so much at that time. Everything came to the point where we had to give up the business of Followers of the Trail. In 1952 we changed it into a colony called Reynolds Hills in order to exist. Those that wanted to stay stayed on and accepted the new ideas. We sold the bungalows that belonged to the camp—that we used to use for accommodations of guests. We sold those bungalows for five hundred dollars apiece and we started to sell the linen, the utensils, everything.

Now it is still a corporation and the grounds belong to the organization. New people that come here are still freer than those that want to have "my" deed and "my" parcel. We still don't have that. We still have the grounds in common. But now if you want to see your friend, you call on the telephone. In those days, we didn't know such a thing. You would go around and take a walk. If you saw somebody in a house, you'd come in and socialize. It was still that feeling that we were always together.

But as new people came in, they came with their own ideas, with their own way of living and manners of association. It's different in that sense. Basically the ideology is the same. A conservative person still wouldn't come here. He would find himself out of place. Not that we are extreme, but this is our way. Even though a lot of people are new, we still can instill in them that feeling and they seem to accept it and participate and help. We carry on whatever we can do under the circumstances.

When we reelect the board, different members accept and they know what they're doing, what they're accepting—all the hardships. They know that they accept to do the work and they're being called upon to give a helping hand. Those that can do it, do it. It just so happens that in the young days we did everything ourselves—there was no question that if we have to paint the pool we have to pay. There were always members, someone that would do it. These same members cannot do it now. They got older.

I maintain that communal living, cooperative living, is very advantageous to the individual providing there is no abuse. To our sorrow, there is a lot of abuse here now. We pay a tremendous price for electricity. So you'll find one who does not give a hoot. You come in the afternoon, the sun is shining, and they have all the lights on. They have basements, the lights are on in the basements from morning until night. You see, this is something that is abuse. We take a moral approach. We talk, we discuss, we stress the point. It angers some people. It's a little friction, but not enough to make you feel bad against one another. These are no major things.

You learn to accept people with all their virtues and vices and you know that this is life. And that enriches you in a way of thinking because no sooner you think of "my own little pile" you're very limited. Then there is the advantage of being with old friends. Some of us are here for over forty years. We are friends.

Your family is close to you very much on the inside, but when you need your family, they're not there. My son would do anything for me, but where is he? He's somewhere in Great Neck, busy with the business. My friends are here. That strengthens the relationship. We know we need each other. I know around here, if something happens, the first thing is you run over to this one, "Do for me this and I'll do for you that," and so on down the line. This place gave us friends. It's a great advantage.

But it's not utopian. Under the capitalist system, you'll never attain that. They'll give you a finger, "Go ahead, organize. Make yourself a colony. Go in business." But when they decide that it's too much, they'll wipe you out. There was, and maybe there still is, a sentiment in the authorities in the town around us, "Oh, these people, they take the law into their own hands." We never go into court. We live here fifty years. How is it possible, in fifty years people should never go to court—not even once? They don't like that. They want us to go to court. They want us to quarrel. They want to justify their jobs. We quarrel, but among ourselves.

The colony was always successful. If you want to compare from when we started to where we are now, it's nothing to compare. When we came here, we had outhouses. When I had to go, I had to run about two blocks down. That's a very important necessity. You can't compare that. We grew with conditions. We cannot stay back where we were. We had to go with the times. The trouble is, in general principles—now I'm not talking just about the colony—the standard of living jumped too high to be able to cope with it. It's a vicious circle.

But the colony accomplished a lot in the sense that our people compared with people I know at a similar age are much more alert, much healthier, much brighter. I have a neighbor, when she saw me come out to go to camp, she said, "Oh, people our age." I said, "What do you mean, people our age? What age?" Their mentality, their way of thinking, is to sit inside and wait—someday to go to the children. That's a routine, whether the children want you or not or you want them or not. Saturday we have to go for supper or they have to come to me for supper. They make a burden for the children to come because this is a routine that keeps them alive.

I don't feel such a thing as "people our age" because I went to live, out to the fresh air, to the sunshine, to discussions. I didn't wait until Sunday when I get up at twelve o'clock and try to read the funnies. All this adds to your physical way of living, and it adds to your spiritual way. People say, "Oh, it isn't what it used to be." It couldn't be what it used to be. There is no such thing as "used to be." Nothing stands still. There are changes and we have to adapt ourselves.

My earlier progressive attitudes don't mellow. When your mind intelligently and emotionally is set for something that is just, it's there. If it mellows, it's sometimes due to other conditions—like physical conditions. I feel I've done all this, I can't do anymore, and sometimes I'm a little disappointed. All this I did, and where is it? What did it bring the youth? What did we prepare for you? But it's not a question of mellowing. I may not agree with the tactics of a certain part of the left, but the ideals are still there. I wouldn't feel that Russia should go back to the czar, but what is the Soviet Union doing now? They incite one against the other. Their greatest leaders were concerned with justice toward the Jews. Lenin was concerned with justice towards the Jews. But, for one reason or another, they incite against Jews. They label it "Zionism" and they say Zionism is against communism, and that's that. This is the leadership. But the basic ideology of communism, of socialism, is always for the benefit of the people, not the leaders. If it's done right, it would be beautiful.

Not a single moment do I regret living the way we did. If you're all of a sudden reborn and you have the choice, you choose to do the thing that you liked all along. The only thing that would stop me eventually coming to Peekskill for the summers is if my health is not very good. When it gets cold, I shrivel up. When it's damp, it's not good. My bones cannot carry heavy coats. I don't need it. My legs cannot drag galoshes. I don't need it. That alone is the reason why Florida is good for senior citizens who would like to make their life easier.

We were pioneers in Florida. We were the first ones from here venturing out. We had been going to Florida quite often for our winter vacations. We liked it and it was beneficial for our health. All along we looked for a life that was outdoors, that was easy, that was good for what ails you. We decided that when Sol was ready to retire, we'd go and make our home there. So in 1962 we decided that we'll make our winter home in Florida.

We came there and met with a lot of friends we had known from the North, people with our ideology—you usually get together that way. We came there and found a Jewish cultural center where we met with the people we were interested to meet, and we decided that people with our economic means cannot possibly afford to come to Florida and pay all these high prices for rentals. So a group of us there decided that we would look for something to buy on a cooperative basis. We had the background for that from the camp. To us, it was not a new venture. On that basis, we started to look for a place. At that time, there was not yet condominiums. It was after we were there already that that new word came into existence.

When we came back to the colony for the summer, people were startled—"You mean to say you're leaving your children and you're going away?" I said right there and then, "Look, if my children would have need to go away from New York, I wouldn't keep them back in any way. What's good for them, is good for them. What's good for us, is good for us." Then when we came and started relating to our friends how we live, how it can be done, and how much easier it is both economically and physically for people our age, little by little, year by year, more families were going down there. But it was a gradual thing. Every once in a while somebody else dared to venture out. As a matter of fact, some people used to keep their apartments in New York to have a home in the North—not to have the feeling that they tore themselves away and made that extreme change. So our friends there are the same people.

We are much richer because of the colony. Our life is much richer. In Florida, individual people come from different places. They don't come as a group that has lived together so many years. They come, they buy into a community, they make friends, I suppose, because human beings need friends. But they haven't got that relationship that we have. People envy us—"You are lucky. You have your friends that you've had all these years." You know, it's not so easy to make new friends for senior citizens. Everybody has his set ways, you never know how to accept the other, you don't know who he is, how you'll be received.

With us, it's like one big family. When we get there, this one calls and that one calls. And who is it? It's the same people. Around where we live, we have in just two square blocks, ten or twelve families from the colony that are together. We grow older regardless of where we are, but this makes it so much easier, more pleasant. You feel so much more secure when you know you're surrounded by friends of such long standing. Also, the cultural life developed a great deal since we're there, so that makes it so much more pleasant. We have the best plays, symphonies, actors—you name it. You can be busy every hour of the day.

But it is not now in Florida what it was eighteen years ago in the sense that when there is an illness in the country, it spreads all over. When there is mugging or other things, it's spreading there too. Senior citizens are robbed. They take advantage of the senior citizens. They take great advantage of the fact that the senior citizens are together, they know where they are, they know that they can get things out of them just to scare them, just to make them feel that they are strong and they can do it. You find now that in the dwellings that senior citizens own, they put on different protection, because of the fact that they take advantage of the senior citizens, particularly women. A lot of women senior citizens are subject to harassment, mugging, being robbed. It's bad.

In certain areas they do a little bit for the senior citizens. They have centers, they have communities where they have a decent life. They can do things, they can enjoy, they can feel that they are not thrown out. But some of them are just sitting around and moping. They have nothing to do and they have no guidance. It's throwing a bone. It's not what it should be. When senior citizens start to be considered a burden, that is a tragedy. And in some areas, the senior citizens are considered a burden by the population because of the fact that they haven't got enough to meet their needs so their lifestyle is such that it doesn't increase the beauty of the surrounding area. But this is something that can be rectified, and it should be rectified.

Most people who have an income that fluctuates know that this is the percentage they make today to meet their needs. For the senior citizen, it's not the same thing. You have an income from when you started to get your social security. It doesn't come up to the increase in prices. Then, because of the influx of so many northerners in Florida, the rentals are very high. You find some of the senior citizens haven't enough left to live on after they pay the rent. This is a serious problem. Of course, there are some people with a little income from other sources—but on social security alone you can't live there. It's very hard.

These people contributed. It's their insurance. They are entitled. They should meet expenses with ease and not have to beg and not have to worry where to take the money to pay for the telephone—because if they have no telephone, then how can they be in contact with people. It's a simple thing. Of course, I'm not going to run the government, but it's quite obvious that when we build airplanes and before you have them ready they're obsolete, all this money is wasted. If we could prevent that, we'd have enough money to meet the needs of the senior citizens.

Of course, we have senior citizens organizations. We are very active in demanding what should be decent. You go to Washington, you knock on the doors, and you see what you can get out of that. The administration should know that these are the people who built the country, these are the people who contributed greatly to the increase of wealth in the country, and these are the people who are entitled to share it according to their needs. This is not done. There is a lack of good organization. Though we have the senior citizen organizations, they function in certain areas, but it is not sufficient. I think there are sixty million senior citizens now. That's a tremendous force. We have a say when we go to vote, providing we are conscious of it, providing we know that this is a weapon and we should use it properly. The representatives should realize this. Meanwhile, this is the only weapon we have.

Some say people in Europe live better, others say they live worse. Everything is relative. Some can live and enjoy with a nice piece of bread and a piece of butter, others must have caviar. You can't judge. I can judge only as much as my intellect can grasp and try to compare from what I read, from what I know, from what they tell me. We know that there are places where there is easier living, so they say. And yet, the easier living is perhaps that the pace is slower. As far as materially, we still have the highest standard of living. But we deserve that—we created it, it's our labor. And we don't share it right. We don't share it equally. We don't have it the way we should. But if you compare it with other countries, this country still has the highest standard of living. How long this situation we're in now will last, this is for us to see.

Under the conditions that we lived in Europe, we grew up early. When you're in a condition that you're always in want, and when you're living in a condition where you see the injustice of nature to man, when the only way you can get something is to become a servant to a more affluent family or you can learn to be a shoemaker's helper, so when you have this situation you begin to think earlier. You think, "What is going to become of me? I'm growing, my father clothes me, gives me food. What then? What then?" When you undertook a trip to America by yourself, not knowing anybody, not knowing what encounter you may have, whom you may meet on the way, what advantage they may take of you—you took all those chances because you wanted to develop, to find out what's in the world, what is it next door that's locked up to me.

Today you don't have to think. My son didn't have to think. He got up and he had everything given to him. Everything was prepared for him. The youth of the United States, even the poor ones, know that they will go to school, and something will be provided for them.

In this country we had the advantage that no war affected us. Except the war for freedom of the slaves, no other war ever affected us. We were always the winners in a sense—there was no destruction of our country. We kept on building, without rebuilding. We've reached a point that it's out of our hands. The world is so divided and the competition between the two systems is so great, they will dismiss the thought that they will hurt the population.

They do things now that are unbelievable. A million things are being discovered. We take poisons and poison the atmosphere for the new generations. Why do we do it? It was discovered and we're stuck with it. We discovered all these chemicals, but it's not in the hands of the people, it's in the hands of the corporations and they don't give a hoot what is going to happen. If you know when you discover a chemical that it is dangerous for the health of the population and, let's assume for the sake of argument, that we must have it because it is needed, then there should simultaneously be built a way of disposing of it so it wouldn't hurt the population.

At present the situation in our country is such that there was never such a tragic, disorganized state as now. There was always respect for law—it meant something. Now when you look around there is no respect for law. You begin to question, "Who are they that make the laws for me? They make it so that I shouldn't have and they should." There is a lot of advancement in this society, but it's wrongly distributed politically and otherwise.

I'll tell you. The way I see it, I don't see any immediate drastic change—call it a revolution. A revolution has to have the basis prepared, a revolution has to have theories. People have to know what they are going to do and how they are going to cope with it. You can't have a revolution with people who from their childhood are brought up with a thought that individually they can be a senator or a president—that all you do is up to you to do it. We bring up our youth as individuals, to think individually. You see what I mean? The people at the head of the government have to realize that if they don't make changes to improve conditions for living—not for wealth, but for safe living—the next thing is the population will reach a stage where it will be like a volcano and it will erupt. It will destroy.

There are so many billions that we spend on armaments and things that get to be obsolete, and all these bureaucrats stuff their pockets instead of seeing that the youth get jobs and feel that they are not nuisances in the society. Either you do it in a democratic way or you'll destroy democracy, and you'll have dictatorship. They'll call it fancy names, but it will be dictatorship. Let's hope for the better way. I'm not out for destruction. Destruction doesn't bring any good. It takes you ten years to build up your home and two hours to destroy it.

Sometimes you figure that you're so helpless, there is nothing you can do. The only thing you can do is hope for the younger generation that is bringing new life into the world. They are beginning to think, "What are you doing to my children, and my children to come?" They will have to take it into their hands. The youth is doing the producing, the inventing, the thinking. And the youth will have to see that it shouldn't get worse.

Sarah A.

Because I spoke Yiddish well, I always treated immigrants the way I would treat my own. I spoke to them in their language. Only I used to think, "Oh, I'm much smarter than them." Actually, I must tell you, the time I changed my way of thinking about immigrants was when I got into the summer camp—Followers of the Trail. You see, I had a white-collar job, so I thought I was King Tut. I thought I knew it all. I knew how to type, English I spoke well—I don't know how well, but I was born here [in the United States].

When I met the others in the camp, all of them practically were needle-trade workers. They all came when they were young—what else could they do? There was no place for them but the shop. They knew already English when I met them, some with an accent, some better, but I still thought I was much smarter than they, that I knew much more than they. And then I went to my first meeting of the members, and was shocked out of my complacency.

I saw the way they conducted a meeting, and I just couldn't believe that these were shop workers with the command of the English language. Those days, I remember, when they used to speak I'd say to myself, "How do they know?" I thought they were greenhorns. You know what a greenhorn is? When you come from the other side, we used to call them greenhorns. But their stock went up in my eyes when I saw how the chairman spoke and what they did when there was a question in the camp. To raise from twenty dollars a week it should be twenty-one dollars there was a fight over the dollar. And how they spoke about it—their logic!

And they had other discussions—talking about operas, which I never even attended in those days, outside of going to Lewisohn Stadium. They went to the stadium every night after their shop work, and they would go and do such things—go to Cooper Union for lectures, and just to educate themselves. But the way they talked about shows and theaters and music and politics and everything in general, I just couldn't believe it. I was just thrown off. That's how it struck me.

They didn't treat me any different. Just sometimes to be snotty, for the fun of it (because at that time I think I was the only one, a Yankee), I would say I'm from the DAR, the Daughters of the [American] Revolution. Because I was born here. But I was always helpful and glad to do anything they asked me. They were glad to get me. They were glad to get members.

Those days, hitchhiking was the style. It was easy and it didn't cost any money. I and my friends used to go practically every weekend to some camps. We were much younger, and naturally we enjoyed it. Then one time we saw an ad in the paper about it—in those days the camp was called Followers of the Trail. It was near New York. I heard of it from my sister because she had a boyfriend at that time who had a tent at Followers of the Trail. So I said to my friend, "Come, let's try it." So we stood in Van Cortlandt Park and we got a ride straight all the way to the bottom of the hill there, and then we walked up and got in. Period.

I never dreamed that I would stay here all these years. I think it was then a Jewish holiday, so I had four days off. We all ate together—it was so good—and we made friends. I enjoyed the communal spirit. One man said, "Why don't you come here steady and become members?" I looked at him. I was a little younger, and I was thinking, "To come here to a place like this and be stuck here for the rest of my life, and not go to other places?" But when we came back again, we decided we could be members and if we wanted to go to another camp for two weeks, we could. In those days I had to consider time. I had a job and I couldn't go when I wanted or get my vacation when I wanted.

Those days, for your tent and everything, I think you had to pay fifty dollars to be a member for the year. We used to get meals and we used to contribute our services. We were the waitresses, and I loved it. I used to get such a kick out of running back and forth, and asking and answering back, and joking. I really enjoyed it very much. In those days we came even by boat and maybe by train. We didn't have all these conveniences that we have now. So I had to run here after work on a Friday, get here, have my supper, and pitch a tent. And I loved it.

I thought I was a millionaire to have the tent—it was ten-by-twelve. I'd put up the flaps and go to sleep. The only furniture I had was like a closet where I hung my clothes and an eggbox, which I covered with material, and the bed. That's all the furniture. I think I put an oilcloth on the floor. And there was a porch outside. So when I got away from the city and into the country, I really loved it, especially helping out and that spirit. If you couldn't do this or that, everybody would just come without thinking twice and help.

To me it was utopian. The community, the togetherness, and having a good time. I never had to think where to go for vacation. You know, it was a problem during the summer, every weekend or so, where to go? When I would go from work, I had no problem where I would go. I would come here, put my flaps up, and take a good deep breath. We were all very close. We'd run into each other's tents or bungalows. We got together two or three times a day—when we ate, when we went down to the pool, and at night we had entertainment. Don't forget, when you're younger, you're running around. Everybody was busy all day. Who ever thought of planting a garden? Nobody would dream of it. Once you had tents, nobody thought of the distance between mine and yours—sometimes there were six tents together and sometimes there were two tents. But that's the way we started out and that's the way we lived. We were always together. Most of us were single, and we didn't need anything.

Don't forget, we're looking back on forty years ago. Lifestyles have changed. When you're older, like now, at this age, I wouldn't want to live in a tent. How could I live in a tent anymore? I wouldn't be able to. Those days in the camp we had one bathroom all the way over there—one for all—and showers were there. And then just one small toilet on the other side for the rest of the whole camp. You can't get along that way anymore. Listen, if the world used electricity for everything, why should we curtail ourselves if we can afford it? We can't bring anything back. That's what life is, and you have to live with what is and make the best of it.

I remember the Paul Robeson concert in Peekskill. I was in a car that was hit. The glass broke on us. Thank goodness no one was hurt. But we saw the faces of those people. A few cars started out from the camp, and I think one bus also. I didn't go in the bus, I went in a private car with somebody. There were stone throwers and the way they looked we thought we'd never get out. When I saw those faces on the road—you know, I never knew what was a Fascist, but they looked just like when you saw pictures of the German Wermacht. And then when we got there, some fellows from here—the younger boys—stayed there to watch to see that we would get through. Then, later, I remember, when we got back to the camp, we had fellows standing on guard. We were afraid they would come to attack. All night, we really were scared.

They called us a Red camp—you know, a Communist camp. The McCarthy period affected us very strongly. I had somebody very close in the family who was a teacher, who was thrown out of the system. He was teaching all this time and he was such a marvelous teacher, such a marvelous guy. I know what they went through, all the interrogation and all of that business. And I knew others, very, very close friends of mine, because I was in that. . . . Most of my friends were in it. So many of them went through all this in the McCarthy period, going through all these questions and answers, and they were always afraid of the FBI. It's a terrible feeling. It's worse than anything. You dream of it at night—that this one's coming to your house and tape recording or whatever.

Now I can't ask for a better life for myself. Here, in Peekskill, I have a bungalow, and I have an apartment in the city. I can afford this. I'm doing well. Of course, I'll say things are good. I can take a trip to Europe even and it wouldn't make such a dent. And I know I have enough to live on because with the pension that I get from Uncle Sam and the union, I have everything that I want.

But when I think of others—what do they have? I have a cousin who is working as long as I, she's a very bright person, only she married early and had a kid, and so forth, so she had to work in the shop. She gets next to nothing. From her line, she gets I think about seventy-three dollars a month. She worked and I worked. Why should she get less? It always bothered me. Why? Why? Why? At this stage of the game, she needs as much as I to live on. Why shouldn't she live and have certain things as I have? Others who live in the South, is the United States good to them? They'll say no. I think the system should be changed. Things aren't correct. I wish I were smart enough to know in which way.

But definitely things have been changing over the last number of years. I would say that it really was due to the left movement, which really brought it through their fighting for shorter hours and everything. If it were not for them, we'd have to wait for years and years to get it. Now it's easier living. But I believe in the principle of it, that people who work should make a living and get the main things. That's what I would stand for always. I know in the USSR things are done this way. But, of course, there is the Jewish question in the USSR. They can't pray, they can't do certain things, they can't go out of the country, they can't write as they please—or if they write they're held in captivity. So knowing this affects me, and I listen.

But I'm not giving up my ideal of what communism is, and what it stands for. If you don't fight for it, you don't get it. But where we were once able to go to rallies and do different things, at this age we can't do it anymore. We can still vote. It's a pity that some of the children don't give a damn.

A lot of the children when they come to the camp now it's to visit their mother or grandmother. They stay two hours or for the day or for the weekend, but then they're glad to get back to their place, because generally they have their own problems.

It's very hard once you have your own life. It's according even to the Bible. They leave their homes and go with their husbands, and that's their life already. That's the way of the world. I don't blame the youth.

Children have to work and make a living, and they really have big problems. They just can't be tied down to their parents. The parents have their own problems, and the children don't have the time. The parents have plenty of time to kill. It will be this way forever after. Especially now, it will be even worse. Would you ever hear of a daughter or son living with their parents? I don't know of any.

Years ago, it was that way. There was more respect then. But, first of all, those years generally they didn't live that long. If they lived to seventy, they were very old. Then they were taken care of all the time, no matter how sick they were. Also, because they died earlier, you didn't hear of all these diseases like cancers and heart conditions. They were all in the house and they were taken care of. You couldn't help it. The grandfathers would talk to the grandchildren, tell them all the little stories. Now they all live separately. But would you dream of changing progress? The girls go to out-of-town colleges, they wouldn't dream of living with their parents. They want their own life. Really, I don't blame them.

Years ago, you were able to have your mother and your grandmother in a three-room apartment. But that's the way we lived then. Now you can't do it anymore. Also, young people don't like old people. They're not pleasant to look at. They see them with a stick, and they feel that they belong to another era altogether. I can understand. When I was young, if somebody was a few years older, I used to feel, "Oh, she's so old." I remember once I had a cold and at the end of the week I was so weak I walked the steps very slowly. I was always a very quick runner on the steps—when I would run, you would think there was a fire. So I said, "My God, if I have to be this way, it doesn't pay to live." I must have been sixteen. That is the way you feel when you're younger. But when you're older you want to live.

Economically, old people are better off now than they were years ago, but they all have the same problem—being alone. Their children are more scattered than they were years ago. Years ago, families were all together, they lived together. But now, one is in California, one is in Europe, one is in Israel. Many women that I know are all by themselves. I know a number of women who are well-off, but they are all alone. They would not dare to go out at night, so they're home with their television.

I think the camp was very successful in this way. I think we're about the only one staying so intact and people are still getting together. That's very important. Being a member of the camp and going to lectures and readings and so forth, naturally it broadened my view of life, which I wouldn't have had if I was just living in one place and just working and coming home.

Considering everything, I think that I've had a pretty good life and enjoyed most things that I like to do. By nature, I am the contented type, but my life helped me to be contented. Of course, I had certain mishaps, but who doesn't go through life without something?

You know, my eyesight isn't good. I had a cataract operation, so certain things I don't see. But I get up and do little odds and ends, and I feel that I'm mighty lucky that I can do all these things in the city and also in the country. Just two years ago, when I would go down the hill to the A & P, I couldn't walk—I had to run. Now my running days are over. My pace is slower. But thank goodness, I can still walk up and down. You know, I walk a little slow. Many times I walk to the A & P just to make it, I should take that walk. Once I go down there and back, I feel that I accomplished something, and then I can start doing anything else I want to do in my house.

And I love my bungalow, my little Shangri-La. When I'm writing to somebody, I say I'm writing from my Shangri-La. I really do. I love it here. I always say this is my best investment. All these years that I enjoyed and made friends and kept busy and had good times—that's what life is.

And if I wanted to complain? To whom shall I complain? Whether there is a God or no God, it wouldn't help me to complain. I just take things as they are and I try to really make the best of it.

Harry S.

I used to close up the store on Saturday at twelve o'clock and I would travel to the camps. There was Camp Nitgedaiget. There was Camp Unity. And then there was Kinderland. The distance was about sixty-five miles from the city. At that time I had a big Nash sedan, and we would come out Saturday and there were no accommodations until Sunday. We would stay on the grounds overnight, we would take out the seats from the car and sleep on the grounds. I used to get disgusted. Saturday and Sunday were my only days to rest. I used to travel and then there was no accommodations. Then I met someone that used to stay in Followers of the Trail.

He was also a member of the club that I belonged to. He told me, "Why do you have to run around and get turned back? Here you can rent a room for the season— they have a main house with some rooms—rent a room there for the season and anytime you want, you know that it's there. You don't have to bring luggage." I went out here and I looked over the place and it looked like a good idea. I rented two rooms—a bedroom and a kitchen. The people were very friendly, and I got right away active in the community because I liked the idea of cooperative living.

I became very active. I had experience running an organization because I was very active in the clubs. I also belonged to the IWO, a fraternal organization. I had organizational ability. Then, you see, this idea of cooperative living just struck me right. I felt that I'm not just doing it for myself, I'm doing it for everybody, for the community.

When I came in in 1936, right away there was the Spanish Civil War. We had the Lincoln Brigade there, it was our baby. We pledged to send an ambulance to Spain to the Republican Army. How did we raise the money? We raised it in small sums, each and every one participated. We used to have meals. Whatever profit we made that used to go to the Spanish War Relief. We had a fellow who would teach tennis and charge fifty cents a lesson and that money would go to Spain. People came to us from the railroad and from Indian Point. We made up that anybody that has a car should bring them here. Instead of taking a taxi, we'd take them back and forth, and charge fifty cents. That money was for Spain. Contributing an ambulance to the Spanish Republican Army feels good up until now. It's already more than forty years, but you still feel a certain satisfaction that you were part of it, that you did something.

The same thing was done for the Russian War Relief. We raised a lot of money. We sent medical books, we sent clothing, and we contributed. We were running around, breaking our backs, collecting clothing, bringing it here and there. And you feel even now that you didn't live only for yourself. This is the satisfaction that you live with as you get older. Even now as I get older, it makes it easier for me because I have that background.

Here I've got to visit somebody that is sick, here I've got to stay with somebody, here I've got to take somebody to the airport. Even people that are not so close to me, I know they are coming to New York by plane, and I know there is a certain feeling that instead of taking a taxi you come and see a face that you know, there's like a friendly hand reaching out to you. This gives you something to look forward to. It gives you satisfaction.

The rate when we started coming here was about seven and a half dollars a week for privileged campers and members. It was the depression years and people didn't have so much money. The reason for the attraction here was we had sport activities—

we had a baseball field, we had two tennis courts, and we had a volleyball court. In those days we had much younger people. As things got better, after the depression already, people got better jobs and they didn't want to come here anymore. Then started the crisis that hit us—beginning with the Paul Robeson concert in 1949. We found out the hatred of the neighbors during the Paul Robeson concert. They knew it was organized and they organized against us. Don't forget that around Peekskill the Ku Klux Klan used to burn crosses. Anybody black was taboo, and besides Robeson was a Communist. The main thing is they worked both. I was on the organization committee of the concert. The first concert was held and disrupted. The second concert had a steering committee to organize the concert. We would meet every week in a different house. We were afraid it would be disrupted.

First there was the question to get a place. After the first concert, we couldn't get a place to have it. There was a builder, a fellow by the name B. He was a liberal Jew, and he had land near Oregon Corners, and he said he's going to give us the land there. He sent in machines to bulldoze it and straighten up the land, and they put up platforms. That was about six miles from here. Naturally, we mobilized and we tried to get everybody to go. It was on a Sunday—it was the weekend of Labor Day—and we mobilized the whole community to go. Of course, we knew there was going to be trouble and we all said no small children should be brought there. Food we brought from our community. There was no water facilities there. We had sodas, we had a lot of sodas, we brought extra boxes of soda. Every car that went, we piled up the trunks with boxes of soda. As we went out, the neighbors that saw us said, "You dirty Communists." They kept on yelling, calling us all kinds of names, "Commies," curse words, "Jew bastard," and everything else. There was that hostile attitude, but we had no hostility to them.

At the beginning the concert was going all right, everything was kept in order, we put up a stand and we gave away soda for people who wanted to drink. The concert itself was really something. You had to witness it to get the enthusiasm of the people. But after the concert—going back—then they started. On the roads they hauled wheelbarrows of rocks and just put them away on the side. You would see the state troopers hold order, they would stay in the line, not to let them go across. But in the back they had the wheelbarrows and rocks, and they would just throw them on the cars as we were passing by. All the windows in my car were smashed. The top of the car was all dented from the rocks that they threw in. Some of the cars were turned over, and the cops were standing there, the state troopers, and they didn't do anything. People came with buses, and they went through the underpasses and there were people on the top with rocks prepared, and they threw down rocks on everybody. When we came back to the camp it was like coming from a funeral, it was a very sad situation. Food was prepared for us to eat, but nobody was able to eat, and all of a sudden we get a telephone call.

We had some scouts going around in bars to see what they planned, what was their next move—so somebody called us up that they heard them say in the bar that they're going to burn down the camp. So we started to alert everybody. I never had any fight with anybody and was never taught to fight or defend myself—I was chairman of the committee organizing to defend the place. I got pipes, half-inch pipes, cut them in pieces and distributed them to people, to go to strategic points to guard and see if anyone comes in, to start to fight with them. I came back about three o'clock in the morning. Nothing happened. I said to myself, "If somebody would have come over to me, they would kill me." I wouldn't even know how to fight. But still there was the spirit, not knowing, you don't even think of yourself, you think of the community. This was the spirit then.

Immediately after that we stopped dealing with Peekskill. We used to buy a lot of merchandise in Peekskill. Orders were given out not to patronize Peekskill. Even my insurance. I had my fire insurance from the bungalow. I called up Miss Moore, and I said, "Cancel the insurance." And I let her know we don't want to have anything to do with Peekskill. It seems that they suffered a lot. They were ashamed, and they didn't even want to talk about it because they claimed they were not responsible for what the hoodlums did. Not only our place, but all the surrounding communities boycotted against Peekskill. They suffered.

After the Paul Robeson affair, the place was branded a Communist camp because we were active. A lot of the so-called liberals shied away. The plain ordinary workers remained. But those others, they didn't want to be associated with it. For instance, in the school system if they thought you were a Communist, they threw you out.

The next couple of years, 1950, 1951, were not going so good anymore, the business was losing money. So we decided to turn the camp into a colony. In other words, to give up the business side of it, each one to do his own cooking in his own bungalows, and the camp bungalows to be sold. We sold all the bungalows that the camp had—we had private bungalows for the members and then we had camp bungalows that we used to rent out for the season or for weekends. We sold those bungalows for five hundred dollars apiece.

When the organization functioned as a camp, the relations was like one family, a very close family. You had to eat in the dining room three times a day. That made the people close. Even now, you see people that you meet twenty or thirty years later, "Oh, you're from the Followers?" They remember you, there was such closeness. It was like a close-knit family. Any time there was a light, it was never a question of being invited or asked to come in. You saw a light, you walked in. Even the outside people that came there for the weekend—those that rented for a day or a weekend or came for the week to stay there—they felt the same way. There were never any locks. Many times it was quite embarrassing—you're getting dressed, and people just walk into your house. They felt like it's one family. Something on the basis of a kibbutz.

People cooperated. The fact of the matter is that you had to contribute, you had to work for the organization. You felt that by your contributing, helping to make profit, the profit was turned over to improve the place. You had to fix the road, you had to put water in, there were a lot of expenses, and that profit was shared indirectly— indirectly you got a share of it—it was put back in the organization.

The spirit then was a little bit different than it is now, although the oldtimers that have been here for years still have the spirit, there's still certain things you can't do. Just to give you an example, we had a little bridge coming through our road. There was a big storm and the bridge broke and the trucks with the food couldn't bring it over to the camp. We had people that formed a human chain, and we carried the food up to the camp until we unloaded all the trucks. That couldn't happen today. Physically, it's an impossibility.

Working for the benefit of others enriched my life. Knowing that you are part of a community, you benefit. You can't only expect to take, you also have to give. You learn to live cooperatively. It's not only what you do, it's what you do for others that gives you satisfaction. Directly you don't benefit, but indirectly there is definitely a great satisfaction.

When I was politically active, at that time don't forget we didn't have any unemployment insurance, we didn't have any Medicare, we didn't have any social security. After going to demonstrations and getting your head chopped when the cops on horses were running after the people, we got unemployment insurance, we got social security, and we got Medicare. It may not be for the best, but we got something we didn't have before. In other words, we accomplished something.

Our main fight was always to have it better for our children. During our lifetime we see that our children live better than we did, and this is an accomplishment—

indirectly. I don't say that we did it, but indirectly they live a better life from the mere fact that we were fighting for it.

Of course we're not as active as we were before. We're much older, but whatever our possibility we do. We want to do something. Every year we make a collection and raise and distribute money to different organizations. The only thing is we don't want to expose ourselves on account of the McCarthy era. We don't know what's going to happen. During the McCarthy era people were afraid of their own shadow. You would get together three or four people in the house, you'd start to discuss politics, and people were afraid to talk. They were afraid to think or talk, because they didn't know who is going to listen. Everybody was afraid. The fact is even now in the Communist Party there are more FBI members than plain ordinary people. People are afraid. In the McCarthy era they were looking out in order to save their own skin. So there is a certain scare, even up to now.

At one time in the camp there was one way of politics—we were all oriented left. Now there is already left, and there is ultraleft, and there is nationalism—pro-Israel and against Israel, but there are no clashes because we don't make any political platforms. I happen to know someone who is an ultraleft man, and I don't object to him because he's of a different political opinion, but I tell him, "Listen, you have your political views, and there are people here of different political views. We don't want to make the social hall the platform for any political ideas." People are old—they are getting excited and they will get a heart attack. We just keep away from politics. You want to discuss personally, all right, but publicly, coming out on the stage and bringing in different parties, we don't do it.

I'll tell you, at one time in order to become a member they used to ask what kind of press are you reading. They wanted them to be reading the progressive press, which was a very foolish thing. A man has got a right to read. A man can be a very nice guy and read the *Daily News,* and a man can be a skunk and read the *Daily World.* It's besides the point. The character of a person does not mean what press he's reading. It's a question what kind of a person he is.

Now the only thing we try to find out is where the man was working, if he's still working, when he was working, what his record was as a union man, whether he was a scab or something like this. We don't want to have any people that would not be harmonious to the organization. This is what we are looking for.

When we were younger, we had certain ideals. We believed in socialism, that that will better the world. We felt the antisemitism going on in the capitalist world would be eliminated and we'll be equal with everybody, with the rest of the world, that there wouldn't be any distinction, Jew or Gentile. I have the same right to live like everybody else. We thought the Soviet Union was different from the capitalist world. But then we got disillusioned with the antisemitism in the Soviet Union.

Before we leaned more toward the Soviet Union, now we lean more toward Israel. The fact of the matter is the changes in Russia that were disclosed after Khrushchev's speech, what the Russians did to the Jewish press and the Jewish literature and how they killed some of the best Jewish writers. Naturally, that affected us and we felt that the only place we can look forward to is Israel. We thought there would be a solution for the Jewish people in Russia, since it's an international group and each one is alike. But it so happens that there is antisemitism. You feel that in Israel it's not the best. I do not believe that the system in Israel is the best there is. I would like to see a more socialist way of living there, but it's still Israel.

In 1966 I took a trip to the Soviet Union. I went there searching. In other words, I couldn't believe—I still thought that a lot of it was slandering. When somebody told me there was antisemitism in the Soviet Union, I didn't want to believe it because our belief was that the Soviet government is based on equality to everybody. I never said I wanted any privilege for the Jewish people. After going to the Soviet Union, I still am not against the system, I am against the people that are running it. I still would like to see that people should not live in poverty and people should be able to get everything they need, they shouldn't be exploited, but the way it's running there is no good. I couldn't believe that under a system of socialism there could be discrimination. I say that anybody that needs help, that stretches out their hand, you should help them. That's been my way of life. That's the way I was brought up by my mother.

I feel that I am healthier in spirit and physically from having an interest in other people, not only living for yourself. You can't have it always your own way. You have to give and take. Give and take. You live with a wife for close to fifty years, we have disagreements many times, but we don't have any fights. After all, no matter what it is, when you go to sleep at night you have to kiss her good night, no question about it. Life is too short. You may as well make the best of it, whatever it is. You've got to take the best out of life that you possibly can. Life is good. It's what you make it. How can life be bad? There's no such thing. If it's bad, you made it bad. To get the best out of life you have to do things for others. By people being selfish, just for themselves, that isn't the best of life.

Morris B.

Starting in the early thirties, maybe even earlier than that, in 1929, '30, when I still worked in the [fur] industry, whatever work there was, running around, being an active participant in various functions, I found out about an organization called Followers of the Trail. It was known as a left-wing camp. Some people called it a Communist camp. I considered myself a left-winger, which meant trying to obtain better conditions for working people, whether it was in my union or other people's. That's what made me a left-winger. I heard of a left-wing camp and prices were cheap—four and a half dollars for a weekend. I came here, spent a couple of weekends, and I enjoyed it. I liked the life here, the lectures, the entertainment. I had friends here. I knew the place quite well.

The Robeson affair was during the period when I used to come up to visit. I wasn't yet a member. Robeson was coming to sing in an open space, where there were literally thousands of people who were coming from all over to hear him. There was a ring of people standing guard, watching that it should not be broken up by hoodlums.

From our union, we had three busloads of people who wanted to come to the Robeson affair. They wanted to come to hear him sing. I had been placed in charge of those three buses to see that they get here and see that they get home. I think it was over a hundred and fifty people—I think it was sixty-some-odd people in each one. My Bess wanted to go too. I said, "No, you are staying home. I don't want you there, I think there might be some trouble." Robeson was known as a left-winger at the time. He was defending the Soviet Union, at every step, whatever he did, but still he was one of the top singers that we've ever heard. She wanted to go, but I said, "No, you better stay home. I'll go. If the press will be there you may hear it on radio." I was damn glad that I did not let her go.

We went through the concert beautifully, but on the way back the whole road from where that took place up until we reached Ossining, wherever there was an overpass on the road there were hoodlums standing on top with mountains of rocks, throwing them at the cars and buses. I had no way to go other than on the main road—Route 9. As we were driving back, there was one fellow sitting next to me— I'll never forget that. This fellow was a member of our union, and he was tall, a six-footer, and he was sitting on the side of the bus, in the front row, and I was on the aisle seat, also in the front row. "Morris," he said to me, "please do me a favor. You know, I'm long-legged. You know I can't sit in that corner. I can't stretch out my legs.

Would you mind swapping seats with me? Give me the aisle seat and I'll take that seat." I said, "Go ahead." I felt that logically he was right. I gave him that seat. As we went along, rocks kept flying towards the buses, and one rock went flying in through the windshield, broke the windshield and hit him in the eye. He was immediately with blood all over him and he began pulling it with his hands. I was afraid he'd ruin the other eye. I ripped off my shirt that I was wearing, tied it around his head and held it as tight as I possibly could, not to allow him to get there with his hands, to ruin his second eye, and I directed the bus driver to go to the hospital. We went in there and he did lose an eye.

I called up Bess, and I said, "Bess, I'm not coming home tonight. The concert is over." She said, "Yes, I just heard it on the radio, everything was fine. It's all over, everybody has left." I said, "Don't believe it. I saw Fascism at work. Don't believe it. I'm OK, there's nothing wrong with me, but one fellow was hit in the eye, and we're at the hospital. I'm going to stay over with friends because we're going to watch the entrances to the camp."

At that time, it was still Followers of the Trail. I came up—I knew some people, one of the business agents from my union had a bungalow here at that time. I came into his bungalow there and I put on a pair of pants that belonged to him and another shirt.

We expected trouble. We were worried that they may come up during the nighttime, from the back and all around. I joined the group and went down to watch the other end, in the back, where they could be coming up. We watched there until about two o'clock in the morning.

BESS: The next day he came back he was covered with glass that was imbedded into the scalp and I sat and picked little tiny slivers, little bits of things, because he couldn't wash his hair without first taking it out. In several hours, we got rid of it.

MORRIS: That was a happening in those days. During the McCarthy period they came in here and they called a number of our people also before the Dies Committee— it was a so-called Un-American Activities Committee. After that, the place was given up and it became Reynolds Hills, where each one owned his own bungalow, and decisions were made that there were no more political activities to go on here at all. As a matter of fact anyone who sold a bungalow and somebody new bought it, he had to appear before a membership committee for approval—that's the system in this colony, that the board has to approve all newcomers to make sure that they're decent people.

Each one is being told this is a community of bungalow owners, you are here to enjoy yourself, you are here to spend a summer vacation in peace and tranquility. We do not know and we don't care whether you are politically active on one side or another. If you are politically active do it where you live, but nothing here. We do not tolerate any political activities. I'm against any kind of activity that is political here—be it good or bad. We don't want to be put on a map that Reynolds Hills people are busy with this and that. We don't want to get on a new list. We know one thing, and I'm convinced of it—there is no McCarthy period now and there is no Un-American Activities Committee now, there is no McCarran business, but I am convinced that lists are still maintained, being built up, and sooner or later when reaction comes in, some organizations are going to be involved badly. And I don't want this organization to be involved.

At our entrance, they had anti-Jewish slogans and anti-Communist slogans, right here at our entrance. In times of reaction, all you need is some guy pulling in with a truck in the width of the entrance and we can't get out. A lot of trouble can occur.

BESS: We had a couple of people who took the *Daily World,* or maybe at that time it was the *Daily Worker,* and went down to the A & P and they put it into the trucks there.

MORRIS: People know that these people are here. They shop there all the time. They know they are from Reynolds Hills. Are we looking for that? I am very much worried, I don't want to get onto any list. I think that the lists continued. I think there are lists being made up continuously.

BESS: But even though politically there is a difference of opinion, it's still a large family. If anyone has a problem, it's our problem just as well. We're all concerned about one another.

MORRIS: There's one thing, that's true. It's a community of friends no matter how we feel politically. I remember an occasion when someone knocked on my door at five o'clock in the morning—politically it was like fire and water between the two of us. I could not stomach their politics. But the guy's sister was sick and I said, "Get a cloth on her and I'll be in front of the door." Within two minutes I was in front of the door and in the next three minutes I shot to the hospital, passing every red light, hoping that a cop would chase me, because if he did he would lead me to the hospital fast. He didn't, but in less than five minutes I was at the hospital and brought her there. We do things for one another knowing that it's one family no matter what.

BESS: And walking around at night, and not worrying about who is going to meet us.

MORRIS: We can walk out of here, twelve, one, two o'clock in the morning. We'll be sitting at a coffee klatch somewheres, walk out one o'clock in the morning and suddenly see someone coming with a flashlight. I am a thousand percent sure that the one who I am going to meet is one who I know and who knows me. No outsiders come in here and we are safe. So far, until now, this place has been the safest in the world. We feel that we are safe. No stranger will ever come up here. It's one family. It's unique in that respect.

That does not mean that people don't have political differences. There are people who have old opinions. There are some people here who are outspoken Socialists, there are some people who are outspoken Communists, and then there are people here who are on the right-wing of the labor movement, who were associated with the old Socialist Party as Socialists, and then there are people who are business people and ex-business people. We're all interested in having a colony where we can get together and have a concert or something going on on Saturday night, folk-dancing on Friday, other things during the week—sometimes we have a reading in the middle of the week when someone reads a section of a book or article and people discuss it, pro and con.

You know, it almost reminds me of the settlements that they have in Israel—the kibbutzim. Where they all work together, produce together. But here only the social life we have is similar to what they have—the cultural and recreational life here is similar to what they have on the kibbutzim in Israel.

This place was started on a shoestring. Young people started hiking and they wound up building something. The Peekskill area was known for having numerous colonies—bungalow colonies—a number of them gave up, they could not make a go of it. I think ours was about the only colony that still exists. It exists over fifty years, and it is making progress continuously. When our people came here, there wasn't a road, it was a path.

There were times I used to think it was Shangri-La. At one time I thought it was so ideal that everybody thinks alike, everybody is wonderful, and then when you get to know people better you get to know that nobody is perfect. No matter where you live, nobody is perfect.

My progressive tendencies, or so-called left-wing tendencies, have left me to a great extent because I felt that the rug was pulled from under me. At one time I believed in a socialist system of society. I looked upon the Soviet Union as the system to be followed by others, that will be followed by others. But the longer I saw this so-called socialism or communism at work, I realized that utopia doesn't exist. Utopia doesn't exist.

Originally, we thought that the muzhiks, or the uneducated Russian who has lived under the czar, he is imbedded with antisemitism and you outroot it. It will take a generation until these people die. The new generation which will grow up under a Communist system or a Soviet system will know better, especially knowing that there is a law against antisemitism on their books. But I see that after three generations—it now is sixty and some odd years after the Revolution—and you still have antisemitism there, and it's tolerated by the government, not only tolerated but sanctioned.

Every Zionist suddenly became a racist, and it's a new coinage of a word. The word Jew is eliminated from criticism in the Soviet Union, it is substituted by Zionist. When they want to say Jew, they say Zionist and with that they are getting away with it. After sixty-three years, I don't believe it anymore. I believe in a democratic system of society. I would believe in a socialist system of society if it can control itself to be socialist in one country. I still believe that the Soviet government, the Soviet system, will never be satisfied with running the Soviet Union alone. They will not be satisfied unless the whole world goes that way. And going that way means to hurt other people, until we can conquer them and rule them. To me, it's not as pure as I thought socialism or communism could be or should be. And I've lost interest in it. I have lost interest in the Soviet Union because my ideals were betrayed. During all these years when I was a lefty, almost ultraleft, I still believed that the Jew has a right to his own country.

My current political beliefs are progressive. I consider myself a progressive. I'm against reaction of any kind—left or right. I believe in a democratic system of society and I would push for all kinds of reforms. Like I once fought for unemployment insurance and social security. I still remember in the thirties when we had over a hundred thousand people in a demonstration fighting for unemployment insurance. And the government heard it, and unemployment insurance came out as a result of these demonstrations. I hate reaction, because I understand it too well. Reaction can come either from the left or from the right. I'm against reaction of any kind—left or right.

Anna T.

One of my brothers was a member of Followers of the Trail Camp. When he got married, he couldn't come during the summer, so he resigned and he left me his membership. I came in on his membership, It was an interesting way to spend the summers. You worked a whole week and you had something to look forward to, to go up to the country for a weekend. It was an interesting life for a worker to have a place to escape from the summer heat of the city.

With the Followers in Ardsley, it wasn't much. But from there, we bought the land in Peekskill, and we made a business out of it. It was a camp. People used to come to register for weekends, or for weeks—for their vacation. Some rented tents for the season. We charged them more than what we charged the members. We weren't prosperous, we just barely made it. But we were eager and we were willing. This was a cooperative endeavor, all working together. There was no question that one does more and one does less. It was beautiful cooperation. People with understanding and experience in their life—these people were all union organizers, strikers, and whatnot. They knew what the score was and they knew this was a beautiful life after a week working in the city. It was an escape.

What other way was there for a worker to get away for a weekend or for a week if you didn't have a place like this? You dind't have money to go somewhere and pay twenty dollars a week. We used to charge our members seven or eight dollars a week with food. Where could you get that? Naturally, we put a lot of work into it. We helped in the kitchen, we helped in the dining room. On Friday nights we used to come here, go into the kitchen and peel potatoes, wash the dishes, set the tables, and everything else—until we got bigger in the business and hired help for each individual part of the work, like cooking or washing dishes or washing floors.

We had a nice following—young, progressive people, educated people with understanding who felt that here was a place for them to be open for discussion of a higher level. We also had people that wanted to achieve. This was the platform for them to learn. Zero Mostel was one of our entertainers. Pete Seeger was one of our entertainers. They started in these camps where people appreciated them and they had an opening. They were free to work and it pulled them up to where they achieved professional stature.

We were in business for a long time. You know why we went out of business? During the McCarthy era, everyone who expressed a more or less broad-minded thought, a progressive thought, was labeled a Communist. During the period of Spain's Civil War, the camp had collected money for an ambulance, so we were branded. During the 1950s the young progressive element—teachers, students, lawyers—

stopped coming little by little because they were afraid. They stopped coming because we were labeled.

When they stopped coming, we couldn't go on with the business. We had a cook, we had a dining room. We had to keep it up. So we had to depend upon a different element—the people that used to go to the mountains, mothers with children. For them you had to have more comfort. We didn't have bungalows with toilets. We had tents. In rainy weather, when we had to go to the bathroom, we went outside to the bathroom. We weren't allowed to have any sinks in the tents. We had one general shower room and one general toilet for men and women—we didn't care, we were young.

There were rumors that it was prohibited to have children if you were a member of the camp. The thing is this—at the time of the depression, it was so hard to push yourself through without thinking of raising a family. What did you want a family for when you hardly had a piece of bread for yourself? Isn't it a crime to bring in a child and make him suffer and not to have enough? That trend lasted for quite a number of years, and some people tried to say that the camp did not recognize children, didn't want any children, and that's why the members of Followers of the Trail didn't have any children. But I think it had to do more with the period of the depression. That's what kept people from having families.

Once we started to sell the camp bungalows, it was a different attitude. If you have a bungalow, it's your place. If I want to mingle, I do. If I don't, I don't. We didn't know of such a thing before. We knew that everything has to be done communally—a concert, we have to be there; a meeting, we have to be there; peeling potatoes, we have to be there. The old timers had a different attitude toward the colony than the newcomers. It was our baby, we raised it, so we had a different feeling. Even in the city, most of us were friends, so wintertime we were together too.

When we started we were poor people. Poor workers. That's why we had to do everything ourselves to bring it up to where it was. And we appreciated it, we lived so communally. When new people came in they can't have that attitude toward communal life that we had. We didn't know any other way. They never knew it. Then a lot of our people got settled in Florida. That started at least fifteen years ago—they started to shuttle back and forth, for the summer here and the winter there. Then, because of advanced age, a lot of people stopped coming back North. They found it too difficult. So there were more bungalows for sale. Now a new element came in—a nice element, a nice element—but they don't somehow click together, mainly politically. The people that are coming now are people with money—$20,000 a bungalow, $25,000 a bungalow. Some are still working, some are retired and have a nice income, like us—I'm not so poor as I was then; I'm not rich because I'm not working for so many years, but I wouldn't say I'm as poor now as when I was working.

Not that the newcomers are worse—they may be more intelligent, more educated one way or the other way. I don't know. But now there's a big rift in this colony politically. If you're for Israel, you're no good. Or, if you read the *Daily World*, you're no good. And we have nothing to do with one another. Why am I going to talk to him? To fight? I can't bring in politics because it's not healthy. Is it good? No it isn't. But that's the way it is. You can't change it.

When it was communal, it was more interesting. It was a united interest, a united effort, a united striving to accomplish something—that's what it was all those years. We weren't anxious to come from New York on a Friday night, roll up our sleeves and go into the kitchen to peel potatoes. Was that an ideal for us? Behind that was the ideal. We all did it together, we all wanted something better. In order to achieve something better, you've got to work communally. I think you can always accomplish more communally—better understanding, more human relationships, without looking down on one another. I don't see any disadvantages in a nice, united communal effort. You can't look down on one another when you work together. If something you're doing is wrong, I correct it without any malicious feelings—because I want you to do better for the community.

But over the years we had a big turnover and there isn't such a united effort as there was or such an amicable crowd that understood one another. Even some people that were here twenty years ago are really not ideologically the same anyway. They claim that the Soviet Union isn't right. They claim that Israel is everything, and that every Jew has to fight for Israel, which we do. But we don't have to say that because it's Israel, everything is right. There is right and wrong. They don't see wrong. If it's Israel, it's right.

I am very happy about the State of Israel—absolutely. I'm not happy with the government, but I am happy with the state. I think we need our own state just as well as any other nationality, but I am not happy with the government—they're not doing the right thing. Zionism does not have to fight socialism, and socialism does not have to fight Zionism. We could have our own country, but we could be on a progressive basis. We have to deal with facts. We can't become a terrorist organization.

We can't occupy land. We have to give up something for the sake of peace. You want to have a land without wars, you have to make peace with the enemy. That's the only thing I'm against, but I'm surely not against the land of Israel.

I still feel my old ideals that I strived for are the correct ones. Striving for a better world, replacing capitalism with something better. But now I have more understanding. I understand the Soviet Union more now than when I came to this country, because then I knew very little of what it stood for. I understand the Revolution in the Soviet Union and the life there more now; for the simple reason that I lived there so little and I understood so little of it that I couldn't assess the big achievement that was won there like the people that really waited for that break. It didn't impress me, because I did not know enough then. As I grew older and became more active in various organizations, and began understanding life—political life, social life, and economic life—I started to understand the significance of the Revolution, what it stood for, and what it stands for now.

I think the Soviet Union stands now for what it stood for then, though other people believe it's not what it's supposed to be. Maybe there are some shortcomings, but I think the life in the Soviet Union—the politics of the Soviet Union—is the future of the world. Each period has its time and one is replacing the other, within time, something will replace capitalism. And within a length of time, whatever replaced capitalism will be replaced, too. The Soviet Union is not Communist yet. Communism will replace the present system of the Soviet Union. When, I don't know, but it can't stay.

In the United States, we are not going to get communism that fast. It will be taken over by the Soviet system—by socialism. You can't get communism before socialism. You start with the fact that the capitalist country, especially our country, is going to the dickens. In every phase of life—economically, socially, materially, every phase. They're just sinking. They don't know what to do to improve it. But the people are not quite ready. You can't make it just because the capitalist system isn't working right, you can't make the masses get up. They have to be educated first. They have to go through a little bit more hell.

We had a much more active element during the depression. People then were fighting for everything. You just couldn't fool them. They knew that they need work and they went on marches to Washington—there was a hunger march. If a grocery raised a penny on a pound of bread, there was a picket line right away, because people were so militant, they were so angry, they were so deprived of a piece of bread that they couldn't afford to let things go against them. The landlord raised a dollar on a month's rent, there was a picket line. During the time after the Second World War people became more or less affluent and the country became—our country, your country—the biggest in the world. They had enough to help everybody else and their own regardless of how many millions of people there were always unemployed. The people forgot about the bad times, because everything was smooth, people made a living. They got cars, and they have houses, and they have good positions, and they have education.

Now they are losing it—the unemployment is tremendous, things are going wrong, our big country is not big anymore. The rest of the world does not accept America as the leader of the world—because she isn't, she is losing ground. The United States is really groping in the dark, from my little point of view. We don't work with a plan. Did you ever hear of a plan in the United States that this five years we are going to do this or that and try to achieve it? They don't work with a plan. There is a depression and you can't meet the city's budget, so you lay off a million workers. What are the workers going to do? They are going to go on relief. That pocket that pays relief has nothing to do with the system of the city to meet the budget, so they don't care. So they close hospitals, they close nurseries, they lay off firemen and policemen. So what happens? There's more robbery, there's more mugging, there's more killing, there's more fires. And when you have a fire, and they need help for a fire someplace else, that help is not there. Why? Because they haven't got enough workers to meet the budget. Is this a plan? Everything is going to the dickens, but the people aren't ready. They still have two cars in the garage and they still have homes and they still have good jobs. Those that haven't, haven't got the leadership—somehow, they lost the leadership.

You don't hear it in the air that people want to revolt or make a picket line because somebody raised the rent. In the old years, there were so many dispossesses from houses—everybody got together. The landlord put out the furniture and the rest of the people got together and put it back in. They're not going to fight it now that much because they are still not that depressed. So you can't get communism in the United States. Forget about it. You can't even get socialism that soon. We have to wait for worse times.

My earlier progressive attitudes are getting stronger as I'm getting older. I'm not more militant. I don't live in a false dream that because I understand the political situation better now I am more active. I'm not. I passed this stage. I can't contribute too much. As much as I can, I do, but it's not too much. I'm not active now, but I understand the political situation now much better, let's say, than I did twenty years ago. I am more assertive with my ideas. I know more what is right and what is wrong. Whether it's in my power to change it is another story.

I enjoy my life now because I have more leisure to myself. Now I don't have to punch a card and I don't have to compete with anybody in the factory anymore, and I don't have to run in the morning in the snow to catch a train. I don't have to do that. I enjoy what I am doing because I'm doing what I want. There are a lot of things I would like to be doing and I don't do, but what I do, I enjoy. I know I'm getting older but I don't feel old. I still have my desire to go and to see and to be entertained and to entertain and live a full life, which I couldn't do when I was younger. I didn't have the money and I didn't have the time.

The camp helped me enjoy my older life. I feel well because I had a healthy life all those years here in the country—living more outdoors and worrying less about what to do and where to go. Otherwise, we probably would have been in the city most of the time. I think it gave us an understanding of how to enjoy our life.

I don't see much of a future for the camp. You've got to have a younger element. As people get older, these people will within time die. We do have a lot of deaths by now—and some will give up because they find it too hard financially or too monotonous. But we need a younger element to perpetuate the camp. I would like to see the colony change to a younger element in order to exist, because the older the people get the less interest they have. How much can you travel back and forth? You reach a certain age, you can't have a car. And without a car—we know what it means without a car—you are lost. But within time, these people will be replaced. I hope that younger people will replace them. It may not be on the same basis that it was built—it couldn't be. They cannot have that feeling of cooperativeness.

We started here from a very, very mediocre endeavor. When we put in a light and a small burning stove, we were already advanced because before we couldn't do it. Then we became so advanced that we were talking about air-conditioners in the houses. So I think we accomplished quite a bit without making plans—five-year plans or three-year plans. We did the things that we could afford at the particular time. If next year we had to do something else, we did something else. We did the most imperative things that we had to do now, and whatever things came along that we could do next year, we did it that way.

The colony was very successful in building up to the extent that we did. I think we were very successful economically and socially—we were having a hell of a time here all the time. Economically, we worked so cooperatively. When money was needed for something, there was no problem that one would give and one wouldn't give. We all shared. Taking the size of the group that we were, in building a beautiful colony like that, I think we were very successful.

I have no regrets. I enjoyed my life here. We had a beautiful life, socially, economically, and spiritually. We had a lovely life here.

Max T.

I met my wife right here in Peekskill on July second, 1933. We got married in 1934. I never heard of this camp before that. We were four men—one was a Spanish fellow who was an automobile mechanic, so he had a car—and we would just ride around. We visited Camp Nitgedaiget maybe once, maybe twice, and some other places. Then someone said, "You know, there is a camp called Followers of the Trail." So we came here and looked around.

It was a rainy, nasty day, and we were hungry. We came into the dining room but it was already after dinner. It so happened that there was a man there who was the manager, and he made sandwiches for us. I found out later that that manager was Anna's brother. She was sitting in the corner, reading a book. I met her and we started to talk. We made a date to meet at a club in the city. Then we made another date, and another date. And it didn't take long—we got married.

Anna and I put a tent up on the other end from where we are now. It was a nine-by-nine floor, about five feet off the ground. We bought a used army tent and put it up there. It was quite convenient. I bought two cell batteries, with a couple of wires, and I made electricity with a little flashlight bulb. So we had sufficient illumination to make the bed or to get dressed or undressed.

We were all attracted to the camp because of its communal life. We lived together, we were in the fresh air together. On the weekends, when we came, there was dancing Saturday nights, there were lectures on Sundays. And people who stayed here during the week didn't idle around either. There were cultural activities for those that stayed during the week—whether they stayed for a week or two or a month. We had the facilities, and a social director, and educational programs.

As far as Anna and I were concerned, we were both working and we found it quite difficult to pay for membership. In the very beginning the dining room was open and they needed waiters, so we volunteered as waiters and we were given our meals free. Then eventually we were also given a dollar for each meal that we served. We became steady waiters—serving five meals during the weekend, and that paid our way of staying here.

The camp was in business for a number of years to be able to pay the mortgage on the land. We used to rent out tents for the weekends and also for weeks or months. We had members and privileged campers, who used to rent places for the entire summer but they were not members. And there were always activities here. When it came Saturday after supper, we had to put the tables to one side in the dining room and wash the floor. There was a little platform in the back of the dining room which we used as a stage, and then we had our entertainment and cultural activities.

The social life was nice, with people of the same ideology—people with the same purpose in life. During the Spanish Civil War, we had groups of people that were formed to collect money to support the Spanish Loyalists. We sent an ambulance to Spain in 1936. In 1941, when the Soviet Union was attacked by Hitler, there was a question of opening up the Second Front. There was a big movement here for opening up the Second Front. Bonds were sold right here from the dining room supporting England, France, and the United States—the so-called democratic countries that were fighting on the side of the Soviet Union. We were buying United States bonds. A lot of people invested an awful lot of money here.

After the War, during the McCarthy era, we noticed that the attendance was becoming less and less in the camp for the simple reason that there was already the stigma that this was a left-wing camp. I remember the Paul Robeson concert in Peekskill. I was there. It was a pogrom. A lot of cars were smashed up. We had to patrol this entire area. For the first two years after it happened, we actually boycotted the Peekskill stores. People were bringing things from New York. We just didn't buy here and that's all there was to it. Not that I mean to say that we didn't have some people that used to shop there anyway, but at least 90 percent didn't. But then, in the third year, we started to come in, and the response on the part of the salesgirls were, "They are coming back."

During the McCarthy period, people were afraid to come here because of the Red Scare. People were scared. For no good reason at all, you were summoned to the Committee to answer questions. Finally, a general of the army destroyed the image of McCarthy, but it was too late for our camp. We saw that we were losing money and people didn't come out anymore, so we decided that it would be the best thing to convert the place into a colony. People started to buy bungalows, to build bigger bungalows, and to put in equipment like running water and toilets.

Sometimes now I wonder which way is better. Today I can sit down at my table in my house and have my lunch and supper in peace. Before, I had to stay in line to enter the dining room and be part of three hundred guests, with all the turmoil. We couldn't take it now. The idea is that when you are young—younger, I should say— you can take the noise of a big crowd much easier than when you become advanced in years. Now I would say that the kind of life we are living under this phase of the colony treats us all very well. I think the choice we made, partly of necessity because of certain circumstances that developed in this country, was also good because of the advancement in age on the part of our members.

As far as sociability is concerned, I think the occasional get-together at the casino, whether it's once a week or twice a week, or for various other functions, is very healthy. It's not repetitious to the extent that we should get on each other's nerves like we used to at the time when we had big crowds three times a day for breakfast, lunch, and supper. So it's pretty good.

Over the years, the membership has changed, also because of circumstances. I remember that the entrance fee for membership in the Followers of the Trail was twenty-five dollars. Then it was fifty dollars. Now, if I'm not mistaken, it's seven hundred fifty dollars. And it might even go up to one thousand dollars. Economically, people that come into this colony at the present time have to be ready to invest quite a sizeable sum of money, beginning with ten thousand to fifteen and sometimes a little bit more than twenty thousand dollars. Naturally, this has to come from families that can afford to do it. Most of the people that come in now are either small businessmen or retired people who have succeeded in accumulating capital. They are giving up their apartments in New York to buy a summer home in our colony, and they buy probably also a condominium in Florida to spend the winter. So, all in all, if you want to buy something here now, you have to be more or less well-heeled.

The camp was very successful originally when all the people that were here were more or less with the same mind and goals. But when people begin to think in different directions, it's already a little different. For some people here now we became a sedate old-age home, where property takes priority over everything that's going on in the world. There are people here now who don't even read the newspaper. They get their checks, they probably get interest from their bank accounts to supplement their income from social security, and they have sufficient money to live on. What are they going to do? Make a revolution? They say, "Am I going to reform the capitalist system? Not necessary. My job is done already. I accumulated money and I'm now living on it. Let my kids worry."

Also, if you are honest about communal living, without taking advantage of one another, it is a wonderful thing. But if one wants to benefit or take advantage, then it's not communal life anymore. That happened here to a certain extent. It happens with some people that don't know what it means to live in a community. In a system of society where dog eats dog, if a group of people get together and want to isolate themselves from the ills of the society that surrounds them, if they can manage it, it's all right. Here we lived for years on a communal basis. At times people began to have differences that one is abusing the other one—that one is using too much electricity, using too much water, this and that. Some said, "Why should I pay for the swimming pool? I don't even go near it." You live in a system where you are forced to pay for what you use, not what you don't use. So you don't want to pay. You see? It's simple. Or, it was pointed out that there is one person that leaves five or six electric heaters on over the winter so as to keep his walls from cracking. That's taking advantage. That's not cooperating. That's being a parasite. But this is a subject for the board of directors to discuss.

Then there are certain improvements to be made in this—colony, if you want to bring it to a certain degree of comfort—the roads that are running through the camp will have to be resurfaced eventually, and the electrical lines will have to be improved in order to put in air conditioning. But this will require money and there are people here that will not be able to meet these obligations. You see, I am satisfied the way it is, but my next door neighbors may not be satisfied the way it is. If they are the majority and they levy a thousand dollar tax on me, I'm choked. I can't afford to do it.

So what's going to happen? Those that cannot afford will eventually go out. Each one will get a deed, they will build the homes to their liking, they'll have the township come in here to clean the roads of snow. I don't see it happening now, but it can happen five years from now, it can happen ten years from now. I don't know when, but it seems to me that this is going to happen. Or, another thing can happen. It can reach a point where everybody will get disgusted to the extent that they will want to sell the whole goddamn thing and forget about it. This can happen also, but it is unlikely.

Politically now, we are also all different. We have reached a stage where our convictions are set. We argue, but each one is entitled to his or her views. We are mature people. You cannot convince anyone to think differently. People with an open mind, who read papers, and follow events will formulate their own outlook on life and see in which direction history is taking people and the world. If I would try to discuss certain subjects with someone without any realization of what the world situation is, it will not hold water. Definitely not. We have to objectively discuss the situation—if you want to discuss it at all—and each one has a right to his own opinion. World history will prove who is right and who is wrong. And that's all there is to it.

When Khrushchev exposed Stalin in 1956 some people here found it very convenient to ease themselves away from the movement. They found an excuse. When the Hitler-Stalin pact was signed, they could not understand it, so that gave them an excuse to say, "Well, look, Stalin made a pact with Hitler—there is no difference." When Khrushchev exposed Stalin and the cult of personality, they didn't understand the implications of it. They found an excuse to ease themselves out from the movement.

About two years ago, we had a cocktail party right in front of the casino. I asked a group of people point blank: Supposing Israel was a socialist country, would you still support it?" They told me yes, and I knew that they are lying. If Israel was a socialist country, they would not support it, because they are social-democrats. They are against socialism.

I can understand the reason why some people became adherents to the formation of Israel, and I am one of those who would like to see Israel prosper and become a haven or a defender of the Jewish people in the world, after what we have found true through the years of antisemitism and the holocaust in Germany. The only thing that is questionable is the foreign policy of Israel, and some people agree with and some people disagree with the foreign policy. I wholeheartedly disagree with the present political policy of Israel. But I would say that Israel has to live—definitely. There is no question about it. On the other hand, Israel has to see that her neighbors should enjoy the same privileges that I would like to see Israel enjoying.

Personally I think—and I base it on analysis by people that know better than I—that the policy that Israel is pursuing now is detrimental to its very existence. I want Israel to exist. So how the hell can I go ahead and support a policy when I know that it will lead to its destruction? How can I support a policy that is looking for expansion of territory and persecution of minorities? To me, it sounds like Hitler started out the same way. I hope I'm wrong, but I don't think I am. They forget that the Palestinians were chased out of there in 1947, I think it was, or in 1948, when Palestine was divided between Israel and the Palestinians. It was a division that was supported in the United Nations. They are afraid that if the PLO will occupy the West Bank there will be a progressive government in there. For that matter, the PLO should be afraid of who will be their neighbor.

According to the *Freiheit*—I don't buy it, it just happend to fall into my hand—there is a very big danger of Fascism in Israel. The *Freiheit* was supposed to be the Jewish organ of the Communist Party, but it has drifted away. If you are an anti-Zionist—if you are against the Zionist ideology—you are antisemitic. That's how they put it. There is the whole thing in a nutshell. When you hear a thing like that, and the editorial says so in the *Freiheit*, how the hell can you agree with it? You just can't. I don't know enough of Lenin to say that Novick, the editor of the *Freiheit*, is misquoting Lenin. But I know he is because I know it on very good authority. He is quoting him out of context, and a lot of times I detect a lot of lies. They say that they are not against the Soviet Union, but if they are not against the Soviet Union, why are they supporting all the reactionary elements who are against the Soviet Union?

Some people become disillusioned because the things that they were fighting for did not happen in their lifetime. They do not understand that history, no matter how fast it moves, is not fast enough to satisfy the short span of an individual's life.

When I left the Soviet Union, I knew exactly what the Revolution was about and what they were trying to do, but I didn't have a chance to actually live under it. Life at that time was hard. It was very hard. The peasants did not cooperate with the Revolution. The middlemen did not cooperate. A lot of people did not cooperate. There were speakers sent to every little hamlet in the Soviet Union to talk to the people, to do propaganda on the part of the Bolsheviks, to explain what the Revolution is. As good as it was, it wasn't good enough because the reality wasn't there yet. You had to wait until it developed.

You know, when you cut up material for a pair of pants you have a piece of cloth. You don't know what the hell it's going to be. It looks good, but maybe it will fit and maybe it won't fit. It takes time. When you put it together, you think it's all right, but no—it's a little bit too long or a little bit too short. I'm simplifying it, but it was the same thing with the Revolution. Some people did not cooperate because they didn't understand what it was. It was unique. There were revolutions before, but they had different characters.

If we had a revolution in this country, with the technological advances that we have, if we went ahead and started working in a socialistic system—in other words, not for private appropriation, but for the good of the people—then we would have absolutely no problem here. We wouldn't have to start from scratch the way they started in Russia. The only thing is, will they give it to you? If a worker owns two or three shares of General Motors, he is psychologically against any changes, because he will lose his stocks. He becomes part owner of the establishment and values property above human beings. When you have an ideology of this sort, then you have to accept the society as it is. But how long can we accept it? Maybe smarter people will come later and say we were wrong and will try to make changes.

We live in a world where there is so much wealth that there is enough for every-body. Why should some expropriate it and squander it while some others find them-selves in dire need and are starving? If you read the *New York Times* you are going to get all this information. And if I am incriminating the *New York Times* for being a radical paper, well, I am not writing the editorials and I am not writing the dis-patches. I am not even a partner to the *New York Times*. I pay a quarter for it and I get my information. Take nuclear power under this system. We live in Peekskill, right near the Indian Point plant. It's dangerous. Definitely dangerous. One engineer right here in the colony said that when they put down the foundation to construct a building, there is already a violation. Once you have that, how the hell can you trust building an atomic energy plant safe enough for the people that work inside and for the sur-rounding area? When there is a question of saving money and cutting corners, you can't. Under a different system of society, where the profit motive is not there, then it's a different orientation. Then it may be safe. Accidents can happen, but not one after another—like we have here Con Edison, and we read about Three Mile Island in Pennsylvania, and somewhere in the West. There's no reason for it.

The government is not too responsible to elderly people. Our mayor's heart is bleeding for me, but he says, "What can I do? I have no money." He has no money to give me an extra five bucks a month I should be able to live a little better? He's concerned for me as a senior citizen who made so many contributions in building up the country and paying taxes? It's a lot of hypocrisy. They are not concerned. They are not concerned for the elderly.

The attitude of young people toward the elderly depends on their understanding of life itself. If they don't understand it, they begin to resent the old people. If I was Bernard Shaw, I would be respected, even if I would express a very unpopular view. But, you see, elderly people are former contributors to society—they helped build society, they were part of it—and as such they should not only be respected, but they should be provided with everything that they need during the period of their golden age. Is it working out like that? But that's the system, and that's the way it is. It's too late for the elderly.

Now I'm seventy-five. Sometimes you want the days to pass fast, and sometimes you say, "Well, it's so late already and I didn't accomplish anything." But, for that matter, I am a retired man. What do I want to accomplish? I'm not building anything. I'm not constructing anything. I retired when I was sixty-two and a half. I retired from the same job that I did ten years before—sewing on a machine, and that's it. I was counting the years, I was counting the months, the weeks, the days, and the hours. I will tell you why. The type of work that I did—handbags—was a means to an end, to get my pay on Friday (or whenever the day was) to meet my expenses and live on it, to buy a book, to buy a record, to buy a stereo. But I was glad to retire for the simple reason that instead of working in a stuffy place with a lot of dust and a lot of roaches—the sanitary conditions were bad—I was able to get out and greet the fresh air.

I know people who are afraid to retire. They don't know how they are going to utilize their leisure time. They may have a point there, but as time goes on they have to realize that eventually they will not be able to do this work anymore. So why not take the best of the good years when you can still do it, instead of reaching a point when you can't do it. Sometimes you get bored. I have plenty of things to do, but sometimes you get bored. I read (not too much now because my eyes are not too good), I listen to music (I have a good stereo in the house), I have a good black and white television, I take pictures once in a while, and I have friends up to the house and I show them my slides, my prints.

Years back we used to take our friends from the camp in the summertime back to New York in the wintertime. It's a little different now because we still go to New York while most of our friends from the camp are going south to Florida. At one time I made an attempt to go to Florida, but it didn't work out. Anna doesn't care for Florida. She doesn't like the whole life there. She likes the four seasons—she likes winter, she likes the snow. You sit in the house and look out of the window, and you enjoy the beauty of black and white. It's beautiful. It's nice.

We have a fine group of people in the place where we live now in Co-op City. We find ourselves very comfortable with them, and they find themselves very comfortable with us. We go to the movies once in a while. You know, at least for me, when you reach a certain age a movie doesn't satisfy you anymore. You want something bigger than that. So you turn to music. Four times a winter we have the broadcast direct from the Metropolitan Opera house on channel thirteen. It comes through beautifully, like sitting in the theater itself. We visit the Metropolitan Museum of Art. We have lectures on art in Co-op City in the library. We have archeological exhibits there. We have lectures on trade unionism. If you want to participate in it, it's all right.

Let's put it this way. If I would say I would like to do mountain climbing, then my age would bother me. But it's not realistic. I'm past the age where I can do that. You have to realize that you just can't do it. So you don't have to feel sorry for yourself. Why didn't I do it thirty years ago, forty years ago? I never feel sorry for myself. Perhaps one time I said to myself, "Maybe I should have done this. Maybe I should have done that." Maybe. And then again, maybe not.

My goal now is only that people should live in a warless society as brothers and sisters. I would not like to be young again now. But it's just that there is so much to expect from the future, I'd hate like hell not to be present to see it.

Reva Y.

I heard about the camp, Followers of the Trail, in 1933. Truthfully speaking, I decided to live here because I met a friend and she told me about a place where you didn't have to do any cooking, where there was a dining room. At that time, I had a bungalow somewhere else, and I had about sixteen friends who used to come without letting me know, and I had to put them up to sleep sometimes overnight. It was much too hard on me. So when my friend told me there was a place where you don't have to cook—you get your meals—we came to see it. Immediately we decided to take a tent. What attracted me most was the dining room, but then, of course, we found a few people that we knew. I wasn't the only one in the camp who belonged to the Party, but I don't know how many did.

We didn't have a nucleus here. I belonged to the Party in New York. You know, at one time the Communist Party had quite a lot of votes.

I used to attend other camps—we had Unity Camp, Camp Nitgedaiget. We used to go there for vacations. But somehow I found more togetherness at Followers of the Trail. Most of our people here were not professionals. The professionals came later. The colony started with trade union people, people that worked in the dress trade or the fur trade. They were seasonal workers. Also it was cheap. You used to pay eight dollars a week and you got your three meals a day and two meals on Sunday. There was a communal dining room. There was a steady cook and a manager, but the waiters were volunteers. I was a waitress, and then we used to get meals free on weekends. We had a big tent, with a three-quarter bed, a dresser, some chairs, and a closet for clothes. We also had a little porch—we'd go up the steps to the porch. It was a nice size tent.

During the McCarthy period, people in the colony had to take out all the books and hide this and that—not to have any Communist materials. We had people coming around here snooping. They more or less knew what it was like here in the colony. During the Spanish Civil War the colony was raising money for an ambulance. We had raffles and we had dinners—whatever way we could raise money, we did. We bought an ambulance and we presented it. But especially after the Paul Robeson concert, they watched the camp. Being a Jewish community and progressive did not help.

I personally was not affected during the McCarthy era, but a lot of my friends were blacklisted. They were in the movie industry in California, and they were blacklisted. They couldn't write on their own name. Some of them even committed suicide. We were very close to the writer's movement. My husband used to write. He wrote for the *Freiheit* and the Jewish magazines, and we used to have a writers' circle in our house. The John Reed Club—American writers on the left—met in our house. Whatever the right cause was, I was for it.

However, now in the colony there are other groupings. It's no longer one complete group of people that formed with the same ideology, the same opinions, the same everything. There are now about three groups. I would say that's due in general to the condition of the country and the world. Politically, we're on opposite sides.

The fact is we have a Jewish newspaper, the *Freiheit,* and we have the *Daily Worker*—the *Daily World* it's called now. Both are supposed to be Communist newspapers, right? But the *Daily World* will attack the *Freiheit.* Why? Because the *Freiheit* comes out with an article where it disagrees with the Soviet Union's position, or is for Israel, or is against the antisemitic books that were published in the Soviet Union.

When Israel came into the picture, that created quite a bit of tension. The opposite side, the anti-Zionists, call everything "Zionist." I'm not a Zionist, I'm a Jew. I am beginning to feel more Jewish than I ever did before because of the conditions in the country. I am being actually provoked, you could say. I am Jewish. You can't take this away—it is my identity, because I am being pointed out all the time. And yet I am not a Zionist. Every Jew is considered a Zionist and that's not so. That is the thing that I actually resent. I think Israel has a right to exist and there is no reason why we have to fight. In 1948, when Israel was formed, at that time I began to feel it had a right to be its own country. But there was a time when I did not feel that way.

It's the Jewishness that took over for me. Disillusionment came after Stalin began to throw people into jails and kill people. When you hear about Jewish writers and about mind doctors, and that Jewish theaters were abolished, and there were no more schools, you become disillusioned. I just read yesterday that they're going to open some Jewish schools in Birobidzhan, which was once a Jewish town. There are fifteen thousand Jews there now and they are going to open schools for them. They have to import all their books. There is not a grammar book, a textbook, in Jewish. Not one book. Now, what happened to all the books? This was a completely Jewish town, everything was Jewish. They abolished the Jewish theater, they abolished the Jewish literature, they abolished Jewish everything. The main disillusionment came during the Stalin period, but even now there are things coming up in the Soviet Union. Antisemitic books are being published there, and they wouldn't dare to publish books like this if the government wouldn't publish them. So this is something that hurts. It's very disappointing—more than disappointing.

Then, there are so many rivalries even in the Communist Party—take the Italian Communist Party and the French Communist Party and the Romanian Communist Party. And then there is China. Two Communist countries, and they are fighting each other. I could not agree with the Cultural Revolution in China. I don't think they were doing the right thing, arresting people and all that. I was at that time against it. There was a lot of disillusionment.

The fact is, I just read an article that last year at Cooper Union there was a gathering of groups—Communists, Socialists, various other groups. And with all the groups, they couldn't come to any kind of place to form one party whereby we would have some sort of vote. We probably don't have the right leadership that could be united and come up with one ideal. I have great regard for the Italian Communist Party, but even there you have the Red Brigades that are doing a lot of damage and are not helping the movement by assassinations and by whatever else they do. They are hurting the Party, hurting the government, hurting the country. There are an awful lot of splinter groups. And this is what the trouble is.

So in the colony we also argue about these things. The communal atmosphere is still present, but a lot of it is missing. A lot of new people came and these people are not the same as the people we had in the beginning. We were pioneers. The relationship is close, but maybe it could be a little closer. There might be better understanding. The colony was successful in bringing people together and forming friendships. There are advantages to communal living as far as togetherness. But we all have our habits and our ways of doing things. We have to be more tolerant of one another. But as you grow older, it's important to have a group of people—not to be alone.

I believe that for elderly people especially it is important to have friends. It's wonderful to have family, but family is not always there. Friends are more important even than family. And this colony achieved that. You have a circle of friends and you are together. No matter what comes, they are there. Let me make this clear. You cannot start getting friends when you're at this age. You have to nourish friends. You have to develop that relationship much younger. My sister did not do this, and now she is lonely. She can make an acquaintance here and there, but that's about all. In order to have friends, you have to start much, much earlier—thirty years before you become a senior citizen. This is my feeling.

If senior citizens could get together and form a colony like this where they could have cultural entertainment and relationships with each other, that would help a lot. But that depends on economic conditions. Don't forget, this is only a summer home. You live here only for four months, and you have to keep up another home. It's quite an expense. In the earlier years, it was much cheaper. In the first place, when we had tents, there was no question. Now we have maintenance—it costs quite a bit of money. I can figure myself about two thousand dollars. If you have to pay that just for four months and you pay rent the rest of the eight months, what do you do then?

The problem for senior citizens now is mostly economic. Some of the senior citizens really don't have enough. The other thing is the fear that they'll live alone, and the fear of getting out of your home. In New York, or wherever you'll be, you're afraid to be on the subway, you're afraid to get out of the house. Senior citizens are prisoners in their own homes, and that's what makes people become senile—they have no friends and they can't communicate.

I think my life is richer than other elderly people—culturally and maybe even physically. Other people are not well. I'm physically pretty well. Part of this comes from the style of living—enjoying life, having a lot of good friends, having a wonderful son, doing the things that you want to do—and being able to do, that's important. I think growing older is also the nature of the person—how you look at things, how you take things. How you take grief has a lot to do with it.

The main thing for the senior citizens, I think, is they should be active. They should meet other people, socialize, and not just stay by themselves. I have different activities in the city and in the colony. In the city there are lectures, concerts, and other things. In the colony I'm busy being on the board. And as chairman of the entertainment committee I have to arrange entertainment for the summer. You have to be occupied. You have to get up in the morning and have things to do—not just to sit.

There are still a lot of problems in this country. The United States is chaotic right now. I went recently to the demonstration against the Indian Point plant. The problems are not all that different than they were before, but there has to be a strong voice to impress the government. The best time in this country was when Roosevelt was president, although I have something against Roosevelt also—that he did not do anything about saving some of the Jews during the holocaust. I remember distinctly, a boat came and was sent back. I was giving birth at the time, because I remember I was in Columbia Presbyterian Hospital and the boat was there all the time. The boat was sent back and what happened is they were all exterminated. A lot more should have been done.

Some of our Jews here didn't do enough either. They could have put more pressure on the government. The mistake was that the Jews in the United States did not believe what was happening. They weren't informed and they just couldn't believe that there could happen things like this—that six million Jews could be exterminated just like this. And maybe that's why there was a lack of initiative of doing something about it. Here and there, there was in the paper something about concentration camps and what was going on. But they just couldn't imagine that children were being taken and thrown right into ovens. Nobody could believe that it could happen in the twentieth century, in the civilized world, so to speak. However, they should have been more aware of it, they should have looked more into it. There was definitely a failure on the part of Jewish organizations. There should have been a stronger voice.

Over the years, even with disillusionment and disappointment, I still consider myself very progressive. My progressiveness didn't mellow or change, only my feelings about the Communist Party, because of the way the Party is, according to my understanding now.

Rochelle G.

We found out about Camp Followers of the Trail when we still lived in the Bronx—it must have been 1938 or '39. There was a man with a candy store on the corner—my husband used to buy from him, and when you buy from someone, you talk to the person. He told us about this camp. It was tents then. We thought it would be a good idea to be able to run away from the city for a while. At that time it took half an hour from where we lived to come to Peekskill.

We rented a tent and we lived in a tent for a summer, and then they proposed us as members. First we became privileged members and then they asked us to become members. At that time, we had a dining room with a manager and people cooperated. That was appealing to me. We used to pay for our meals and we had nothing in the house. We lived on this site without water. Then they had water put in, but they didn't allow water inside, so we had water outside.

Little by little it evolved into self-housekeeping. Now it's a different system altogether. It became like a village. Each minds his own business and doesn't interfere with somebody else. We were younger then, so you really can't compare the way we felt at that time and the way we feel now.

Over the years here, we became bourgeois. We became very, very selfish. I really don't know the reasons. Part of it was looking into other people's pots—what they have. Maybe they have a little bit more than I have. And I think the composition of the place changed, too. We had here in the beginning a real working group. In the beginning a businessman or somebody like that couldn't get in. It was very work conscious. Now we have socially conscious snobs. Communal living would be good to an extent if like people lived communally. But if you take a group of people that have very little in common in many respects—like culturally and in other ways—and throw them together, I don't think there is a big advantage. One is against the other. It was a wonderful thing, if something happened to someone you were able to say, "Hey, can I do something for you? Can I help you?" This was a sample of people getting together and living together—learning from one another, tolerating one another, living and sharing, and partaking.

Each individual still has a certain past here in the camp. It's our past and our present, and our future—because of our past. Because we lived here, we spent a different type of life. Now the life has changed, but the past has not left us completely. If you look at it from that point of view, it's part of you. It's not something that I used and throw it away. It's part of your body. Some of your blood is in here. I cleared the grounds here. I took sick from here.

In those early times in the camp, there were different causes. There was unemployment, there was hunger, there was the Spanish Civil War, Mussolini, Hitler. You know, it was a different feeling. During the Spanish Civil War, we demonstrated. At that time, we let off a lot of steam. It really had no affect on politics, but not to do it would be wrong, too. We had to show them that there is a certain amount of resentment in a certain group of people. It wasn't only the Jewish people or the immigrants. Many people were in favor of the Spanish Revolution at that time, and not only for that. At that time we thought—and I still think—that the existence of the Soviet Union is very important. Because otherwise, with this technology and with everything else, I don't know how far the money makers would go. You know? The world doesn't know.

World War II was a shock. I went through a lot with World War I. There were refugees, and seeing people devastated, losing their lives, the pogroms at that time after World War I, and then the Civil War. It was a very traumatic experience for me. And to face a repetition of it, it was very, very bad. That's how I felt. I was really put out completely. We found out about the holocaust very late. It came so late that we couldn't react emotionally to it. It's still an emotional experience to visualize— sometimes I visualize myself, that I am the one being marched, nude. Men are not very nice to men—to their own species. Not nice at all. It's the desire of aggrandizement, the desire to supersede the others. Basically I cannot understand it. I really don't. We have something in us where compassion and other things go away and just the beast is there. I don't exclude myself. Maybe I'm that way, too. I hope not, but how can I tell what circumstances might be? Man is capable of doing it.

The Jews here didn't know. We didn't know. We were too busy. The active people were too busy saving the world. So we didn't know the particulars. We knew that certain refugees came from Germany, but we didn't know about the crematoriums. We didn't know. Maybe if we knew we would have made more of a noise. Demonstrations to Roosevelt. But what could we do? Roosevelt acted very badly.

We didn't know about the holocaust, but Roosevelt knew. He knew about it. There was a deal that had to be made with the trucks. We found out later on. They wanted too much of a price for it. If they would have come to the Jewish community, they would have given any price. To save people, they would have given any price. But the holocaust wasn't the first time. If you read Jewish history, one time or another there is an eruption of some kind against the Jews. The best thing is to arm them— let them die at least like people, like soldiers.

At the time of the Russian Revolution, I thought they would solve the problem of Jews being persecuted, being excluded from many things, not being accepted in the society, being ignored as a people, being a pariah of society, being the scapegoat of society. I knew that because Jews were a minority they were very prone to persecution, to be a scapegoat of society, to divert the anger of the pent-up emotions or suppressions of the masses. So they directed it out, and it was organized in this manner from those that are in power. They wanted to perpetuate their power at the expense of a small, helpless people. But I thought the Revolution would solve the problem by education, by enlightening people, by eliminating not only the profit system but the parasitic exploitation. In fact, the Jews took a very, very important and leading part in the Russian Revolution. So for a while I was very much impressed by it. I never belonged to any party, but my leanings were intellectually there.

I'm much less politically involved than I was. The change came because of the Soviet Union. The Jews again became to an extent a scapegoat. They singled out the Jews as a people under suspicion of creating a fifth column there. And that's as a result of their policies. Naturally, I resent it greatly.

I'm afraid I will sound very reactionary, but I have learned from experience that Jewish people—no matter what they do, they don't gain anything. Maybe a temporary relief for a day or two. And then there is not one thing but another thing. They are after our destruction. We are living in a jungle, surrounded by beasts, and we might as well put up a stand, we might as well say, "Our cage is such and such, but while I have it I'm not going to surrender it." That is my feeling. Some people think I am a reactionary as far as that is concerned.

But it never entered my mind that changing or escaping from being Jewish will better me in any way. Culturally, I feel we have a very rich heritage and a rich culture. I, as a representative, wouldn't want to be one to change or modify it in any way, to obliterate it. I feel sometimes that we are the Christs of the society. That Christ was really symbolic.

My life here in this country was turmoil, adaptation, and struggle. There was happiness here and there, of course. You know, you live. But as a whole, maybe I accomplished more than I would have accomplished under similar circumstances in Europe because I had better opportunities here. In Europe, I was dependent. Here, I became a person. I got my education here. I started to function as a human being and as an individual. But, as a whole, whatever you attain, you have a price you pay for it. Transplanting to a new land is a very difficult process. Learning a new language, new customs, new behaviors, and other things. It's difficult. You come and you have to start working, and you have to do this and you have to do that. It's a hard process. But I assimilated here. I'm not a European anymore.

Harry G.

One of my friends was a member of Followers of the Trail Camp. He took us out for a weekend and we fell in love with it because of the way this community was running and the friendships. Also, it was very cheap at that time—for eighteen dollars or seventeen dollars a week we got food and lodging and everything. It was an escape for me. I came home from a day's work or a week's work, and I came here to the country. You looked forward to it. You have to have something to look forward to. You have to have something in front of you.

The camp has changed a lot. Physically, it changed for the better—better houses, we have a swimming pool, we have a lot more necessities. But spiritually, it also changed a lot. It was more spiritual here before. We used to fight for freedom, we were fighting for the coal miners, we were fighting to support the Spanish Civil War, we supported a lot of things here. Everything was different. Now there is a different mixture of people. Some of them are extreme revolutionists, some of them are extremely against revolution.

During the Spanish war, we collected money. Three people from my club volunteered to go to Spain to the Lincoln Brigade. One of my dearest friends was killed there. There were two brothers—the father had a tool shop and they used to fix bicycles and some other things. The two brothers were my friends. They both enlisted in the Brigade. One got killed and one came back. Another one of my friends came back with one leg. I couldn't go myself because my father died and I had to support the family. Also, I was married then, so I couldn't do it.

Then Pearl Harbor was in 1941. I was working in a grocery in New York parttime. I really wanted to enlist. When Hitler wrote *Mein Kampf*, I read it and saw that he was against the Jewish people. We knew what was happening, but we couldn't do anything. We didn't have any leaders at that time in the United States. If we would have had stronger leaders in the United States among the Jewish people—more militant Jewish leaders—maybe we would have saved a lot of Jewish people. Another thing with the holocaust was that no matter how much we knew, we couldn't foresee or foretell that certain things would happen—the slaughter.

I wanted to enlist after Pearl Harbor, partly for patriotism to the Jewish people and partly for patriotism to the United States. Shirley was always against it. I couldn't convince her. But when I was drafted, I had to go. I went to the draft board, but they rejected me because of my eyes. That's why I didn't go. But I was very active in the

Russian War Relief, selling bonds, collecting food, and trying to do whatever I could to the best of my capability.

I was always sympathetic to the Soviet Union. We were disillusioned in the beginning by the Hitler-Stalin pact, but the Communist Party sent a lot of speakers to our clubs and organizations to prove that the pact between Stalin and Hitler was a necessity. We see now that it wasn't a necessity, because when Stalin made the pact with Hitler, Hitler was free to go further into Poland. Maybe he wouldn't have gone there.

But I was sympathetic to the Soviet Union up until 1956. Then my attitude changed entirely. The background of the Russian people was always antisemitic, right back to when the czar was there, but when the Revolution broke out, when the Bolsheviks came in, the barrier disappeared a little bit. But when Stalin came and antisemitism came out again, naturally my opinion changed. I became disillusioned with the Soviet Union on account of antisemitism.

I feel very hurt by this. I feel very hurt. You know, Hitler killed us—he killed six million Jewish people and he killed maybe twenty million Russians in the Soviet Union. Under Stalin, right after the War, there was the second holocaust. Hitler killed us bodily—he exterminated us. Stalin took away our souls. He killed our culture. He killed our best writers, he closed the Jewish schools, he destroyed the Jewish books, everything. The Jewish culture almost was exterminated. A people can't live without culture. We have no grammar in the Soviet Union, we have no schools, we have no theaters—we have maybe a vaudeville or two. We haven't got any teachers. They abolished everything. A people without a culture is dead. So we have two holocausts. There used to be a saying, "When you scratch a Russian, you'll find an antisemite." They always used the Jews as scapegoats, even under the czar. The Soviet Union does the same thing, because there is something basically wrong under their socialism. I figured that with a Socialist government, a Communist government, antisemitism could never exist. It couldn't. The Soviet Union will never be Communist as long as antisemites will be in the Soviet Union. That's why we are not so friendly to the Soviet Union now. I would support the Soviet Union if they would take those antisemites and put them where they belong.

We became more Jewish-conscious since 1948, when Israel became a state. We did whatever we could. Right away we went to collect money, we spoke to people, we did whatever was possible for Israel. The Jewish state was so important because when

Hitler tried to exterminate the Jewish people and they were running, they didn't have a place to run. Hitler spread out and they had no place to go. The United States, England, and other countries wouldn't let them in. If we would have had Israel at that time—if we would have had our own country—thousands and thousands of Jewish people would have been saved.

I would say that 90 percent of the people in the colony here agree with or have sympathy for Israel. A small percent, who are Communists or so-called Communists, are old-fashioned and they cannot adapt themselves to the new times. They can't see what's taking place in the Soviet Union. They can't see any change. I have pity for those people because they can't adapt themselves and they have no place to go. They're not religious and they're not strictly Communists. So they're miserable. They're pathetic, in other words. The situation changed.

The sun doesn't always shine. Sometimes you have the moon, and sometimes it's cloudy all night. Life without problems doesn't exist. As long as you're alive, you have problems—problems which you can avoid, problems which you can't avoid, problems which are serious, and problems which are foolish. The main problem that arises about the Soviet Union now is antisemitism. But there are always problems. When you go to school, you have problems in playing with the children, they don't want to take you on the team—it's a problem. When you get older, you have a problem in getting a girl to go out—it's a problem. You get married—there are problems. When you get older, you have different problems. You would like to go out somewhere and you can't do it. You would like to play ball and you can't. There are always problems. Anybody that tells you he hasn't got problems is absolutely insane.

But I had a big advantage in coming to the United States. When I came here I was like a new-born man, with food and clothing . . . and even sneakers. We struggled but struggling helps. You learn from experience. You learn from people, from the surroundings. You learn a lot of things. But I wouldn't want to be young again and go through what I went through. I'd like to be healthy now, that's all.

I worked hard all my life and I'm comfortable. I get social security, I have a few dollars saved up. There are two basic things in life when you get older—food and shelter. Under Hoover, we had a lot of evictions in the United States, especially in New York. If you didn't pay the rent, they'd throw you out. We didn't have any food and we didn't get subsidies like now. The only thing was you could get food on food lines. They had kitchens and they'd give you a plate of soup and a slice of bread. Roosevelt turned the country the other way. America was ripe—seven million people unemployed, walking around, sleeping in parks, selling apples, eating garbage. The United States made big concessions—she gave grants, she gave doles, she introduced social security, unemployment insurance. Now we have a better old age system.

I get my social security check. I get my few extra dollars I put in, and that's all. I just want to enjoy myself, take it easy, have good meals, go to bed, go to see a picture, go to see a show. I don't have to go out to make a living anymore.

Florence M.

It was like a retreat, it was a place out of heaven—it was a haven here after a whole week working coming here on Friday. Everyone accepted you with open arms. Everyone looked on life the same, we had the same interests. The major change is that more people of better means are coming in and they don't care how much it costs them. They don't want to do what we used to come and do ourselves. That's why it's getting harder and harder to be here. But even with this, we still help out one another, we are concerned with one another, and this plays a great part in a human being's life. When you come here you feel that you're not alone. Even though I have no relations here, I feel that I'm among family. I feel that I'm not lost. I never feel lonely and I feel young.

Except that when I was young I overcame everything very fast. It's when you get older that things stay with you, they linger with you. Sometimes it's good to reminisce, but not all the time. Very seldom do I think about the past. I like to think about the future. Jack and I went through an awful lot of hardship in this country. We worked in factories, we were not skilled workers, we were small wage earners, and it was season work. Jack gave all his life to the movement, he used to speak on the corners for hours, and I followed him. And that's what I regret now. I should have gone to college and I regret it to this very day. I went to the Jefferson School, workers' school, and I took courses there. I took American history, the ABCs of communism, political courses, which I had no use out of it. We gave away our young lives for nothing. If we wouldn't give up our lives for being active in the movement, we would be monetary-wise much better off and not struggle the way we struggled. We should have thought about ourselves a little bit.

Self-preservation—that's what I taught my Harold. When Harold got older, I said, "Harold, you come first. Self-preservation. When you know you're not hungry, you'll be able to fight for better things in life. You'll be able to do what you want." From my experience I taught my son, "You come first." Self-preservation.

I would still fight for better conditions for the people of the world. I would, because it's in me. But I would not shackle my life in the factory. I wouldn't have gone to the workers' school. I should have gone to university and studied something and had an easier life. The same is with Jack. He wanted to be a pharmacist, and he studied pharmacy in the home. He landed in a factory, because they needed people in the factories to organize the factories.

I still believe there are changes that could be made that there should be a better world—abolish war, abolish unemployment, better housing, more hospitals, more schools—that would be a better world. But I don't believe in revolution. I believe in evolution.

To me, Soviet Russia was a utopia, and now it's nothing. I can't forgive them that in a country where each and everyone should be equal, they single out the Jews and they are tormenting them, took away from them their culture. How can a people live without their culture? I can't forgive them for that and I never will.

I think the working man lives here nicer than in any other part of the world. Look at me, I'm a small wage earner. The two of us, we made very little. I haven't got luxuries—diamonds or mink coats or cars or whatever, but I have enough to exist, to go to the theater, go to the ballet or to a concert.

There are people that are worse off than I am and have less than I. I do look at the South Bronx, where people have no homes and things like this, and there are other places, let's say in the South, where they are still very, very poor, and there is no excuse that in a country of wealth people should struggle like this.

Bertha S.

Summers we used to take our children to a farm. Whatever money it was—maybe fifty dollars for the summer—we used to pay it out weekly. Years later, when things were better, a friend I had from the shop where I was working asked me if I wanted to buy something in the country. She was a member of Reynolds Hills Colony, and she told me there were houses available. I came out to see, and I liked it. We were glad to buy.

That was in 1955 and times were better then. You know, we were two people working at that time, so we were able to afford it. We paid nine hundred dollars for the frame of our ten-by-twenty bungalow. Then the year after, we started building it up. Little by little, we built it up. We took out of the bank. We felt we are building this little house, and it's ours.

My first impression was that the colony was like one big family. I'm here now twenty-five years, and I know we were one big family. It was mostly Jewish, but we never made a difference here, Jewish or non-Jewish. We had one member who was not Jewish when I came, but we didn't discriminate. There was no difference then in politics or in work. We all did the same things. It was like one big family and this was to my liking.

I always found it special. I used to come for weekends and when I went home I was heartbroken that I had to leave my little cottage. Memories remain with me. Once we all did the same work, everyone was a friend. But it's not the same. It cannot be the same because people changed their political views.

I mellowed with age. What I strived for before, if I didn't accomplish it, I let it go. I feel you have to mellow with the trend, the way it goes. If there is any change, you have to do what you should because you can't live as a fanatic. My views changed. I'm thinking more of Israel. Since we got our Jewish country in Israel, I feel like supporting it.

Some of the people in the colony here don't have that feeling. Sometimes there is a controversy. There is a left and a right here. I am changed to the right. Those people who are left, they don't live with the times. I would call them back numbers.

I can't live the fanatic way. We once thought that a Socialist country was free. But we found out it's not so free. For these fanatics, they don't think that way. This is a controversy. Some people would like to bring lecturers to the colony to tell the people how good the Soviet Union is. We bring a lecturer here on an Israeli topic and they come up and say that Israel is Fascism and they call people the worst names. But that you can't help because people are people and they react to their feelings.

I always want to see both sides, and the truth. These here fanatics, they see one side and no truth. They believe in what was fifty or sixty years ago. They feel that if you support Israel you are already a Zionist. I don't have to be a Zionist to support Israel. You know what I mean? I feel that I want to support it. And this is what we have here. But otherwise I don't fight with no one. They have a right to their belief and I have a right to mine.

Feigl Y.

We found out about the Reynolds Hills Colony already in the fifties. We found out from friends. There were several bungalows for sale then. We liked one, and we took it for five hundred dollars—we paid it out. You see, I lived in a small town in

Europe. We were surrounded by woods and forests in my town. I loved the countryside. Whenever spring came, I used to sit by the machine and say, "Oh, how I would want to be now in the country." When I had the chance to buy a bungalow for five hundred dollars I grabbed it.

But at that time, we were like one family. If anything happened, good or bad, everybody was interested. We were all workers coming from the shop to rest up on a weekend. Now anybody comes in. We had no rich people here before. Now those that want to sell are anxious to sell, and we haven't got as many restrictions anymore. The element changed. We have manufacturers now, we have intellectuals, so-called—lawyers, doctors. The new people are strangers to me. We say hello and goodbye but I have nothing in common with them. Nothing. I liked it better before. But the spirit is still there. My spirit is good. My spirit is young. I'm still progressive. I'm disillusioned in many things, but I wouldn't give up my ideals for a better world.

Once we thought that the Soviet Union is going to be an example for good, and then we were disappointed. In the beginning it was very nice in the Soviet Union, especially for Jewish people. They abolished pogroms, they abolished antisemitism. But years later, Stalin came to power and it was no good. There is a lot of antisemitism there now. I am very, very much Jewish. I always was, from my youngest days. When I worked in a shop I wouldn't let any Gentile insult me because I'm Jewish. I would always stand up for it. I love Jewish literature, Jewish history, Jewish culture—because it has a lot to give. Now, I suppose, I'm very much pro-Israel.

But, I'll tell you, I still love America. I think it's the best country in the world, except we elect the wrong people—grafters, people that don't care for anybody. If people would have the sense to elect the right people, we could have heaven in this country.

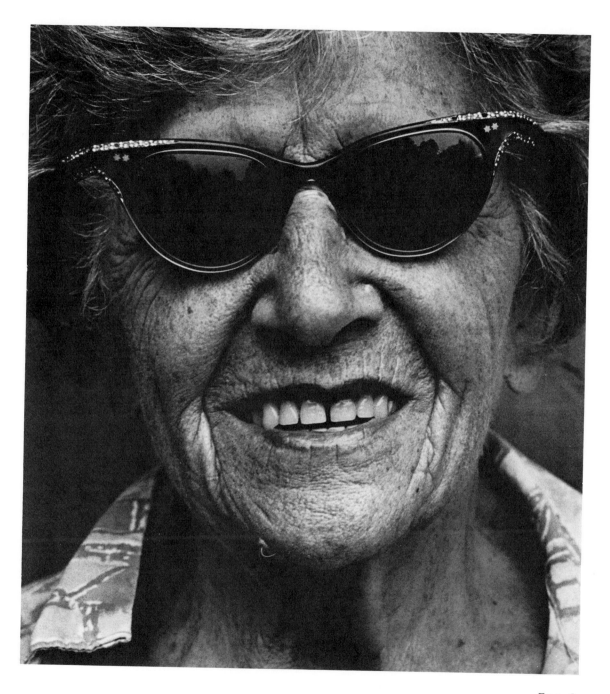

Fanny O.

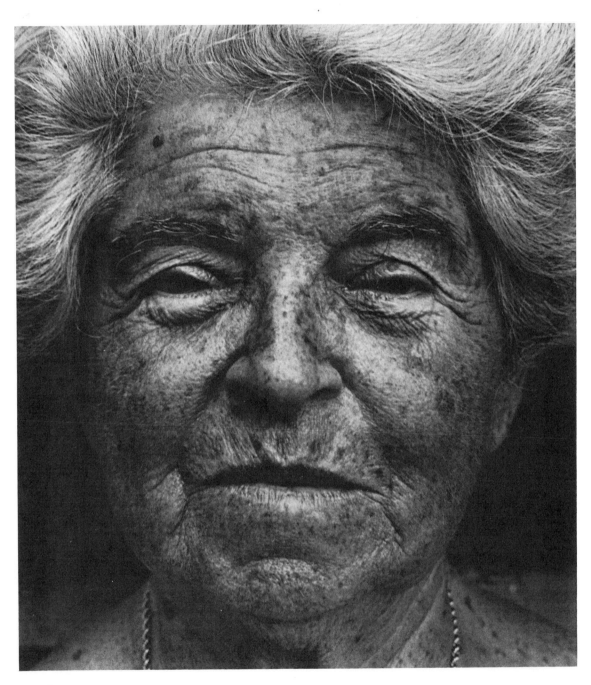

Sarah C.

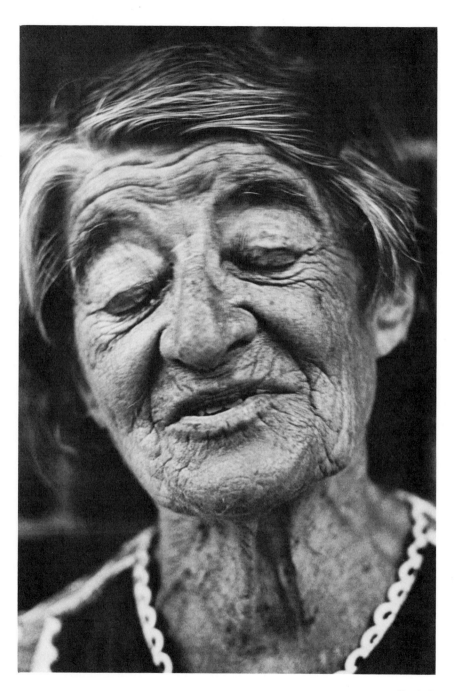

Sarah A.

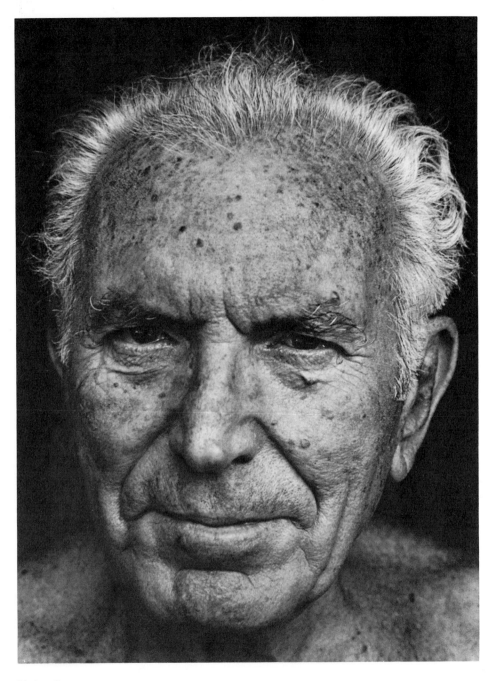

Nathan R.

A Note on the Interviews

All of the interviews were conducted between May and September 1980. They varied in length from two hours to twelve hours. The shorter interviews were usually done in one sitting, rarely more than two. The longer interviews were done in as many as six sittings. I worked from a questionnaire that was constantly revised and amended. Rather than guiding my subjects, I listened, often allowing them to stray far from my line of questioning. This method enabled me to identify important aspects of a person's life, which I could then come back to later in the interview. It also provided me with a wealth of information and detail.

After the interviews were recorded, they were transcribed word for word. The transcripts were then edited into narrative form. First, my questions were removed, allowing the Followers to tell their stories without interruption, as well as enabling the reader to experience their lives more directly. Without the questions, the Followers were talking to everyone, not only to me.

Second, the Followers' life stories were edited chronologically, beginning with their young lives in Europe and ending with reflections upon aging in America. While perhaps not the most creative form of presentation, the straightforward, logical progression easily conveys the evolution of each of the Followers' lives.

Third, each of the Followers' narratives was divided into three parts—"Europe," "America," and "A Shtetl on a Hill." This allows the reader to absorb completely and compare immediately each of the Followers' three major experiences, avoiding what can sometimes be the tedious work of reading one's life story from start to finish. At the same time, this chronologically staggered collective autobiography reinforces the Followers' ideological principles while it preserves their presence as individuals.

Finally, the language that the Followers used to tell their stories is respected. For example, "My father was by profession a cantor" could have been reshuffled. Leaving the Followers' language as it was presented, however, helps the reader hear the Followers.

FIRST ANNUAL COLOR LIGHT BALL

given by the

Prospect Workers Club

SATURDAY **8** MARCH
Evening 1930

At HOLLYWOOD GARDENS

896 Prospect Ave. (Bet. 161st & 162nd Sts.) Bronx

ADMISSION 75c.   464   (Union Band)

THE BUILDERS

We are the builders,
We build the future,
The future world lies in our hands.
We swing our hammers,
We use our weapons,
Against our foe in every land.
And we the workers,
Who are the builders,
We fight, we do not fear to die.
All power and freedom unto the workers
Is our defiant battle cry

I

UNITY CAMP

A Resting Place for Proletarians

—:—

COMRADE KRANESS musical director, requests that all comrades who play a musical instrument should bring them to camp.

A Class Is Being Formed!

—:—

DIRECTIONS:
From Grand Central or 125th St. to Wingdale, N. Y.

By Bus:
From 1800 Seventh Avenue, corner 110th St. Fridays at 6.30 P. M., Saturdays 1:30 Sunday at 9 a. m.

TELEPHONES:
MONUMENT 0111
or STUYVESANT 8774

2

REGISTER NOW BEFORE IT IS LATE!

UNITY CAMP

WINGDALE, N. Y.
CAMP PHONE WINGDALE, N. Y. 51

A COOPERATIVE CAMP FOR WORKERS

Gather Strength for the Looming Fight!

Good Food, Comradely Atmosphere Proletarian Sports, Recreation and Cultural Activities. Bathing, Boating, and Fishing in Lake Unity.

Register Now for July 4th
CARNIVAL, BALL, MUSIC AND DRAMATICS

Register at once at

1800 Seventh Avenue, New York City, Tek Monument 0111 or at the Barber Shop, 30 Union Square. Tel. Stuyvesant 8774.

Our buses leave 1800 Seventh Avenue, Corner 110th St. Every Fri. 6:30 P. M. Sat. 1.P. M. Mon. 12 noon.

OR BY TRAIN FROM GRAND CENTRAL TO WINGDALE, N. Y.

3

RED FRONT

OUR BATTLE IS GREAT, OUR FIGHTING IS VITAL
PROLETRIAN CAMPS MAKE US READY AND STRONG
PROLETARIAN CULTURE, SPORT AND RECITAL
TEACH US TO FIGHT WITH A SONG
COME TO WOCOLONA
COME TO NITGEDAIGET
COME TO UNITY AND KINDERLAND—
THEY ARE ALL WITHIN THE REACH OF YOUR HAND

Automobiles leave for Camp Unity every day 9 to 10 a.m. and 2:30 p.m. from 143 E. 103rd St.

FRIDAY—9 to 10 a. m. and 6 p. m.
SATURDAY—9 a. m. to 10 a. m. and 5 p. m.
SUNDAY—9 a. m. to 10 a. m.

We also take passengers to Kinderland
Headquarters for Children—143 E. 103rd St.

for information call at the office of all 4 camps
32 UNION SQUARE, ROOM 505, TEL. STuy. 9-6332

4

5

6

Announcement on Opening of Co-Operative Camps

Nitgedaiget and Unity

For the Season 1932

The approaching camp season in this period of ever worsening crisis brought sharply before the Board of Directors of Camps Nitgedaiget and Unity the following problems: How to make the camps available to and usable by thousands of workers who want and need its services and benefits at this time more than ever before, but who, because of terrific wage slashes and unemployment, cannot pay the usual camp rates and are therefore condemned to stew in the heat of the city instead of being able to recuperate in the freshness of the country.

The first reaction of the Board of Directors was to reduce the rates sharply, the suggestion being made that $13 a week be fixed as the total charge. But investigation proved that even the small sum of $13 a week was more than the average worker could afford to pay in this time of unemployment and wage cuts.

The Board started with this principle: That under any and all circumstances Camps Nitgedaiget and Unity must be made available to the greatest number of workers, even though they may have to get along without some of the conveniences of service that they have had in the past along with camping.

Carrying out this purpose the Board of Directors, supported solidly by the membership, therefore decided that the camps should be opened this season on the following basis: rooms in the hotel, bungalows of various sizes and tents shall be rented to workers and their families at rates ranging from a minimum of $15 to a maximum of $85 PER SEASON; weekly rates $3 per person to $6 maximum rate per family; single day rates, $0.75 per night; two-day week-end, $1.25.

Of course, these rates do not include food, although they do include electricity and a supply of linen. Arrangements are being completed whereby food can be purchased at city prices, and conveniences for cooking made available.

Above all, it must be remembered that the cultural activities which are the basis of camp life will be maintained.

This plan goes into effect after the July 4 week-end. This week-end is being run on the old basis for the purpose of affording as many workers and their families as possible in order that they may have the opportunity to make proper selection and definite arrangements to rent the bungalows, rooms and tents for the future.

Rates for this week-end are $2.50 for one day and $2 for each additional day thereafter, including food and lodging.

We are certain that the workers will appreciate and understand this step of putting the camps within reach of the broadest strata of the workers. Workers, these are your camps. Take advantage of this opportunity to use them to the utmost extent.

Read our regular ad for further information.

Camping as Our Ideal

"Camping as Our Ideal," written by Bella S., served as the Followers' founding manifesto.

For the last few years a new movement has developed—Camping. This movement began to spread far and wide. Like a ball of fire it rolled and the easiest inflammable spots caught it. People of big cities like New York and the like, who have been spending their best days in the shops and factories, began to feel that the oxygen in the air was diminishing and the relief was to turn to Mother Nature.

In those days, when camping was yet in its infantile stage, a number of young people organized themselves into a hiking group. Once they rested in the lap of Mother Nature, they decided to start camping. The above mentioned group, however, is no other than the present "Followers of the Trail."

We, the "Followers of the Trail," began to spend our best leisure time out in the open, close to Mother Nature's shrine, bathing our bodies in the silver rays of the sun, drinking to intoxication the air which is full of perfume from the plants and flowers surrounding us. We danced, played, sang like children freed from obligation. With all the joy Mother Nature gave us, a question, however, aroused before us: "Is this all we want and should do in our leisure time?" And the answer came in the negative.

"It is true," we said, "in the lap of nature we are children, but we are also children of a definite class—the working class. As devoted children we dare not forget the duties we owe to our class."

We at once realized that we are to set up a new form of living different from that of the city—the cooperative form—where we can do away with little individual matters. A form of living which should give us spare time for various activities. We also realized that with our bodies rested, minds fresh and clear, we can more readily help to promote the struggle we left behind us in the city.

Again, another question occurs, "But how are we to do it? Here where nature is so mild, so motherly tender to us, where the reaction can be nothing else but gentleness and tenderness." To that we answer, "Yes, we can and should do things beneficial to our class as well as ourselves. As a group we can and should help organize workers' cultural centers. We can and should help keep up the struggle through our press and see that our press is kept going, for we as a nucleus of the whole are the ones to keep it going."

We out here in the lap of Mother Nature, freed from the poisons of the city can more readily crystallize our aims, our ideals, bring ourselves up to the level of some of our dreams.

Our ideal, therefore, of camping is and should be a combination of both conscientiousness as members of a definite class and outdoor activities.

Bella S.

Notes

Introduction

1. Studs Terkel, *Working: People Talk about What They Do All Day and How They Feel about What They Do* (New York: Pantheon, 1974).

2. Irving Howe, *World of Our Fathers: The Journey of the Eastern European Jews to America and the Life They Found and Made* (New York: Harcourt Brace Jovanovich, 1976).

3. Oscar Handlin, *The Uprooted: The Epic Story of the Great Migrations that Made the American People* (1951; Boston: Atlantic, Little Brown, 1973); Moses Rischin, *The Promised City: New York's Jews, 1870–1914* (1962; New York: Harper & Row, 1970).

4. Nell Irvin Painter, *The Narrative of Hosea Hudson* (Cambridge: Harvard University Press, 1979). See also James Barrett and Robert Ruck, eds., *Steve Nelson: American Radical* (Pittsburgh: University of Pittsburgh Press, 1981); Vivian Gornick, *The Romance of American Communism* (New York: Basic Books, 1977); Kenneth Kahn, *Joe Rapoport: The Life of a Jewish Radical* (Philadelphia: Temple University Press, 1981).

5. Jacob Riis, *The Making of an American* (New York: Macmillan, 1901); Mary Antin, *The Promised Land* (Boston: Houghton Mifflin, 1912); S. S. McClure, *My Autobiography* (New York: Frederick A. Stokes, 1914); Edward Steiner, *From Alien to Citizen: The Story of My Life in America* (New York: F. H. Revel, 1914); Marcus Ravage, *An American in the Making: The Life Story of an Immigrant* (New York: Harper & Brothers, 1917); Edward Bok, *The Americanization of Edward Bok: The Autobiography of a Dutch Boy Fifty Years After* (New York: Charles Scribner's Sons, 1920).

Chapter One

1. Statistical information cited can be found in "International Migration and Naturalization," *Historical Statistics of the United States: Colonial Times to 1970*, part 1 (Washington, D.C.: U.S. Dept. of Commerce, Bureau of the Census, 1975), pp. 105–20.

2. Ibid.

3. According to the *Oxford English Dictionary* a *fellow traveler* is "one who sympathizes with the Communist Movement without actually being a member." The word assumed its political meaning when first used by Leon Trotsky to describe "non-communist writers sympathizing with the Revolution." The Russian word for fellow traveler is *poputchik*. See *Oxford English Dictionary*, s.v. "fellow traveler."

4. Simon Dubnow, "Pogroms and Revolution in Russia (1902–1907)," *History of the Jews: From the Congress of Vienna to the Emergence of Hitler*, vol. 5, trans. Moshe Spiegel (New York: Thomas Yosseloff, 1973), pp. 716–47.

5. Arthur Liebman, *Jews and the Left* (New York: John Wiley & Sons, 1979), p. 30.

6. Philip S. Foner, *The Fur and Leather Workers Union: A Story of Dramatic Struggles and Achievements* (Newark, N.J.: Nordan, 1950), p. 123.

7. The story of the political struggle in the needle-trade industry is one of complexity and intrigue. There is a considerable amount of work that deals with the subject. For more on these union battles and the TUEL (as of August 1929, the Trade Union Unity League) involvement, see Theodore Draper, *The Roots of American Communism* (New York: Viking, 1957), p. 314; Theodore Draper, *American Communism and Soviet Russia: The Formative Period* (New York: Viking, 1960), pp. 64–95; Melech Epstein, *The Jew and Communism: The Story of Early Communist Victories and Ultimate Defeats in the Jewish Community, U.S.A.* (New York: Trade Union Sponsoring Committee, 1969), pp. 121–43 and 236–42; Foner, pp. 122–54 and 343; William Z. Foster, *History of the Communist Party of the United States* (1952; New York: Greenwood, 1968), pp. 202–10 and 252–55; Irving Howe and Lewis Coser, *The American Communist Party: A Critical History* (1957; New York: DaCapo, 1974), pp. 236–72; and Liebman, pp. 207–82.

8. Irving Howe, *World of Our Fathers: The Journey of the Eastern European Jews to America and the Life They Found and Made* (New York: Harcourt Brace Jovanovich, 1976), p. 335.

9. Foner, p. 244.

10. Foner, pp. 180, 233–44.

11. For more on the *Forward* and the *Freiheit*, see Epstein, pp. 98–104; Foner, pp. 126–29; and Liebman, pp. 325–56.

12. See Draper, *Roots*, pp. 237–62; Foster, pp. 186–95; and Benjamin Gitlow, *I Confess* (New York: E. P. Dutton, 1939), pp. 132–62. On page 133, Gitlow explains how the Geese were named: "The name 'Goose Caucus' originated in the course of a stormy debate, when William Dunne, exasperated by Jakira's [member of the Russian Federation] unceasing and persistent stuttering, interjected, 'Jakira, you make me sick; you cackle like a goose.' And Amter, springing to the defense of his fellow factionalist, retorted, 'But the Geese saved Rome and we shall yet save the party,' while Lovestone, counter attacking with ridicule, shouted back, 'All right, then; from now on you are the Goose Caucus!'"

13. Epstein, pp. 110–12; Gitlow, pp. 160–62. Moissaye J. Olgin was a member of the Socialist Party until the creation of the Communist Party in 1919, at which time he began to be influential in the Communist Party. He wrote *The Soul of the Russian Revolution*. For a "Portrait in Miniature" of Olgin, see Epstein, pp. 382–89.

14. Statement of the Political Committee of the Communist Party of the U.S.A., "The Class Character of the Palestine Revolt and Its International Political Significances," *Daily Worker*, August 30, 1929, pp. 1, 5; see related article, "Jewish Workers Join Arabs in War on Zionism," on pp. 1, 2, 5; see also Epstein, pp. 223–33; and Liebman, pp. 348–49.

15. Moissaye J. Olgin, "A Model of a Militant Progressive Union," *Jubilee Journal* (New York, January 23 and 24, 1937), p. 65, issued at the Twenty-fifth Anniversary of the Furriers' Joint Council; Foner, pp. 126–29, for discussion of the connection between the *Freiheit* and the Furriers. "A Yiddish paper was needed which would expose the role of the *Forward* and its right-wing allies in the union leadership. It was needed to clarify the issues and problems of the workers, and to present the rank-and-file program without distortion. To meet this need, the *Freiheit* appeared on April 22, 1922" (Foner, p. 126). "The *Freiheit* . . . had proved an indispensable ally in their [Furriers] bitter battles against gangsterism, the employers and the right-wing officials" (Foner, p. 242).

16. Robert Kent, "Singing for the 'Daily': Workers of Different Races, Nationalities and Trades Compose New *Daily Worker* Chorus," *Daily Worker*, January 17, 1945, p. 5, includes photograph of "revolutionary chorus in rehearsal."

17. Moissaye J. Olgin, "Mass Work Among National Groups," speech delivered at the Tenth Convention of the Communist Party, New York State, May 20–23, 1938; published in *Proceedings, Tenth Convention, Communist Party, New York State, November 1938)*, p. 282. See also Foster, p. 317: "But the most clear headed and energetic in the fight for a real people's culture were the Communists and other lefts, including Art Young, Robert Minor, Michael Gold, William Gropper, Fred Ellis and Moissaye J. Olgin."

18. Paul Novick, "The Distorted '*World of Our Fathers*,' A Critique of Irving Howe's Book," review of *World of Our Fathers* by Irving Howe, *Morning Freiheit* (1977), p. 28. The review originally appeared in the *Freiheit*. This reprint was translated from Yiddish by Sid Resnick.

19. Paul Novick, interviewed on March 15, 1985, pp. 5, 10, 15. The circulation for both newspapers in 1930, the *Freiheit*'s peak, was: *Freiheit*, 64,500; *Forward*, 175,000–200,000 (Liebman, pp. 326 and 346).

20. Liebman, p. 345.

21. Liebman, p. 350.

22. R. Saltzman, "Notes on the History of the Jewish American Section of the International Workers' Order," *Our People: The Jew in America* (New York: Co-operative Book League, Jewish American Section, IWO, 1944), p. 154.

23. Saltzman, p. 154.

24. *A New Workers' Stronghold: What is the International Workers' Order, and Why Every Worker Should Join It* (New York: National Executive Committee, IWO, 1930), pp. 9, 10, 11, 12.

25. *Workers' Stronghold*, pp. 14, 15.

26. *Youth Section, International Workers' Order, Insurance, Dramatics, Athletics, Cultural, Social Activities* (New York: National Youth Committee, IWO, 1932), pp. 4, 5, 7.

27. *Youth Section*, pp. 4, 7, 8.

28. Most of the information on the clubs comes from an interview with Harry Schoenbach, a member of the Prospect Workers' Club. For more on clubs, see Epstein, pp. 207–09.

29. See appendix 2, fig. 1.

30. *Daily Worker*, July 12, 1930, p. 5. See appendix 2, fig. 2.

31. *Daily Worker*, July 1, 1930, p. 3. See appendix 2, fig. 3.

32. *Daily Worker*, September 14, 1931, p. 2. See appendix 2, fig. 4.

33. *Daily Worker*, June 14, 1932, p. 2. See appendix 2, fig. 5.

34. Clement Wood, *Bernarr Macfadden, A Study In Success* (1929; New York: Beekman, 1974).

35. Wood, p. 1.

36. Bernarr Macfadden, *Building of Vital Power: Deep Breathing and a Complete System for Strengthening the Heart, Lungs, Stomach, and All the Great Vital Organs* (New York: Physical Culture Publishing, 1904), pp. 41–44.

37. Bernarr Macfadden, *The Virile Powers of Superb Manhood: How Developed, How Lost, How Regained* (New York: Physical Culture Publishing, 1900), p. 161.

38. Macfadden, *Building of Vital Power*, p. 15.

39. Macfadden, *Building of Vital Power*, p. 203.

40. Macfadden, *The Virile Powers*, p. 4.

41. See appendix 3.

42. *Daily Worker*, August 4, 1933, p. 3. See appendix 2, fig. 6.

43. *Daily Worker*, July 1, 1932, p. 2. See appendix 2, fig. 7. The statement in fig. 7 appeared one season before the Followers placed their first advertisement in the *Daily Worker*. The statement indicates the increased demand being made for affordable vacation spots for workers. The Followers attempted to meet this demand, creating an additional workers' camp with consistently less expensive rates than those of other camps.

Bibliography

Abramson, Harold J. "Assimilation and Pluralism." In *Harvard Encyclopedia of American Ethnic Groups,* pp. 150–60. *See* Thernstrom et al.

Antin, Mary. *From Plotzk to Boston.* Boston: W. B. Clarke, 1899.

———. *The Promised Land.* Boston: Houghton Mifflin, 1912.

Barrett, James and Robert Ruck, eds. *Steve Nelson: American Radical.* Pittsburgh: University of Pittsburgh Press, 1981.

Barth, Fredrik. *Ethnic Groups and Boundaries: The Social Organization of Cultural Differences.* Boston: Little Brown, 1969.

Bernard, William. "Immigration: History of U.S. Policy." In *Harvard Encyclopedia of American Ethnic Groups,* pp. 486–95. *See* Thernstrom et al.

Blasing, Mutlu Konuk. *The Art of Life: Studies in American Autobiographical Literature.* Austin: University of Texas Press, 1977.

Blythe, Ronald. *The View in Winter: Reflections on Old Age.* New York: Harcourt Brace Jovanovich, 1979.

Boelhower, William. *Immigrant Autobiography in the United States: Four Versions of the American Self.* Verona: Essedue Edizione, 1982.

Bok, Edward. *The Americanization of Edward Bok: The Autobiography of a Dutch Boy Fifty Years After.* New York: Charles Scribner's Sons, 1920.

Bourne, Randolph. *The Radical Will: Selected Writings, 1911–1918.* Ed. Olaf Hansens. New York: Urizon, 1977.

Brody, David. "Labor." In *Harvard Encyclopedia of American Ethnic Groups,* pp. 609–18. *See* Thernstrom et al.

Browder, Earl. *Communism in the United States.* New York: International Publishers, 1935.

———. *The Communist Party U.S.A.: Its History, Role and Organization.* New York: Workers Library Publishers, 1941.

Bruss, Elizabeth. *Autobiographical Acts: The Changing Situation of a Literary Genre.* Baltimore: Johns Hopkins University Press, 1976.

Buckley, Jerome. *The Turning Key: Autobiography and the Subjective Impulse Since 1800*. Cambridge: Harvard University Press, 1984.

Buhle, Paul. "Jews and American Communism: The Cultural Question." *Radical History Review* 23 (1980), pp. 8–33.

———. "Historians and American Communism: An Agenda." *International Labor and Working Class History* 20 (Fall 1981), pp. 38–45.

Cahan, Abraham. *The Rise of David Levinsky*. New York: Harper & Brothers, 1917.

———. *The Education of Abraham Cahan*. Trans. Leon Stein et al. Philadelphia: Jewish Publication Society of America, 1969.

———. *Yekl and the Imported Bridegroom and Other Stories of the New York Ghetto*. New York: Dover, 1970.

Cannon, James P. *The First Ten Years of American Communism: Report of a Participant*. New York: Lyle Stuart, 1962.

Cantor, Milton. *The Divided Left: American Radicalism, 1900–1975*. New York: Hill and Wang, 1978.

Charney, George. *A Long Journey*. New York: Quadrangle, 1972.

Couser, Thomas. *American Autobiography: The Prophetic Mode*. Amherst: University of Massachusetts Press, 1979.

Dearborn, Mary. *Pocahontas's Daughters: Gender and Ethnicity in American Culture*. New York: Oxford University Press, 1986.

Draper, Theodore. *The Roots of American Communism*. New York: Viking, 1957.

———. *American Communism and Soviet Russia: The Formative Period*. New York: Viking, 1960.

———. "American Communism Revisited." *New York Review of Books*, May 9, 1985, pp. 32–37.

———. "The Popular Front Revisited." *New York Review of Books*, May 30, 1985, pp. 44–50.

Easterlin, Richard. "Immigration: Economic and Social Characteristics." In *Harvard Encyclopedia of American Ethnic Groups*, pp. 476–86. *See* Thernstrom et al.

Epstein, Melech. *Jewish Labor in U.S.A., 1882–1914: An Industrial, Political and Cultural History of the Jewish Labor Movement*. New York: Trade Union Sponsoring Committee, 1950.

———. *The Jew and Communism, 1919–1941: The Story of Early Communist Victories and Ultimate Defeats in the Jewish Community, U.S.A.* New York: Trade Union Sponsoring Committee, 1959.

Fink, Gary M., ed. *Labor Unions*. Westport, Conn.: Greenwood, 1977.

Fishman, Joshua. "Language Maintenance." In *Harvard Encyclopedia of American Ethnic Groups*, pp. 629–38. *See* Thernstrom et al.

Foner, Philip S. *The Fur and Leather Workers Union: A Story of Dramatic Struggles and Achievements*. Newark: Nordan, 1950.

Foster, William Z. *History of the Communist Party of the United States.* 1952. New York: Greenwood, 1968.

Frisch, Michael. "The Memory of History." *Radical History Review* 25 (1981), pp. 9–23.

Gans, Herbert J. "Symbolic Ethnicity." In *The Making of Americans: Essays in Honor of David Riesman,* ed. Herbert Gans et al., pp. 193–220. Philadelphia: University of Pennsylvania Press, 1979.

Gitlow, Benjamin. *I Confess: The Truth About American Communism.* New York: E. P. Dutton, 1939.

Glazer, Nathan. *The Social Basis of American Communism.* New York: Harcourt, Brace & World, 1961.

Gleason, Philip. "The Melting Pot: Symbol of Fusion or Confusion." *American Quarterly* 16 (1964), pp. 20–46.

———. "Confusion Compounded: The Melting Pot in the 1960s and 1970s." *Ethnicity* (March 1979), pp. 10–20.

Gold, Michel. *Jews Without Money.* New York: H. Liveright, 1935.

Gordon, Milton. *Assimilation in American Life: The Role of Race, Religion, and National Origins.* New York: Oxford University Press, 1964.

Goren, Arthur. "Jews." In *Harvard Encyclopedia of American Ethnic Groups,* pp. 671–91. *See* Thernstrom et al.

Gornick, Vivian. *The Romance of American Communism.* New York: Basic Books, 1977.

Grele, Ronald. "A Surmisable Variety: Interdisciplinarity and Oral Testimony." *American Quarterly* 27 (1975), pp. 275–95.

Grestle, Gary. "Mission from Moscow: American Communism in the 1930s." *Reviews in American History* 12 (December 1984), pp. 559–66.

Gwaltney, John. *Drylongso: A Self-Portrait of Black America.* New York: Random House, 1980.

Handlin, Oscar. *Boston's Immigrants, 1760–1865: A Study in Acculturation.* 1941. Cambridge: Harvard University Press, 1959.

———. *The Uprooted: The Epic Story of the Great Migrations that Made the American People.* 1951. Boston: Atlantic, Little Brown, 1973.

Handlin, Oscar, ed. *Immigration as a Factor in American History.* Englewood Cliffs: Prentice-Hall, 1959.

Hansen, Marcus. *The Atlantic Migration, 1607–1910: A History of the Continuing Settlement of the United States.* Cambridge: Harvard University Press, 1940.

———. *The Immigrant in American History.* Cambridge: Harvard University Press, 1940.

Hapgood, Hutchins. *The Spirit of the Ghetto: Studies of the Jewish Quarter in New York.* New York: Funk and Wagnalls, 1902.

Harrington, Mona. "Loyalties: Dual and Divided." In *Harvard Encyclopedia of American Ethnic Groups,* pp. 676–86. *See* Thernstrom et al.

Haywood, Harry. *Black Bolshevik: Autobiography of an Afro-American Communist.* Chicago: Liberator Press, 1978.

Herberg, Will. "The Jewish Labor Movement in the United States." *American Jewish Yearbook* 53 (1952), pp. 3–76.

Higham, John. *Strangers in the Land: Patterns of American Nativism, 1860–1925.* 1955. New York: Atheneum, 1963.

———. *Send These to Me: Jews and Other Immigrants in Urban America.* New York: Atheneum, 1975.

Howe, Irving. *World of Our Fathers: The Journey of the Eastern European Jews to America and the Life They Found and Made.* New York: Harcourt Brace Jovanovich, 1976.

Howe, Irving and Lewis Coser. *The American Communist Party: A Critical History.* 1957. New York: Da Capo Press, 1976.

Howe, Irving and Kenneth Libo, eds. *How We Lived: A Documentary History of Immigrant Jews in America, 1880–1930.* New York: R. Marek, 1979.

Isserman, Maurice. *Which Side Were You On? The American Communist Party During the Second World War.* Middletown: Wesleyan University Press, 1982.

Iversen, Robert. *The Communists and the Schools.* New York: Harcourt Brace, 1959.

Jones, Maldwyn. *American Immigration.* Chicago: University of Chicago Press, 1960.

Kahn, Kenneth. *Joe Rapoport: The Life of a Jewish Radical.* Philadelphia: Temple University Press, 1981.

Kallen, Horace. *Culture and Democracy in the United States: Studies in the Group Psychology of the American Peoples.* New York: Boni and Liveright, 1924.

Klehr, Harvey. *The Heyday of American Communism.* New York: Basic Books, 1984.

Liebman, Arthur. *Jews and the Left.* New York: John Wiley & Sons, 1979.

Macfadden, Bernarr. *The Virile Powers of Superb Manhood: How Developed, How Lost, How Regained.* New York: Physical Culture Publishing, 1900.

———. *Strength from Eating: How and What to Eat and Drink to Develop the Highest Degree of Health and Strength.* New York: Physical Culture Publishing, 1901.

———. *Building of Vital Power: Deep Breathing and a Complete System for Strengthening the Heart, Lungs, Stomach and All the Great Vital Organs.* New York: Physical Culture Publishing, 1904.

———. *The Book of Health.* New York: Macfadden Publications, 1926.

———. *Strengthening the Nerves.* New York: Macfadden Publications, 1928.

Markowitz, Norman. "Frozen Vision: A Cold Warrior's History of Communists in the 1930s." *Political Affairs* (May 1984), pp. 38–40.

Meyer, Frank. *The Moulding of Communists: The Training of the Communist Cadre.* New York: Harcourt Brace, 1961.

Meyer, Stephen, III. *The Five Dollar Day: Labor, Management, and Social Control in the Ford Motor Company.* Albany: SUNY Press, 1981.

McClure, S. S. *My Autobiography.* New York: Frederick A. Stokes, 1914.

Naison, Mark. *Communists in Harlem During the Depression.* Urbana: University of Illinois Press, 1983.

Novack, Michael. "Pluralism: A Humanistic Perspective." In *Harvard Encyclopedia of American Ethnic Groups*, pp. 772–81. *See* Thernstrom et al.

Olney, James, ed. *Autobiography, Essays Theoretical and Critical*. Princeton: Princeton University Press, 1980.

Painter, Nell Irvin. *The Narrative of Hosea Hudson*. Cambridge: Harvard University Press, 1979.

Pascal, Roy. *Design and Truth in Autobiography*. New York: Garland Publishing, 1985.

Peterson, William. "Concepts of Ethnicity." In *Harvard Encyclopedia of American Ethnic Groups*, pp. 234–42. *See* Thernstrom et al.

Ravage, Marcus. *An American in the Making: The Life Story of an Immigrant*. New York: Harper & Brothers, 1917.

Richmond, Al. *A Long View from the Left*. Boston: Houghton Mifflin, 1972.

Riis, Jacob. *How the Other Half Lives: Studies Among the Tenements of New York*. New York: Scribner's Sons, 1890.

———. *The Making of an American*. New York: Macmillan, 1901.

Rischin, Moses. *The Promised City: New York's Jews, 1870–1914*. 1962. New York: Harper & Row, 1970.

Rosengarten, Theodore. *All God's Dangers: The Life of Nate Shaw*. New York: Alfred Knopf, 1974.

Rosenzweig, Roy. "Oral History and the Old Left." *International Labor and Working Class History* (Fall 1984), pp. 27–38.

Rossiter, Clinton. *Marxism: The View from America*. New York: Harcourt Brace, 1960.

Roosevelt, Theodore. *American Ideals and Other Essays, Social and Political*. New York: G. Putnam's Sons, 1897.

———. *Fear God and Take Your Own Part*. New York: G. H. Doran, 1916.

Roth, Henry. *Call It Sleep*. New York: R. O. Ballow, 1934.

Roy, Ralph. *Communism and the Churches*. New York: Harcourt Brace, 1960.

Sanders, Ronald. *The Downtown Jews: Portraits of an Immigrant Generation*. New York: Harper and Row, 1969.

Shannon, David. *The Decline of American Communism: A History of the Communist Party of the United States Since 1945*. New York: Harcourt Brace, 1959.

Sollors, Werner. "Theory of American Ethnicity, or '?s Ethnic? / Ti and American / Ti, De or United (W) States S S1 and Theor?'" *American Quarterly* 33 (1981), pp. 278–81.

———. "Literature and Ethnicity." In *Harvard Encyclopedia of American Ethnic Groups*, pp. 657–65. *See* Thernstrom et al.

———. *Beyond Ethnicity: Consent and Descent in American Culture*. New York: Oxford University Press, 1986.

Starobin, Joseph R. *American Communism in Crisis, 1943–1957*. Cambridge: Harvard University Press, 1972.

Stein, Gertrude. *The Making of Americans: The Hersland Family*. New York: Harcourt, Brace, 1934.

Steiner, Edward. *From Alien to Citizen: The Story of My Life in America.* New York: F. H. Revel, 1914.

Stone, Albert E. *Autobiographical Occasions and Original Acts: Versions of American Identity from Henry Adams to Nate Shaw.* Philadelphia: University of Pennsylvania Press, 1982.

Stone, Albert E., ed. *The American Autobiography: A Collection of Critical Essays.* Englewood Cliffs: Prentice Hall, 1981.

Terkel, Studs. *Hard Times: An Oral History of the Great Depression.* New York: Pantheon, 1970.

———. *Working: People Talk About What They Do All Day and How They Feel About What They Do.* New York: Pantheon, 1974.

———. *"The Good War": An Oral History of World War II.* New York: Pantheon, 1984.

Thernstrom, Stephan. *Poverty and Progress: Social Mobility in a Nineteenth Century City.* New York: Atheneum, 1970.

———. *The Other Bostonians: Poverty and Progress in the American Metropolis, 1880–1970.* Cambridge: Harvard University Press, 1973.

Thernstrom, Stephan et al., eds., *Harvard Encyclopedia of American Ethnic Groups.* Cambridge: Harvard University Press, 1980.

Waltzer, Kenneth. "The New History of American Communism." *Reviews in American History* 11 (June 1983), pp. 259–67.

Waltzer, Michael. "Pluralism: A Political Perspective." In *Harvard Encyclopedia of American Ethnic Groups,* pp. 781–87. *See* Thernstrom et al.

Ward, David. *Cities and Immigrants: A Geography of Change in Nineteenth Century America.* New York: Oxford University Press, 1971.

———. "Immigration: Settlement Patterns and Distribution." In *Harvard Encyclopedia of American Ethnic Groups,* pp. 496–508. *See* Thernstrom et al.

Wood, Clement. *Bernarr Macfadden, A Study in Success.* 1929. New York: Beekman, 1974.

Yezierska, Anzia. *Bread Givers: A Struggle Between a Father of the Old World and a Daughter of the New.* New York: Doubleday, Page, 1925.

Zangwill, Israel. *The Melting Pot: A Drama in Four Acts.* 1909. New York: Arno Press, 1975 [1914 edition]. Play first performed October 5, 1908, in Washington, D.C.

Miscellaneous Materials

Daily Worker.

Jubilee Journal: Issued at the Twenty-fifth Anniversary of the Furrier's Joint Council of New York, 1912–1937. New York: Signal Press, 1937.

Proceedings, Tenth Convention, Communist Party, New York State, May 20–23, 1938. New York: New York State Committee, Communist Party, 1938.

A New Workers' Stronghold: What is the International Workers' Order, and Why Every Worker Should Join It. New York: National Executive Committee, IWO, 1930.

Youth Section, International Workers' Order, Insurance, Dramatics, Athletics, Cultural, Social Activities. New York: National Youth Committee, IWO, 1932.

Report of the Immigration Commission: Statements and Recommendations Submitted by Societies and Organizations Interested in the Subject of Immigration. Vol. 41. Washington, D.C.: Government Printing Office, 1911.

Index

Morris H.